THE JEWS'
STATE

THE JEWS' STATE

THEODOR HERZL

A CRITICAL ENGLISH TRANSLATION

translated and with an introduction by

Henk Overberg

JASON ARONSON INC.
Northvale, New Jersey
Jerusalem

This book was set in 11 pt. Berkeley Book by Alabama Book Composition of Deatsville, Alabama and printed and bound by Book-mart Press of North Bergen, New Jersey.

10   9   8   7   6   5   4   3   2   1

Library of Congress Cataloging-in-Publication Data

Herzl, Theodor, 1860–1904.
    [Judenstaat. English]
    The Jews' State / by Theodor Herzl ; a Critical English
Translation by Henk Overberg.
        p. cm.
    Includes bibliographical references and index.
    ISBN 0–7657–5973–X (alk. paper)
    1. Zionism. I. Overberg, Henk. II. Title.
DS149.H514   1997
320.54′095694—dc21   96-40904

Manufactured in the United States of America. Jason Aronson Inc. offers books and cassettes. For information and catalog write to Jason Aronson Inc., 230 Livingston Street, Northvale, New Jersey 07647.

Contents

A Note
from the Translator

Citations in German from *Der Judenstaat* in Part I are based on the 13th edition of the work, published by Jüdischer Verlag, Berlin (year unknown), and reprinted by the Jewish Publishing House, Jerusalem, 1975. Citations in English from *The Jews' State* in the introduction have used my own translation. No page references for *Judenstaat* or *The Jews' State* quotes have been given. Page references to citations from Herzl's original German diaries and letters refer to the Propyläen/Ullstein critical edition in seven volumes (Vienna and Berlin, 1983–1996). References have been made thus: BT2:305, which stands for *Briefe und Tagebücher*, Volume 2, page 305. Each citation has also been given in English, taken from the edition by Raphael Patai (New York, Herzl Press, 1960), thus P1:85, which means *The Complete Diaries of Theodor Herzl*, Volume 1, page 85.

Preface

The Jews' State is one hundred years old. The work is both catalyst and prophecy. Catalyst: speaking both to Jews and to the international community, it virtually launched the modern debate about a modern state for Jews. Prophecy: it foretold the entire scope of this debate, its timing, its spread, its nature, its parameters. It is all there in embryo for us to read and ponder. The little book continues to inform conceptions and arguments about the position of Jews in their state and in the world, and about the relationship between Jews and their fellow human beings. In a very real sense, it still deeply guides how we view the contemporary Middle East.

Translated and retranslated countless times and into many languages since it was published, this present translation is one of only three English translations that have been attempted in the century since its first publication, the first English translation in twenty-five years. Its concerns are both text and context. Though the text has been with us ever since its publication, it is the context that needs recreating. The experience of the world and the Jewish community during the last century, the salience of antisemitism, the Holocaust, the formation and development of the state of Israel, the troubled existence of the Jewish state ever since its inception, the continuing Jewish diaspora and its relationship with state and world: these are among the factors that have created distance between us and the

world in which *The Jews' State* was created. The common understandings which Theodor Herzl assumed in his readers have dissipated and
vanished, and with them a sense of his book's import and impact. These
understandings need to be retrieved and recreated.

The present edition is therefore an attempt both at presentation
and retrieval: presentation of the text in the language of today;
retrieval of the context which gave rise to it. This dual function
informs the three main parts of this edition. Its first part is about
context: it is in the form of an introduction to the setting in which
The Jews' State was written. After a section on the circumstances
which gave rise to the work, it gives an account of the ideological
and social worlds in which Herzl worked and wrote, the Jewish
world and the mainstream world, and it argues that Herzl's interaction with both these worlds rests on some complex attitudes on his
part in which approval, compliance, critique, and rejection all
played a role. There follows a section on *The Jews' State* itself, which
picks up on the main themes that occupied Herzl, and discusses
their scope and treatment. This first part finishes with a description
of the initial impact of *The Jews' State* on Herzl's world.

The second part of this edition offers a presentation of the text
itself, in the form of a translation which attempts to recreate in a
modern idiom the content of the work as well as some of the
peculiarities of Herzl's style. The third part of this edition consists of
a critical glossary, dealing with some salient issues in translation, as
well as the explanation of a number of terms and allusions in the
text, whose meaning is not immediately obvious to modern readers.
The edition closes with a bibliography.

The preparation of the present edition took some two years, and
the writing was done in Melbourne, Jerusalem and Vienna. I have
great pleasure in acknowledging a debt of gratitude to people and
institutions in each of these cities.

My colleagues Klaus Hermes and Uldis Ozolins at Deakin
University helped me in a number of discussions concerning
difficult translation problems and unusual sociological concepts.

Bernard Hacourt from the Catholic University of Louvain, who was on leave to Deakin University, provided material about nineteenth-century Belgium necessary to explain certain allusions by Herzl in *The Jews' State*. Kathryn Thaniel contributed the translation from Latin of Justinian's *Institutiones*. The staffs of the libraries of Deakin, Monash and Melbourne Universities, as well as of Corpus Christi Theological College in Melbourne, were unfailingly helpful in locating material.

I am thankful to Moshe and Bruria Schaerf in Jerusalem for their kind hospitality, their very careful reading of preliminary drafts of the book, and their many valuable suggestions. Much interest in the work was shown by Michael Heymann and Josef Wenkert of the Central Zionist Archives, to whose mixture of critical and encouraging response the work owes a great deal. Chaja Harel was kind enough to set up a number of meetings. I am indebted to Robert Wistrich and Claude Klein of the Hebrew University who gave of their time and knowledge to clarify some difficult issues. The director of the Central Zionist Archives, Yoram Mayorek, and his staff, were unfailing in their courtesy and their efficiency in locating material. In addition, it was a pleasure to work at the National Library of Israel, and the Archives of the *Kultusgemeine* of Vienna, both at Givat Ram, Jerusalem.

My studies in Vienna brought me into contact with Adolf Gaisbauer of the Austrian State Archives and Norbert Leser of the University of Vienna, both of whom gave freely of their detailed knowledge of the history of the late Habsburg Empire. A free-ranging discussion with Jacob Allerhand of Vienna University in the congenial atmosphere of the Café Sacher tied up a number of frayed ends. Gerhard Milchram of the Jewish Welcoming Service provided an overview of Herzl studies in German-speaking universities as well as some normally inaccessible material. The efficiency and courtesy of the staff of the Österreichische Nationalbibliothek was exemplary.

The research and writing were greatly facilitated by a research grant from the Faculty of Arts of my university, Deakin University,

Melbourne, Australia, which provided an indispensable and generous financial backing.

My wife Janet was my constant personal and intellectual compan-
ion throughout all stages of the writing, and it is to her that I would
like to dedicate this book.

Henk Overberg
June 1996

Theodor Herzl:
The Jews' State

An Introduction

Theodor Herzl published Der Judenstaat *with the Viennese publisher Max Breitenstein on February 14, 1896.*

Title and Genesis

THE TITLE

The very title of the work, *Der Judenstaat*, requires comment. *Judenstaat* is a compound noun consisting of two nouns, *Jude* and *Staat*. The first of the constituent nouns of this compound could either be singular or plural, so that the literal rendition of *Der Judenstaat* in English is either *The Jew State* or *The Jews' State*. The rendition *The Jews' State* is the common Hebrew rendition of the title, *Medinat Hayehudim*, and this, too, is the rendition which David Vital recommends in his monumental history of Zionism (Vital, 1975). Sylvie d'Avigdor's English translation, which appeared in 1896 during Herzl's lifetime, renders the title as *A Jewish State*, and it is under this title—changed by Israel Cohen to *The Jewish State* (1934)—that the work has become generally known in the English-speaking world.

However, the rendering of *Der Judenstaat* as *The Jewish State* has two shortcomings. The first of these refers to the fact that Herzl really does not conceptualize his proposed state as anything particularly Jewish: the nature of his state is fully derived from general Western and European conceptions of the state. What he has in mind is not a state that is Jewish in nature, structure or tradition, but that it is a modern state based on conceptions of modern sociology, economy, technology and law, in which Jews can live as full-fledged citizens: a state *for* Jews, in fact. All the main features of the Jews' State, of which Herzl is so proud, are sourced in conceptions of national life current in Herzl's time: the seven-hour working day, the *alliance par le travail*, women's work, the constitutional basis, the arrangements about the transfer of property and the status of personal property in the new state. Conversely, Herzl makes it clear that what might be considered specifically Jewish in his new state—matters of personal morality, faith and religious organization—is going to be kept firmly within the personal domain and outside the public domain:

> *Werden wir also am Ende eine Theokratie haben? Nein! Der Glaube hält uns zusammen, die Wissenschaft macht uns frei. Wir werden daher theokratische Velleitäten unserer Geistlichen gar nicht aufkommen lassen. Wir werden sie in ihren Tempeln festzuhalten wissen . . . In den Staat . . . haben sie nichts dreinzureden, denn sie werden äußere und innere Schwierigkeiten heraufbeschwören.*

> Will we end up having a theocracy? No! Faith will hold us together, science makes us free. We will not even allow the theocratic inclinations of our spiritual leaders to raise their ugly heads. We will know how to keep them in their temples. . . . They have no say in the state which treats them with deference, for they will only conjure up external and internal difficulties.

Herzl indeed is supremely indifferent to the role of religion in personal life, as is clear both from his letters (Pawel, 1989:181) and from *The Jews' State*:

> *Wir wollen drüben jeden nach seiner Fasson selig werden lassen. Auch und vor allem unsere teuern Freidenker, unser unsterbliches Heer, das für die Menschheit immer neue Gebiete erobert.*

Over there we would like everybody to gain his eternal happiness in his own way. That includes our precious free thinkers, our immortal army, which will conquer ever new lands for humanity.

As one commentator sums up: "*Herzls 'Judenstaat' war kein 'jüdischer' Staat, sondern ein moderner Staat, ein Gebilde aus Zweckmäßigkeit und Technik*" [Herzl's "Jews' State" was no "Jewish State," but a modern state, a concept based on clear aims and technology] (Gaisbauer, 1988:91; see also Vital, 1975:260). It is "inspired by modern secular ideals rather than any messianic dream of restoring the ancient Kingdom of David and its sacral splendor" (Wistrich, 1989:452). Indeed, Herzl, unlike his Viennese contemporary Nathan Birnbaum, was not interested in arguments about the nature of Jewish culture and religion and their relationship to a state. "There was to be nothing especially Jewish about the Jewish state he hoped to create; there would be no common language, not even Hebrew. The state was to be an open, pluralist society, but not a particularly Jewish one" (Pauley, 1992:55). It is not the *state* which was to be Jewish, in fact, but its *population*. The semantic difference between "Jewish State" and "Jews' State" may be a fine one, but it has been stated that this "fine semantic difference [has] exerted considerable influence on the direction and course of the World Zionist movement" (Patai, 1971:629). It is not without interest that the most recent French translation by Claude Klein (1990) refers to the works as *L'état des Juifs* rather than the traditional *L'état juif*, and that Klein offers an apologia analogous to my own (Herzl/Klein, 1990:8–11).

The second shortcoming in the term "Jewish State" refers to the fact that the word *Judenstaat*, much like "Jew State," is clearly a pejorative term. It has something of the insult about it and it is meant to shock. Herzl is quite aware of this, and alludes to the pejorative connotations of his title in the work itself:

Durch die bisherigen Vorbemerkungen wollte ich nur in aller Eile den ersten Schwarm von Einwendungen abwehren, den schon das Wort "Judenstaat" hervorrufen muß.

> With the above introductory remarks I have aimed to deflect the
> swarm of objections which the very term "Jews' State" is likely to
> evoke.

Yet he deliberately takes this word with the insulting connotations
on board and specifically makes it his aim to turn this expression of
insult into a word of honor. Herzl means there to be a measure of
provocation, a challenge to the world in his use of the word
Judenstaat: by using the term he wants to confront the world with its
own prejudices and unfairness. The issue becomes clearer still if we
consider the way he launched his newspaper *Die Welt* in 1897,
calling it a *Judenblatt*—a Jew(s') paper—or in Pawel's rather rougher
translation, a "Jew rag" (Pawel, 1989:323), and then justifying his
use of the term *Judenblatt* in its very first issue in these terms:

> *Unsere Wochenschrift ist ein "Judenblatt." Wir nehmen dieses Wort, das
> ein Schimpf sein soll, und wollen daraus ein Wort der Ehre machen. (Die
> Welt, 4 June 1897)*

> Our weekly is a "Jew Paper." We take this word on board, which is
> supposed to be curse, and want to turn it into a word of honor.

It must be said, however, that Herzl must have been aware of
Sylvie d'Avigdor's translation of his work as *A Jewish State*. He
certainly raised no objection to the English title which she finally
adopted (21 May 1896; BT2:346, P1:354).

The present edition of *Der Judenstaat* will, however, follow the
original nomenclature and Vital's (Vital, 1975) recommendation and
refer in English to the work as *The Jews' State*.

HERZL'S LIFE

At the time of the publication of *The Jews' State*, Herzl already had a
considerable reputation. He was born of liberal Jewish parents in

Pest (a component town of the later Budapest) on 2 May 1860, and moved with his family to Vienna in 1878 in order to take full advantage of the educational and social opportunities the Austro-Hungarian capital had to offer. University studies in law were followed by a short career in a legal office in the provinces. Although the legal knowledge Herzl acquired was later to be of use when working out the legal implications of founding a state, Herzl saw his immediate ambitions as lying in the field of literary production. A number of theater pieces flowed from his pen, some deemed good enough to be given at the Burgtheater in Vienna, and even in Berlin and New York, but his dramas were to give him only limited personal satisfaction and public acclaim. Gradually transferring his activities to journalism, Herzl in 1891 took up the post of Paris correspondent of the most important Viennese daily newspaper, the *Neue Freie Presse*, whilst continuing his literary career. *The Jews' State* was written during his period in Paris. The public reactions to the book, and the commitments that began to emerge from its publication for Herzl as organizer of Jewish community activities, led him to ask his employer to appoint him to the prestigious position of *feuilleton*-editor with the *Neue Freie Presse*, a position which kept him in Vienna, and enabled him to elicit contributions from eminent writers of the day for the newspaper on a range of important political and cultural issues. Despite the immense workload which came to him as a result of his newfound Zionist interests, Herzl continued his job at the *Neue Freie Presse*, but his literary career was for all intents and purposes put on the backburner, only to surface occasionally with a further play, and in 1902 more significantly with the Zionist novel *Altneuland* (Old New Land), which forms an imaginative description of life in a future state run by Jews. Herzl died on 3 July 1904.

GENESIS OF *THE JEWS' STATE*

Herzl first mentions *The Jews' State* by name in his diary entry for 3 June 1895, calling it his "political treatise" (BT2:67, P1:30), and most of the drafting was done in Paris in the three-week period that followed. He seems to have realized that he had hit on a momentous undertaking, important enough for him to start keeping a diary of his activities and thoughts, focused specifically on enabling future generations to trace the work he was embarking on. This is the famous start to his diary:

> *Ich arbeite seit einiger Zeit an einem Werk, das von unendlicher Größe ist. Ich weiß heute nicht, ob ich es ausführen werde. Es sieht aus wie ein mächtiger Traum . . . Titel: Das gelobte Land!* (Whitsun, 1895; BT2:43)

For some time past I have been occupied with a work of infinite grandeur. At the moment I do not know whether I shall carry it through. It looks like a mighty dream. Title: The Promised Land! (P1:3)

How *'unendlich' groß* [infinitely grand] this work appeared to him is evident a few days later:

> *Ich glaube, für mich hat das Leben aufgehört und die Weltgeschichte begonnen.* (16 June 1895; BT2:131)

I believe that for me life has ended and world history has begun. (P1:105)

During these three weeks he felt as if he had lost his mental balance and worked as if in a creative trance; it was a period of "crisis" (Pawel, 1989:238) for him, "an acute manic episode" (Pawel, 1989:226–231); Chouraqui speaks of a "month of exaltation" (Chouraqui, 1970:93); Wistrich (1989:443) calls it a "semi-mystical state of ecstacy and possession":

> *Diese Aufschreibungen sind mir keine Arbeit, sondern eine Erleichterung. Ich schreibe mir die Gedanken los, die heraufsteigen wie Luftblasen in*

einer Retorte und schließlich das Gefäß sprengen würden, wenn sie keinen Abzug fänden. (12 June 1895; BT2:122)

For me these notes are not work, but only relief. I am writing myself free of the ideas which rise like bubbles in a retort and would finally burst the container if they find no outlet. (P1:93)

Only ten days later he felt he had regained some sort of equilibrium (22 June 1895; BT2:152, P1:128). Where the thoughts came to him too rapidly to put down in an orderly fashion, he recorded them willy-nilly, so that we can follow quite closely the arguments, ideologies, and positions as they occurred to him. The complete corpus of entries for June 1895 reads virtually like a first draft for the work which he continued to shape for the rest of the year and published the following February. The diary came to constitute a detailed record of the typical pattern of Herzl's life as it was to develop following the publication of *The Jews' State*. This pattern encompassed first his writing, then his rounds of canvassing ideas with important people both Jewish and non-Jewish, then his experience of the general disinterest of these people and his coping with the resultant disappointment, then his switch to woo the Jewish communities, then the Zionist Congresses. The whole cycle would then renew itself.

HERZL'S MOTIVATION

In the important initial entries in his diary, Herzl stresses that what got him started on *The Jews' State* was his personal experience as the butt of antisemitic name calling and prejudice, and his realization that this experience was general and experienced by every member of the Jewish community to a greater or lesser extent. This was what he termed the *Judennot*—the plight of the Jews, and his claim as to the motivation it gave him to write will be examined in some detail below. Nevertheless, this does not quite answer the question why he, in fact, started writing the book in 1895, when, by his own admission, he had been aware of the *Judennot* for well over a decade. This time lag is more of biographical than of critical interest, and it would seem that other factors, more personal and down-to-earth rather than altruistic, have to be brought into play to explain the sudden surge of writing in 1895 that resulted in *The Jews' State*.

The first of these seems to have to do with aspects of Herzl's character: the peculiar mixture in the man of extreme clarity and personal vanity. By 1895 he had put well over a decade of his life into trying to make a literary reputation through his plays. None of them had, after initial reception, maintained themselves on the stage, and it may have started to dawn on him that if he was going to make his mark in life he would have to do so differently. Indeed, he himself is quite clear that his motivation in writing *The Jews' State* is not exclusively to ameliorate the suffering of the Jews: it is also an avenue of bolstering his self-esteem and satisfying his vanity which had been denied him through the lukewarm reception of his plays:

> *Und eigentlich bin ich darin noch immer der Dramatiker. Ich nehme arme, verlumpte Leute von der Straße, stecke sie in herrliche Gewänder und lasse sie vor der Welt ein wunderbares von mir ersonnenes Schauspiel aufführen. Ich operiere nicht mehr mit einzelnen Personen, sondern mit Massen: der Clerus, das Heer, die Verwaltung, die Akademie etc,—für mich lauter Massenunitäten. (11 June 1895; BT2:99)*

> Come to think of it, in all this I am still the dramatist. I pick poor people in rags off the streets, put gorgeous costumes on them, and have them perform for the world a wonderful pageant of my composition. I no longer operate with individuals, but with masses: the clergy, the army, the administration, the academy, etc., all of them mass units to me. (P1:67)

He sees himself finding a new stage with new characters to manipulate and direct, and he is honest enough to see that here lies part of the satisfaction he is experiencing in writing *The Jews' State*. Whether people consider his plan mad or not, he derives considerable satisfaction from the thought that this mad plan will be the "*Gegenstand großmächtiger diplomatischer Schritte* [the object of diplomatic activity by the great powers]" (26 June 1896; BT2:383, P1:395). It will lead him to the mightiest on earth, to the privilege of an hourlong private audience with the Kaiser (9 October 1898; BT2:638, P2:697; and 19 October 1898; BT2:671, P2:726), and the enjoyment of seeing the astonishment of the Kaiser's entourage as he, the "*unbekannte Jude im bügerlichen Rock* [the unknown Jew in civil dress]," enters the imperial apartments. He loves being received like royalty, whether on the railway station at Sofia (17 June 1896; BT2:358, P1:368) or in Rehovoth (29 October 1898; BT2:677, P2:742). Herzl, the man of the theater, saw the opportunity to turn politics into theater, with himself at the center of things (see Benjamin cited in Stewart, 1974:201). Those who knew him have commented on this personal need in him, and how the new object of his writing promised satisfaction where the old object had failed. Here are some views of Arthur Schnitzler, who saw him regularly during this time and observed him with the intuition of the poet. "*Kann in H.s Gesellschaft nicht wirklich warm werden; mich eigentlich nicht einmal annähemd wohl fühlen* [I cannot warm to H.'s company; I do not feel at ease with him at all]" (Schnitzler, 29 March 1895; 1989:132). Herzl has "*im Gespräch stetes Bedürfnis, sich geltend zu machen* [the constant need to dominate the conversation]" (Schnitzler, 31 August 1894; 1989:86); he cannot stand Herzl, "*sein gewichtiges Sprechen mit den großen Augen zum Schluss jedes Satzes irritiert mich* [I am irritated by his pompous manner of speaking with the wide open eyes after every sentence]" (Schnitzler, 11 September 1894; 1989:87). Since the publication of *The Jews' State* Herzl parades around town "*mit einem gewissen Gefühl der Verpflichtung, offiziell sowohl zu den Makkabäern in die Burg als ins jüdische Restaurant* [with a unmistakable air that the world is obligated to him, whether in an official capacity at a performance of the 'Maccabees' at the

Burg-Theatre or at the Jewish restaurant]" (Schnitzler, 19 April 1896; 1989:185). Karl Kraus also picked this up. He turned his attention to Herzl in 1898, dismissing him as the King of Zion with a nice turn of phrase:

> Es wird wohl selten noch einen Souverän von so ausgesprochenem feuilletonistischem Talent gegeben haben wie den König von Zion. Unbotmäßige Vasallen gewinnt er durch ein paar graziöse Beobachtungen, und wenn er über abendländische Angelegenheiten, als da sind . . . zu plaudem beginnt, fliegen ihm die Herzen aller Untertanen zu (Karl Kraus in Die Waage, 15 January 1898, in Kraus, 1979:151–152).

> There can seldom have been a sovereign with such a pronounced talent as a feuilletonist as the King of Zion. He wins over insubordinate vassals to his side by a couple of gracious remarks, and when he starts talking about such general concerns as are around, the hearts of all his subjects flock to him

Chaim Weizmann, who worked with him over a number of Zionist Congresses, makes essentially the same point, albeit without Kraus's malice:

> He had excessive respect for the Jewish clergy, born not of intimacy but of distance . . . His leaning toward clericalism distressed us, so did the touch of Byzantinism in his manner. Almost from the outset a kind of court sprang up about him, of worshipers who pretended to guard him from too close contact with the mob. I am compelled to say that certain elements in his bearing invited such an attitude. (Weizmann, 1966:45)

Apart from the failure of his latest play, *Das Neue Ghetto* (The New Ghetto), and the finally recognized need to change the direction of his life, there was the Dreyfus case in Paris (Stewart, 1974:163–167). Ever since Jacob de Haas published Herzl's biography in 1927 (Haas, 1927:50–52), it has been assumed that the

Dreyfus case deeply influenced Herzl to begin his Zionist writing, yet modern scholars have demonstrated that there is no connection (see Wistrich, 1989:441–442), and even de Haas wrote as early as 1904 that "Herzl has not confessed to what particular incident the publication of his 'Jewish State' in the winter of 1895 was due. He was in Paris at the time, and was no doubt moved by the Dreyfus affair" (Singer et al, 1904:VI.370). Herzl himself mentioned the Dreyfus affair in his diary only on 17 November 1895, a full year after the trial had been concluded and nine months after Dreyfus' official degradation on 5 January 1895 (BT2:278, P1:273).

More to the point of the starting time of *The Jews' State* may be that Herzl's father-in-law Jacob Naschauer had died on 3 January 1894, releasing an inheritance to him of about half a million guilders (a quarter of a million dollars today); so he suddenly gained considerable financial independence, and found himself in a position to devote both time and financial resources to his new-found political activity (Pawel, 1989:195–197). He had also sent his family home from Paris early in 1895, staying back on his own, which gave him time and leisure to write. He himself only returned to Vienna to live with his family in April 1896. From Vienna he was well-placed to turn from publication of *The Jews' State* to the organization of the Zionist Congresses.

The Jewish Context

THE TRADITION OF ZION

Although the term *Zionism* did not enter public discourse until the end of the ninteenth century, a selection of the cluster of the meanings later to be encapsulated in the term had been a part of Jewish community consciousness since time immemorial. Originally the term *Zion* merely denoted a hill just outside the confines of the old city walls in Jerusalem, and this is still one of its meanings. It is first mentioned in the Book of Psalms (137:1–6):

> By the rivers of Babylon we sat down and wept when we remembered Zion. There on the willow-trees we hung up our harps, for there those who carried us off demanded music and singing, and our captors called on us to be merry: "Sing us one of the songs of Zion." How could we sing the Lord's song in a foreign land? If I forget you, O Jerusalem, let my right hand wither away; let my tongue cling to the roof of my mouth if I do not remember you, if I do not set Jerusalem above my highest joy (*The New English Bible*, 1970:I.865–866).

This first reference, born in the captivity of the Jewish people in Babylon, serves both as presentation and representation; it is both denotation and symbol. It denotes the hill in Jerusalem and its immediate surroundings, but in addition symbolizes the longing of the Jewish community in captivity for a return to Zion. With these geographical, religious and psychological dimensions, the term *Zion* has remained current within Jewish communities throughout the Diaspora, and has been used in both religious and secular contexts (Israel Pocket Library, 1973:1).

In the nineteenth century the concept of Zion came to be associated with the settlement activities of Jewish persons in Palestine and with the ideologies, individuals and societies that were connected with these activities. The settlement activities in question were basically threefold in character. There were firstly those concerned with building accommodation for local Jewish residents of Palestine as well as for prospective settlers: Yemin Moshe, the "Windmill" settlement in Jerusalem, started by Moses Montefiore in 1860, is an example of this. Secondly, there was an increasing stream of agricultural settlements which was meant to encourage the emigration of Jewish groups to Palestine. The first of these settlements went back to 1860 and was sponsored not by an individual, but by a Jewish group from Frankfurt-on-the-Oder in Prussia: the *Kolonisationsverein für Palästina* [Society for the Colonization of Palestine]. The Frankfurt group had some eminent members: both Moses Hess and Rabbi Hirsch Kalischer worked for it (Patai, 1971:201). The third type of settlement activity had to do with the establishment of educational institutions. This activity can be traced back to 1857, when the Edel-Lämel school was established in Jerusalem, again by a group, this time from Austria (Jonas, 1923:419). This school was later to be taken over by the *Hilfsverein der Deutschen Juden* [Society to Assist German Jews], which continued establishing new schools, ranging from kindergartens to secondary colleges. The language of instruction at the kindergarten level was Hebrew, but at the higher levels the students were taught in German (Jonas, 1923:419). The most important work in the establishment of educational institutions, however, originated in France, under the auspices of the *Alliance Israélite Universelle* [Universal Israelite Alliance], which had been founded in 1860 in Paris by Adolphe Crémieux. The first educational venture of the Alliance in Palestine was an agricultural school near Jaffa, the Mikve Yisrael School, but soon other schools were established in other towns (Patai, 1971:356). The Alliance schools, which spread throughout Palestine from the 1880s onwards, were for a long time the only modern schools in Palestine specifically for Jews. Their language of instruction was French, and their curriculum was oriented toward Paris. So in terms of establishing a Jewish national consciousness they did not mean a great deal:

> *Sie hatten nicht die Tendenz, die Juden zu bodenständigen, land- und volksverbundenen Elementen heranzuziehen, sondern nur dazu, daß die irgendwo ihren Unterhalt fänden. (Jonas, 1923:419)*

> They did not aim at educating Jews into elements with a local orientation who would consider themselves tied to their land and their people, but merely that they would find a livelihood somewhere.

German Jews came to regard them with suspicion as *"nur ein Glied in der imperialistischen Kulturpropaganda Frankreichs im Vorderen Orient* [merely a link in the imperialist cultural propaganda of France in the Near East]" (Jonas, 1923:419). French Jews for their part returned the compliment: "The circumstance that many of the Zionist leaders had been raised or educated in Germany . . . only served to deepen . . . suspicions" (Patai, 1971:350; Rinott, 1986:295). Hence the imperialist competition between nations which characterized Europe in the late 19th century was to some extent replicated in these Jewish educational endeavors in Palestine.

In the Zionist historical literature this tradition is usually referred to as the philanthrophic tradition, for it was characteristic of this tradition that the work done was in the nature of what Sir Karl Popper would have called piecemeal social engineering, without any thought to nationbuilding or the creation of a specific Jewish polity.

It was in large measure, but not exclusively, sponsored by wealthy Jews who made available their resources, and used their political contacts in order to get isolated and individual projects off the ground. Baron Maurice de Hirsch, whom Herzl went to see in Paris on 2 June 1895 as he was writing *The Jews' State*, was a perfect representative of this tradition. Not only was he in the habit of making regular contributions to the *Alliance Israélite Universelle*; he had also founded his own *Jewish Colonization Association* in 1891 to promote agricultural settlements in Palestine. Edmond de Rothschild, whom Herzl called "the philanthropic Zionist," (19 July 1896; BT2:411, P1:428), and with whom he had a long meeting on 19 July 1896 (BT2:409, P1:426ff), was another example. Both these men were sounded out by Herzl to see whether their philanthropy could be stretched to political support for a new state for Jews. Both these encounters remained without immediate practical issue. If the meeting with Hirsch (see Pawel, 1989:218–222), whom Herzl had called "*nur ein Philanthrop, ein Peabody*" [a philanthropist, a peabody] (24 May 1895; BT2:54, P1:16), was saved by the civility and the politeness of the Baron, his meeting with Rothschild must have been quite difficult, judging by the irritation Herzl later showed in his diary: "Twice Edmond R. said: '*Il ne faut pas avoir les yeux plus gros que le ventre* [Your eyes should not be bigger than your stomach].' That, I believe, is the extent of his philosophical insight" (20 July 1896; BT2:413, P1:430). Yet the two meetings did confirm Herzl's deepest suspicions about the philanthropic movement. In *The Jews' State*, in an important diatribe, Herzl characterizes it as a barely concealed form of antisemitism:

> *Noch mehr Vorteil als die christlichen Bürger würden die "Assimilierten" von der Entfernung der stammestreuen Juden haben. Denn die Assimilierten werden die beunruhigende, unberechenbare, unvermeidliche Konkurrenz des jüdischen Proletariats los, das durch politischen Druck und wirtschaftliche Not von Ort zu Ort, von Land zu Land geworfen wird. Dieses schwebende Proletariat würde festgemacht werden. Jetzt können*

*manche christliche Staatsbürger—man nennt sie Antisemiten—sich
gegen die Einwanderung fremder Juden sträuben. Die israelitischen
Staatsbürger können das nicht, obwohl sie viel schwerer betroffen sind;
denn auf sie drückt zunächst der Wettbewerb gleichartiger wirtschaftlicher
Individuen, die zudem auch noch den Antisemitismus importieren oder den
vorhandenen verschärfen. Es ist ein heimlicher Jammer der Assimilierten,
der sich in "wohltätigen" Unternehmungen Luft macht. Sie gründen
Auswanderungsvereine für zureisende Juden. Diese Erscheinung enthält
einen Gegensinn, den man komisch finden könnte, wenn es sich nicht um
leidende Menschen handelte. Einzelne dieser Unterstützungsvereine sind
nicht für, sondern gegen die verfolgten Juden da. Die Ärmsten sollen nur
recht schnell, recht weit weggeschafft werden. Und so entdeckt man bei
aufmerksamer Betrachtung, daß mancher scheinbare Judenfreund nur ein
als Wohltäter verkleideter Antisemit jüdischen Ursprungs ist.*

Getting rid of the Jews who remain true to their group would be even
more advantageous to assimilated Jews than to Christian citizens, for
assimilated Jews would no longer have to cope with the worrisome,
inevitable, incalculable competition of the Jewish proletariat, thrown
about from place to place and country to country by political
pressure and economic distress. This floating proletariat would
become tied to one place. At present many Christian citizens—
commonly known as antisemites—are in a position to protest against
the immigration of foreign Jews. The Israelite citizens cannot do so,
even though they are the more heavily affected, because they are in
competition with their own economic kind, who, apart from everything else, are responsible for importing antisemitism from abroad or
even for increasing local antisemitism. This is the lament of assimilated Jews, to which they then give expression in "philanthropic"
projects. They establish emigration societies for immigrating Jews.
This phenomenon is a paradox which might even be funny, were it
not that suffering human beings are involved. In offering assistance
some of these societies do not work for but rather against persecuted
Jews. The poorest among these must be taken away, very quickly and
very far. Indeed, when you go into it carefully you realize that many

a would-be friend of the Jews is no more than an antisemite of Jewish background in disguise.

Certainly strong words: many a seeming friend of the Jews is an antisemite in disguise; no matter if they are Jews themselves: then they are merely antisemitic Jews. Herzl charges that a large number of wealthy assimilated Jews promote these settlement activities merely to rid themselves and their countries of their objectionable poorer brethren. In this way they ingratiate themselves with their gentile compatriots, and in effect do the dirty work for the antisemites. Indeed, they may well even decide to torpedo Herzl's own efforts to establish a state for Jews. In Herzl's advocacy of a state for Jews there is an element of scarcely contained threat toward the wealthy Jewish philanthropists: they will risk being unmasked for what they are if they refuse to make the financial contributions toward his enterprise which he will no doubt ask of them:

> *Finden aber diese (die großen Finanzjuden) mit ihrer Lage ganz zufriedenen Herren sich nicht bewogen, etwas für ihre Stammesbrüder zu tun, die man mit Unrecht für die großen Vermögen einzelner verantwortlich macht, so wird die Verwirklichung dieses Planes Gelegenheit geben, eine reinliche Scheidung zwischen ihnen und dem übrigen Teile des Judentums durchzuführen.*

These gentlemen may be quite happy with the present situation, but if we cannot get them to do something for their blood brothers who are always held responsible for the large wealth of a few, then the realization of this plan will provide the opportunity to draw a clear division between them and the rest of the Jewish community.

One wonders how the aristocratic Rothschild and the exquisitely polished Hirsch would have reacted to this paragraph. What is clear is that Herzl's experiences with the rich and famous Jews, and his conclusion that they might by and large be antisemites anyway, were instrumental in his abandoning his courtship of them. It led him to being suspicious of any settlement program which was not solidly based on the existence of a specific polity for Jews. In Pawel's enlightening phrase: Herzl's mission was about "politics and power" (Pawel, 1989:337).

The bulk of European Jewry in Herzl's time lived in Czarist Russia, and they lived under the worst conditions. The waves of pogroms, which were to become an ever more insistent feature of Jewish community existence in Czarist Russia, led to the political and ideological activity of Leo Pinsker, a Jewish medical doctor in Odessa. Deeply disturbed by the pogroms in his home city in 1871 and again in 1881, he made a trip around Europe, visiting many eminent Jews to sound them out about the possibility of mass emigration of Jews to Palestine. Encouraged to set down his views in writing, he wrote the pamphlet *Autoemanzipation—Mahnruf an seine Stammesgenossen von einem russischen Juden* [Autoemancipation—a warning of a Russian Jew to his brethern] in 1882 (Pinsker, 1913). In this he argued that the main issue underlying popular feeling against Jews was that they were an alien element in every nation, and they would be subject to discrimination and persecution even where they had equal civic status. The only way out was mass emigration to Palestine. By his own admission, Herzl only got to know Pinsker's writing when *The Jews' State* was on its way to the bookshops, and his comment (10 February 1896; BT2:300, P1:299) to the effect that, had he known of the existence of this pamphlet, he would not have bothered writing *The Jews' State*, is an indication of how much of what Herzl was to say later had already been canvassed by Pinsker fourteen years earlier. *Autoemanzipation* quickly became well-known in Jewish circles within Russia, and motivated a number of them to form the emigration society of the *Hibbat Zion* [Love of Zion], whose members became known as the *Hovevei Zion* [Lovers of Zion]. *Hibbat Zion* provided the impetus for the pioneering work of the *Bilu* workers, who founded a number of Jewish settlements in Palestine in the 1880s (Patai, 1971:139). The movement also went international: there was an early *Hibbat Zion* in Warsaw, there soon was another in London (Schoeps, 1987:133). In Vienna the first *Hibbat Zion* group, calling itself *Ahavat Zion* [Love of Zion] was formed in May 1882 by Reuben Bierer, a doctor from Lemberg (Lvov) in the provinces who had come to Vienna for further study. The European movement gained further strength and profile through the publicity engendered by a conference it organized in Kattowitz (Katowice) from 6 to 12 November 1884. How quickly the movement gained in strength in the first ten years is indicated by Nathan Birnbaum, who reported the existence of groups in Berlin, London, Edinburgh, Paris, and New York, as well as a number of Austrian groups coordinated in Vienna (Birnbaum, 1893:26).

The *Ahavat Zion* in Vienna counted among its members a number of students, who on 23 March 1883 branched off to form their own society, calling it the *Kadimah*, the name meaning both "eastward" and "forward". The early years of the *Kadimah* have been researched in detail by Julius Schoeps, on whose work the following presentation is based (Schoeps, 1987). In the words of Isidor Schalit, one of its original members, "*Kadimah hat zwei Bedeutungen: Ostwärts gegen die Assimilation und für nationale Arbeit und Kadimah vorwärts gegen Orthodoxie und für Fortschritt* [*Kadimah* has two meanings: eastward against assimilation and for national activities and forward against orthodoxy and for progress]" (cited in Schoeps, 1987:115). Police regulations in Vienna at the time forbade the formation of societies with national aspirations for minorities, so in order to be eligible for incorporation at all, the *Kadimah* cloaked its aims in literary and scientific objectives: "*die Pflege der Literatur und Wissenschaft des Judentums mit Ausschluß jeder politischen Tendenz* [the fostering of the literature and science of Jewry with the exclusion of any political orientation]" (cited in Schoeps, 1987:115). It was in this form that the new society was advertised on the notice boards at Vienna University:

Denn nur aus den reichen Schätzen der jüdischen Literatur wird die Jugend Liebe zum jüdischen Volk lernen und nur aus den unerschöpflichen Quellen der Geschichte des Judentums wird sie nützliche und fruchtbrin-

gende Lehren für die Zukunft des jüdischen Volkes ziehen können' (*Kadimah,*
1933:18).

For only by contact with the rich treasures of Jewish literature will
our youth learn to love the Jewish people, and only from the
inexhaustible springs of the history of Jewry will it gain useful and
fruitful lessons for the future of the Jewish people.

Yet *Kadimah's* activities soon showed that this professed cultural
orientation was nothing more than a veneer for political objectives.
The group took up contact with Pinsker and made him an honorary
member of the society; in return, he sent them 180 copies of his
Autoemanzipation, so the *Kadimah* were well aware of this publication and its arguments. Publicity for the society was in the hands of
Nathan Birnbaum, who in 1884 in a pamphlet entitled *Die Assimilationssucht* [The Desire to Assimilate] wrote:

Die Wiedergewinnung eines nationalen Mittelpunktes ist die einzige Hoffnung
des jüdischen Volkes, sie ist die einzige absolute Rettung. . . . Mit dem
Wiedergewinnen einer Heimat würde der jetzige Judenhaß in seiner spezifi-
schen Gestalt vom Erdboden verschwinden, die ganze Judenheit würde nach
langen und bangen Jahrtausenden schweren Alpdrucks wieder aufatmen
(Birnbaum, 1884:14–15).

Regaining a national center is the only hope of the Jewish people; it
is the only absolute salvation. With the reclaiming of a home country
the present hatred of the Jews in its specific form would vanish from
the earth, and the whole of Jewry would breathe again after the long
and frightful nightmare of thousands of years.

This paragraph, in effect, foreshadows Herzl's later positions in
The Jews' State in their most important dimensions because it
predicates the end of the general hatred of the Jews on national
rather than philanthropic action. But Birnbaum lacks Herzl's consis-
tency, for even as late as 1893 Birnbaum talks about a field to

till—*Ackerbau*—as the true basis of Jewish communal life (Birnbaum, 1893:12).

In 1885 Birnbaum went so far as to establish a journal, naming it *Selbstemanzipation* [The Emancipation of the Self], a name clearly modelled on the title of Pinsker's pamphlet. The issue of 2 September 1885 then reiterated the aims of the *Kadimah* quite clearly: there is *"nur eine nationale Lösung der Judenfrage . . . Die antisemitischen Drangsäle sind die Wehen, die der Wiedergeburt unserer Nation vorangehen . . . die Realisierung der jüdisch-nationalen Ideen wird ja endlich ganz die Quelle des Unglücks stopfen"* (*Selbstemanzipation*, 2 September 1885, p.1) [there is only a national solution to the issue of the Jews. The antisemitic persecution is the pain which precedes the rebirth of our nation . . . . the realization of Jewish-national concepts will finally fully block the spring of our misfortune]. Indeed, to Nathan Birnbaum belongs the honor of first using the word *zionistisch*—in the issue of 1 April 1890, and later the word *Zionismus* in the issue of 16 May 1890—"the only solid achievement of his career," in Pawel's rather dismissive assessment (Pawel, 1989:271). However, the term must have been in common use among members of the *Kadimah* before this, for, as the research of Schoeps has shown, Reuben Bierer had used the formula *zionistischer Brudergruß* [brotherly Zionist greeting] in a letter to the *Kadimah* of 9 December 1888 (Schoeps, 1987:127). Herzl first used the term in *The Jews' State*.

Although the primary focus of the *Kadimah* was the development among Jewish students of an interest in Jewish national life, much of their concern in the early 1890s seems to have been taken up with their day-to-day experiences of antisemitism in the Vienna of the day. For the *Kadimah* this preoccupation with antisemitism centered in the first instance around the issue of how, as a Jewish student society, it was to relate to other university fraternities. In practical terms the issue focused on the rights of its members to challenge members of other fraternities to fight duels. The denial of this right was meant as an insult, and was regarded by Jewish students as a serious expression of anti-Jewish discrimination. In 1896 a German-speaking nationalist fraternity at Vienna University, the *Deutschnationale Studentenschaft* [National German Student Society] in a decision known as the Waidhofen Decision (11 March 1896; for text see Schnitzler, 1968:360), went so far as to declare Jewish students "*wehr- und charakterlos* [without character and unsuited to defend their own honor]"; as Jews they could simply never be in a position where they might have to protect their honor (not having any), hence they were to be denied the right to fight duels. The immediate concern may have been one of honor and insult; the long-ranging implication of the decision was to deny Jewish students entry into the professions or the reserve officer corps after their student days were over (Schoeps, 1987:128–132). Schitzler (1968:155–156) and Herzl (14 March 1896; BT2:310, P1:310–311) both spoke out strongly against the Waidhofen Decision, and both worried about it as a further instance of antisemitism on the march in Vienna.

Although Herzl had been in contact with eminent French Jews and the chief rabbi of Vienna, Moritz Güdemann, as he was writing his *Jews' State*, he seems to have known relatively little of the tradition and the development of the *Hibbat Zion* and the *Kadimah*. Before 1896 he had never heard of Pinsker. Yet on the other hand, the publication of *The Jews' State* hit the *Kadimah* like a bombshell, and it was the *Kadimah* who then sought out Herzl. They invited him to address their meetings, feted him as a new Jewish leader, and finally helped him set up the structures that led to the calling of the first Zionist Congress. Herzl welcomed all this attention, which was very useful to him at the time; later he distanced himself from the *Kadimah*. At the time of the Zionist Congresses he had a particularly rough time with Nathan Birnbaum, who not unreasonably wanted to claim some of the credit for setting in motion Zionist discourse and the new Zionist movement. Herzl's references to him in his diaries are rather ascerbic (10 March 1897; BT2:485–486, P2:519 and 3 September 1897; BT2:541, P2:584).

THE TRADITION OF ASSIMILATION

The tradition of Zion, with its philanthropic work of the rich Jewish financiers as well as the settlement activities of the groups and societies, represents but one stream in the Jewish tradition with which Herzl felt he had to come to terms in *The Jews' State*. There was, however, in addition, another Jewish community tradition, which had been developing ever since the end of the 18th century. It hooked into the European Enlightenment of the 18th century: thinkers like the French *philosophes* and the German *Aufklärer* had started to look at notions of the separation of the state from the Christian Church, of the secular from the religious domain in public life. Out of this political exploration developed conceptions of civil equality for all the citizens in states based on secular rather than Christian-religious tenets. This stream of thought was to have a complex effect on the civic status of Jewish communities.

On the one hand it clearly carried the message that Jews everywhere should have the same civil and political rights of other citizens, or to put it differently, that Jewishness was simply an irrelevant condition when considering a person's civil and political status. Hence it offered Jews the opportunity of full emancipation from the ghetto existence into which they had been driven by centuries of social discrimination, and it held out the promise of full assimilation into the national community.

There was a catch, however. As a corollary the Enlightenment took to stigmatizing the time-honored ghetto existence of Jews as evidence of the benighted past, and expected Jews to assimilate into mainstream societies, that is, to become indistinguishable from other citizens. The first practical political expression of this stream of thought was the US Declaration of Independence of 1776, which led the way in the civil emancipation of Jews in that country (Gaisbauer, 1988:11). The French National Assembly granted full civil rights to Jews on 27 September 1791 (*Selbstemanzipation*, 16 October 1891,

p. 1), the Dutch followed suit in 1796. Then throughout the 19th century virtually all European countries followed these examples: Italy in 1861, the Balkan countries after the Congress of Berlin in 1878, Russia as late as the revolution of 1917 (Patai, 1971:288). The first of the German states to grant Jews civil and political equality was Prussia in 1822 (Hellendal, 1973:110). Full political emancipation of Jews throughout all German lands came in the wake of unification: the North German Confederation, which preceded it, had granted Jews civil equality in 1869 (Sondheimer, 1906:89), and the Empire simply followed suit. Austria had made a first attempt in 1848 after the revolution; the law was subsequently revoked, then finally Jews were granted full civil equality and religious freedom in the new constitution of the Dual Monarchy of 21 December 1867 (articles 2 and 14) (Gaisbauer, 1988:11). By the time that Herzl published *The Jews' State*, the emancipation of Jews, that is, "the removal of civic, political and economic restrictions imposed on Jews" (Patai, 1971:288) had been guaranteed by law in the United States as well as most European nations.

It took little time for the Jewish communities to realize the full impact of this emancipation. In Vienna the initial reaction of the Jewish community was euphoric, if we are to believe its president at the time, Josef Wertheimer, who exulted in *Die Neuzeit* (1868:19):

Ich will die düstern Bilder einer traurigen Zeit, in welcher ich mein Amt antrat, nicht heraufbeschwören, nicht gedenken . . . der Versagung aller Bürger- und Menschenrechte. Nein, ich will an diesem Tage . . . nur bei der herangebrochenen schönen Zeit verweilen. In diesen letzten Tagen sind durch die Sanktionierung der Grundrechte auch die letzten Reste einer mittelalterlichen Gesetzgebung für uns gefallen. Frei sind uns alle Bahnen geworden, offen sind uns alle Kronländer . . . , zugänglich ist uns jede Stellung geworden. Wir, die einst Geächteten und Verachteten, sind die Beachteten und Geachteten geworden. Dass ich dies erlebt, das erfüllt mein Herz mit großer und dankbarer Freude.

I do not want to conjure up the somber pictures of that sad era, in which I started my professional career, or call to mind the denial of all human and political rights. No, on this day I want to think of the beautiful times which have now dawned. In the last few days the last remains of medieval legislation have vanished—for us, too—through the granting of the basic rights. All avenues have become free for us, all Crown Lands have become open for us, all public positions have become accessible to us. We, who were once outlawed and despised, have become persons of honor and note. It fills my heart with gratitude and great joy that I have experienced this.

He had a point. The Jews of the Austro-Hungarian Empire, so long restricted in their movements and social opportunities, now began a wholesale migration to Vienna in search of the good life. This was to leave an indelible imprint on Viennese society: the number of Jews in Vienna, which had stood at 72,588 in 1880 had risen to 149,926 by 1900 and topped the 175,000 mark by 1910 (Pauley, 1992:23). They had come for a tertiary education and social advancement: although only about one in ten Viennese were Jewish, a third of all Viennese matriculants (*Abiturienten*) were Jewish (Beller, 1986:29). Herzl was quite right with his repeatedly stated claim that this emancipation and migration led the Jewish community to become very good at producing a vast reservoir of "middle range intellectuals," but he did his community less than justice by ignoring the truly astounding Jewish cultural and intellectual elite of Vienna, which virtually exploded out of this vast reservoir within a generation, and which stands comparison with any group in any epoch: the poets Arthur Schnitzler, Hugo von Hofmannsthal, Karl Kraus, Franz Werfel, and Stefan Zweig; the academics Ludwig Wittgenstein, Ludwig Gumplowicz, Sigmund Freud, Martin Buber, and later Karl Popper; the musicians Gustav Mahler, Arnold Schönberg, Bruno Walter, and Selma Kurz; Theodor Gomperz, Otto Weininger, Joseph Roth, David Vogel, Albert Ehrenstein. The list is seemingly endless, and the Jewish contribution to Viennese cultural life at the time stands supreme. It is a measure of the stature of the man that in these circles Herzl held his own, be it as playwright, as the brilliant Paris correspondent to the *Neue Freie Presse*, or finally as the feuilleton editor of the same paper. Stefan Zweig (1948:44) once said that nine-tenths of Vienna's nineteenth-century culture depended on the Jews, and Beller has commented (1986:28): "At the strategic points in Viennese culture, Jews did predominate."

There was, however, a price to be paid for all this emancipation and brilliance in mainstream society. This price was hotly debated, both among Jews and in the general community, and at one level, Herzl's *Jews' State* is one component of this debate. Whatever the disadvantages of the traditional ghetto-existence of Jewish communities in Europe, and they were many, the daily struggle for survival of the ghetto in the face of a hostile world did serve over the centuries to strengthen the bonds of communality and the sense of peoplehood among Jews. Jewish existence, in terms of sheer community discipline and survival, partly but significantly found its definition in terms of opposition to the outside world, and the ghetto was both the geographical location and the symbol of this opposition. In contrast to this, what the emancipation movement encouraged or, stronger still, demanded, was Jewish acceptance of community not in the sense of specific historical ethno-religious community, but in the sense of secular national community. To put it differently, Jews living in Germany, Austria, and France were to be precisely that: German, Austrian or French citizens of the Jewish persuasion, whose reference was to be the national group of the state of which they were citizens, and only that. In such a socio-ideological framework, the concept of Jews as a separate entity and of Jewishness as a point of reference for community identification became of questionable validity. French Jewish intellectuals had been expressing this in the following terms:

> *Vient enfin le grand siècle de la libre pensée: le voltairianisme . . . La Révolution française, exécutant des décrets des philosophes, donne aux*

Juifs droits de patrie pleine et entière en France, et à sa suite, dans les pays de civilisation . . . En brisant la barrière de séparation entre le Juif et le Chrétien, elle met un terme à l'histoire du peuple juif. A partir du 28 septembre 1791, il n'y a plus de place à une histoire des Juifs en France; il n'y a qu'une histoire du Judaïsme français, comme il y a une histoire du Calvinisme, ou du Luthéranisme français, rien d'autre et rien de plus (Darmesteter, 1892:188–189)

Finally the great century of free thought, of Voltairianism, arrives on the scene . . . Putting into practice the decrees of the *philosophes*, the French Revolution gives Jews full and entire civil rights in France and subsequently in all civilized countries. By breaking the barrier between Christian and Jew, it effectively puts an end to the history of the Jewish people. Since 28 September 1791, there has been no more room for a history of the Jews in France; there is room only for a history of French Judaism, just as there is a history of French Calvinism, or of French Lutheranism, nothing more and nothing less.

Jews were now to be fully part of the French, or of their respective national polity; and it became a non sequitur to conceptualize their community existence in terms of a Jewish national group. That was assimilation ideology, pure and simple, and many Jews not only came to see their existential situation simply in these terms but welcomed this development with open arms. In the words of the French Jewish historian Théodor Reinach:

Le Juif émancipé réussit à concilier l'attachement à son antique tradition religieuse avec les devoirs que lui imposent les progrès de la civilisation et sa qualité de citoyen dans les divers pays qui l'ont affranchi . . . Il n'est pas vrai qu'un "patriotisme" spécial et tout négatif, la haine du gentil, s'oppose dans la conscience du juif actuel à l'éclosion vraie et sincère du patriotisme civique. Certes il a fallu du temps pour qu'un race, ayant de brillants souvenirs d'indépendance et de grandeur politique, consentît à abandonner ses espérances et ses revendications, pour que le judaïsme, cessant d'être une nation, se résignât à ne plus être qu'une communauté

religieuse. Cette transformation nécessaire s'est accomplie cependent.
(Reinach, 1884:XIV.385)

The emancipated Jew has successfully reconciled attachment to his
ancient religious tradition with the duties imposed upon him by the
progress of civilization and his status as a citizen of the various
countries that have enfranchised him . . . It is not true that a
special, quite negative "patriotism"—hatred of the gentile—closes
the conscience of the Jew to true and sincere patriotism. It is true that
some time was needed before a race possessed of such brilliant
memories of independence and political greatness agreed to abandon
its hopes and claims, before Judaism, having ceased to be a nation,
resigned itself to be no more than a religious community. However,
this necessary change has been accomplished.

Insofar as the Jewish community as a community had any
existence at all, it was to be the existence of a religious community.
This is how the German Rabbi Sondheimer from Heidelberg saw the
emancipated existence of his community:

*Durch die reichen Verkehrsmittel der Gegenwart und den literarischen
Austausch ihrer Geisteserzeugnisse reichen sich die Juden aller Länder die
Hände, um unbeschadet ihrer innigsten und treuesten Hingabe an das
Vaterland, in dem sie wohnen, dem Judentum die Anerkennung zu
erringen, welche ihm als einer uralten und mit der menschlichen Vernunft
durchaus übereinstimmenden Religion gebührt. Mehr und mehr werden
die weltgeschichtlichen Grundsätze des Judentums, der Glaube an den
Einzigen, Einigen, Ewigen und die Betätigung wahrer Menschenliebe zur
Geltung gelangen; heilige Aufgabe der Juden aber ist es, die Gotteslehre in
Haus, Schule und Synagoge mit aller Kraft und Treue zu pflegen und mit
aller Liebe im Leben zu bewähren. Durch die Treue gegen die Gotteslehre
hat sich das große Wunder der Erhaltung Israels vollzogen; in ihr ist der
Fortbestand der Juden als eines Religionsvolkes verbürgt; diese Treue
macht uns zufrieden, froh und glücklich, und durch sie werden wir
beitragen zur Herbeiführung der messianischen Zeit, in welcher Gott als
der Eine und sein Name als der Einzige allüberall wird erkannt und*

verehrt und alle Menschen in Frieden und Liebe miteinander leben werden (Sondheimer, 1906:93).

By means of the rich communication network of the present and the literary exchange of their intellectual creations, Jews of all countries link hands, to express without danger their innermost and faithful love for the country in which they live, and to attain the recognition for Jewry which is in keeping with its ancient status as a religion based on human reason. Increasingly, the world-historical bases of Judaism will be respected: its faith in the one, only, eternal [God], and the practice of true humanity. However, it remains the sacred task of the Jews to practice God's teaching in the home, at school and in the synagogue; and to lovingly preserve it throughout life. Through faithful observance of the word of God the great miracle of Israel's survival has been accomplished; in it lies the guarantee of the continuation of the Jews as a religious people; this faith makes us content, glad, and happy, and through it we will contribute to the coming of the time of the Messiah, when the one God and His only name will everywhere be recognized and revered, and when all human beings will live together in peace and love.

This then was the price of emancipation: the abandonment of any definition of Jewish communal life and aspirations that went beyond religious contexts. Emancipation led to a *"Reduzierung des Judentums auf ein nur-religiöses Phänomen* [reduction of Judaism to an exclusively religious phenomenon]" (Gaisbauer 1988:13); Jews were transformed into mere *"Deutsche, Slaven, Magyaren . . . mosaischer Konfession* [Germans, Slavs, Hungarians . . . of the Mosaic faith]" (Birnbaum, 1884:1). Whether this was a price worth paying for civil emancipation became an ever more hotly debated question as the nineteenth century was drawing to its close, in Vienna as much as everywhere else. Karl Kraus certainly thought so, and he reserved some of his special venom for Herzl and the Zionists who rejected Jewish assimilation into the mainstream of Habsburg society:

Herzl ist der Führer des Zionismus, und sein Schauspiel [Das neue Ghetto] ist, wenn es auch kein Wegweiser nach Palästina genannt werden kann, gewiß aus der Gefühlssphäre dieser Bewegung geboren. Die furchtlose Ehrlichkeit, die er von den Juden verlangt, daß sie Farbe bekennen, sie spricht laut und deutlich auch aus dem Neuen Ghetto. Hier predigt der fanatische Stolz des Antiassimilanten, die Juden bleiben unter Deutschen und Slaven ein fremdes Element, sozusagen ein Stück Fleisch im Holze der anderen Nationen. Aber neben den Zionisten, die mit schönem Eifer an einen historischen Irrtum so kostbares Gefühlsmaterial verschwenden, gibt es aber immer noch so verstockte Europäer unter den modernen Juden, die, weil ihnen aus den heute noch schlecht beleuchteten Niederungen des Wienertums zeitweise "Hinaus mit euch Juden!" zugerufen wird, durchaus nicht geneigt sind, entrüstet zu erwidern: "Jawohl, hinaus mit uns Juden!" Man denke nur, der Umstand, daß in Wien eine Partei von Dummköpfen ephemeren Terrorismus ausübt und daß noch nicht überall Verständnis für speziale Kämpfe anzutreffen ist, hat die meisten unter den Juden noch immer nicht veranlaßt, Sehnsucht nach dem Gelobten Lande zu empfinden, und es gibt solche, die geradeaus erklären, daß der Judenstaat auf der Basis der Anerkennung und der Bejahung des antisemitischen Vorurteils aufgebaut sei! (Karl Kraus, Wiener Brief, in Breslauer Zeitung, 16 January 1898, in Kraus, 1979:157)

Herzl is the leader of Zionism, and his drama was certainly conceived in the emotional world of this movement, even though in fairness it cannot truly be called a guide to Palestine. That fearless honesty which requires Jews to show their true colors speaks loudly and clearly in this *New Ghetto*. It is a sermon born of the fanatical pride of the anti-assimilationist; that Jews are and will remain an alien element among Germans and Slavs, a piece of meat among the wood of the other nations, so to speak. But side by side with the Zionists, who so diligently waste such precious feelings on a historical mistake, there are still obdurate Europeans among modern Jews, who have no inclination at all to answer the call of the most benighted echelons of the Viennese lower classes, "Away with the Jews," with their own indignant "Yes, away with us Jews." Just consider that even though in Vienna a party of blockheads practices some terrorism here and there and even though there is not always a general understanding of the social processes, all this has still not led Jews to develop a longing for the Promised Land, and there are even those who maintain without hesitation that the Jews' State has been built on the basic prejudice that antisemitism is somehow both proper and legitimate.

Not attempting to score a point or run a movement, but more interested in writing books, Arthur Schnitzler was more balanced in his views than either Herzl or Kraus. He devoted an entire novel, *Der Weg ins Freie* [The Road to Freedom] (1898), to the Jewish debate between the assimilationists and the Zionists. The assimilationist Jewish poet Heinrich explains:

> *Mein . . . Instinkt sagt mir untrüglich, daß hier, gerade hier meine Heimat ist und nicht in irgend einem Land, das ich nicht kenne, das mir nach den Schilderungen nicht in geringsten zusagt und das mir gewisse Leute jetzt als Vaterland einreden wollen, mit der Begründung, daß meine Urahnen vor einigen tausend Jahren gerade von dort aus in die Welt verstreut worden sind.*

My instinct tells me without fail that my home is here, right here, and not in some country or other that I am not familiar with, depicted in terms that do not appeal to me in the slightest and which certain people want to hold up to me as my fatherland, the reason being that a couple thousand years ago my forebears were dispersed around the world precisely from there.

His Zionist friend Leo, who also speaks of his experiences at the Basel Congress, answers in the following terms:

> *Ihr Blick in diesen Dingen ist doch ein wenig beschränkt. Sie denken immer an sich und an dem nebensächlichen Umstand... daß Sie ein Dichter sind, der zufällig, weil er in einem deutschen Land geboren, in deutscher Sprache und, weil er in Österreich lebt, über österreichische Menschen und Verhältnisse schreibt. Es handelt sich aber in erster Linie gar nicht um Sie*

und auch nicht um mich, auch nicht um die paar jüdischen Beamten, die
nicht avancieren, die paar jüdischen Freiwilligen, die nicht Offiziere
werden, die jüdischen Dozenten, die man nicht oder verspätet zu
Professoren macht, —das sind lauter Unannehmlichkeiten zweiten Ranges
sozusagen; es handelt sich hier um ganz andere Menschen, die Sie nicht
genau oder gar nicht kennen, und um Schicksale, über die Sie, ich
versichere Sie... trotz der Verpflichtung, die Sie eigentlich dazu hätten,
noch nicht gründlich genug nachgedacht haben. (Schnitzler, n.d.: 126–
127)

Yet your view of these matters is rather narrow. You are always
thinking of yourself, and of the secondary circumstance that you are
a poet who, because you happen to have been born in a German
country, writes in the German language, and who, because you have
been born in Austria, writes about Austrian people and conditions.
But in the first instance you and I are not all that important; neither
are the few Jewish officials who cannot get promotion, nor the Jewish
volunteers who don't become army officers, nor the Jewish tutors
whose promotion to professor is either delayed or does not happen at
all. All of those are unpleasant experiences but they are really of
secondary importance; the real issue concerns other people whom
you do not know very well, if at all, and destinies which, I assure you,
you have not thought through properly, despite the fact that you
really have an obligation to do so.

One way of making sense of this paradoxical situation of being
emancipated, yet at the same time having lost traditional Jewish
identity, was to take a symbolic view: to see the very condition of
emancipation as the fulfillment of the messianic promise. The
salvation of the Jews had taken effect through their emancipation,
the Messiah had arrived in the guise of civil emancipation. This was
expressed with great clarity by Vienna's chief rabbi Adolf Jellinek on
the occasion of the seventieth birthday of the same Josef Wertheimer
who had greeted Jewish emancipation in Austria so positively two
years earlier:

Als der Gefeierte die Schmach seiner Brüder in Österreich schilderte,
durfte er es nicht wagen seinen Namen zu nennen, und nun hat Gott eine
Zeit anbrechen lassen, in welcher die Schmach Ägyptens von den Juden in
Österreich abgewälzt wurde. Er schrieb für das Recht seiner Glaubens-
genossen, Grund und Boden auf heimatlicher Erde zu erwerben, und nun
ist er Zeuge, wie sie Häuser und Paläste bauen. Er kämpfte für das, was
im "halben Schekel" bildlich ausgedrückt ist, für gleiche Rechte und gleiche
Pflichten im Staate, und Gott ließ ihn mit eigenen Augen sehen, wie ein
Grundrecht für alle Söhne Österreichs Geltung hat. Kann es einen
schönern Beweis göttlicher Liebe und Treue geben als wenn die teuersten
Ideale unserer Jugend in unserem Alter verkörpert und verwirklicht
werden. (Jellinek, 1870:6–7)

When the man we honor here today was writing about the suffering
of his brothers in Austria, he could not even risk mentioning his
name, and now God has given us a new era, in which the suffering
of Egypt has been lifted from the Jews in Austria. He advocated the
right of his coreligionists to acquire land and estate on the soil of their
homeland, and now he is a witness how they build homes and
palaces. He fought for those things symbolized in the "half shekel":
equal rights and equal duties in the state; and God has allowed him
to see how one constitution now treats all Austria's sons equally. Is
there a more beautiful sign of God's love and troth than seeing the
ideals of our youth realized in our old age?

Not surprisingly, emancipated Jews who held the above beliefs
were likely to be disturbed when confronted with Jewish claims that
stressed Jewish uniqueness. They would regard such claims not
merely as antiquated ideas of a benighted bygone age, but rather as
as positively dangerous, calculated to stir latent forces of antisemitism in society if pursued with too much vigor. The Viennese Jewish
author George Clare recalls his father's fury when as a young boy he
inadvertently reminded his father of the latter's ghetto origins by
calling him *Tate* in public one day. By extension, he asks us to
understand the worries which Moritz Benedikt, owner of the *Neue*

Freie Presse, had with his *feuilletonist* Theodor Herzl, once Herzl went off on the Zionist track:

> Benedikt . . . could only see good [in Austria-Hungary]. Like many thousands of assimilated Jews, Benedikt shrank from the Jews of the eastern ghettos, so uncouth with their Yiddish language, their beards, side-curls and strange garments. The westernized Jews regarded their mere existence as a threat to their own status, and when reminded by the single word, *Tate*, that they belonged to the same people as those others, those primitives, they hit out, like Father, in despair. (Clare, 1982:88)

ZION, ASSIMILATION, AND HERZL

Herzl had a thorough knowledge of these arguments of the assimilated Jews and rejected them:

> *Ernster wäre der Einwand, daß ich den Antisemiten zur Hilfe komme, wenn ich uns ein Volk, e i n Volk nenne. Daß ich die Assimilierung der Juden, wo sie sich vollziehen will, hindere, und wo sie sich vollzogen hat, nachträglich gefährde, soweit ich als einsamer Schriftsteller überhaupt etwas zu hindern oder zu gefährden vermag.*
>
> *Dieser Einwand wird namentlich in Frankreich hervorkommen. Ich erwarte ihn auch an andern Orten, will aber nur den französischen Juden im voraus antworten, weil sie das stärkste Beispiel liefern.*

A more serious objection would be that by calling Jews a people, or rather *one* people, I am giving a boost to the antisemites; that I am hindering the assimilation of Jews where it is about to occur; or that I am endangering in retrospect the position of those Jews already assimilated—as if one solitary writer is in a position to seriously hinder or endanger anything at all.

This objection is likely to come in the first instance from France. I also expect it from other places, but I will answer the French Jews in anticipation, because they provide the most striking example.

His reasons for the rejection were twofold. First of all, he regarded assimilation as simply impossible, for mainstream society would simply not tolerate successfully emancipated Jews: no matter how well they tried, they would always be denied full equality of status. Indeed, as the tendency would be for emancipated Jews with their diligence and their intelligence to rise up the social ladder in the professions, general hatred against the Jews in society would merely increase. As Shlomo Avineri has pointed out, in Herzl's view emancipation did not alleviate antisemitism, it caused it (Avineri, 1981:93). Here are Herzl's words in *The Jews State*:

> *Ich sprach schon von unserer "Assimilierung". Ich sage keinen Augenblick, daß ich sie wünsche. Unsere Volkspersönlichkeit ist geschichtlich zu berühmt und trotz aller Erniedrigungen zu hoch, als daß ihr Untergang zu wünschen wäre. Aber vielleicht könnten wir überall in den uns umgebenden Völkern spurlos aufgehen, wenn man uns nur zwei Generationen hindurch in Ruhe ließe. Man wird uns nicht in Ruhe lassen. Nach kurzen Perioden der Duldsamkeit erwacht immer und immer wieder die Feindseligkeit gegen uns. Unser Wohlergehen scheint etwas Aufreizendes zu enthalten, weil die Welt seit vielen Jahrhunderten gewohnt war, in uns die Verächtlichsten unter den Armen zu sehen. Dabei bemerkt man aus Unwissenheit oder Engherzigkeit nicht, daß unser Wohlergehen uns als Juden schwächt und unsere Besonderheiten auslöscht. Nur der Druck preßt uns wieder an den alten Stamm, nur der Haß unserer Umgebung macht uns wieder zu Fremden.*

I have already mentioned our "assimilation." I do not say for a moment that I want it. Our national character is historically too famous and, despite all humiliation, too proud to wish for its demise. But perhaps we could merge without a trace into the peoples around us if we were left in peace for a couple of generations. They will not leave us in peace. After short spells of tolerance the hostility against us awakens anew. There seems to be something in our prosperity that irritates people, because the world has been accustomed to seeing us as the most despised among the poor. At the same time they do not notice, whether from ignorance or narrow-mindedness, that our prosperity weakens us as Jews and dissipates our character. Only pressure keeps us close to the old tribe, only the hatred that surrounds us turns us into strangers.

His second reason cut even deeper. It was that the price of assimilation was simply too high: Jews would have to give up their existence as Jews; Jews that were assimilated were simply not Jews any longer. He saw them all around him in France: "israelitische Franzosen" he called them, but not Jews. For people like that, the whole debate about a state for Jews was simply irrelevant, for they were no longer Jews. He expected no help from these assimilated Jews for his plans; worse still, as we have seen, he fully expected conspiracies by these wealthy assimilated Jews to torpedo his plans. Hence on both these two scores—the loss of Jewish identity and the paradox of emancipation—assimilation was impossible as a solution to the Jewish dilemma. Antisemitic outbursts in society simply could not be controlled or stopped.

So now we can assess how Herzl stands in the Jewish tradition as he knew it. The particularist tradition as represented in Vienna by the *Kadimah* was right insofar as it anticipated a separate Jewish existence and worked towards it, even though in Herzl's eyes it fell short of clearly spelling out the need for a Jewish polity. The assimilationist position, however, was to lead inevitably to loss of identity and persecution. Ever unsure of themselves, assimilated Jews became increasingly worried by expressions of Jewish particularism, which they saw as endangering their precious-won emancipated position. The German historian Zmarzlik was to write in 1970:

Ihre Haltung [blieb] von dem Bestreben bestimmt, provozierendes Auftreten zu vermeiden. Wieweit das faktisch geglückt ist, wird sich kaum ermitteln lassen. Doch ist eindeutig nachzuweisen, daß entschiedene Äußerungen jüdischen Erwähltheitsbewußtseins, die hin und wieder laut wurden, und die Belebung des jüdischen Selbstgefühls durch die zionistische Bewegung Theodor

Herzls von der ganz überwiegenden Mehrheit der Juden mit geradezu ängstlicher Sorge betrachtet und als unerwünschte Störung des Assimilationsprozesses zurückgewiesen wurden. (Zmarzlik, 1970:44)

Their attitude was determined by their aim to avoid provocative behavior. To what extent that aim was realized is difficult to assess today. But it can be clearly demonstrated that decisive expressions of Jewish uniqueness, which rose to the surface now and then, and the awakening of Jewish consciousness through the Zionist movement of Theodor Herzl were regarded by the vast majority of Jews with great anxiety, and were dismissed by them as undesirable disturbances of the assimilation process.

So the contribution the Jewish tradition made to Herzl's thought is in the form of a predicament: the settlement movement, on the one hand, did not go far enough in terms of his political ambitions, and was polluted by antisemitic Jews; and the emancipation movement, on the other hand, simply rested on a paradox that caused Jews to lose their very Jewish identity yet did not alleviate their suffering. The *Judenfrage*, however, was not only related to Jewish traditions. It also had to do with tendencies in mainstream German and European thought. Herzl knew he was not only a Jew: he was proud of his roots in the Austrian and European mainstream, and keen to be an actor in mainstream society. Indeed, without his consciousness of himself as an Austro-German, it is unlikely that he would have written *The Jews' State*. The next section examines the contribution of contemporary mainstream ideologies to Herzl's *Jews' State*.

The
European Context

Der Gedanke, den ich in dieser Schrift ausführe, ist ein uralter. Es ist die Herstellung des Judenstaates.
Die Welt widerhallt vom Geschrei gegen die Juden, und das weckt den eingeschlummerten Gedanken auf.

The concept with which I am dealing in this paper is very old. It is the establishment of the Jews' State.
The world resounds with clamor against Jews, and that arouses this concept out of its sleep.

Thus the first two sentences of *The Jews' State*. They are significant, both for what they say, and what they leave unsaid. Herzl here characterizes the work he is about to start—establishing a state for the Jews—as a *reaction*: a reaction against the tradition of antisemitism in Europe with which he had become very familiar over the years, both through his readings and his personal experiences. But in the Europe of his day, and more precisely in the Austria of his day, the personalities, motivations, aims and characteristics involved in antisemitic ideologies operated in fields that went beyond what the antisemitism he knew actually encompassed. In the German-speaking lands, the whole antisemitic movement was embedded in a vast and complex spectrum of late nineteenth-century cultural and political

41

ideologies: in nationalism, in the myth of the *Volk* and the equation of nation and *Volk*, in the ideology of race, in the quest for the survival of nations, in notions of national and racial adaptation to new realities. Herzl's roots in this intellectual and social climate go deeper than mere reaction: he was educated in it and worked within it. The claims he makes about the Jews as a *Volk*, about their right to nation and state, about the place of this nation among other nations, about the Jewish renaissance and regeneration which nationhood will bring forth: all these are embedded in his detailed knowledge of this political tradition, his willingness to work within its demands and structures, and his legitimation of its nature, even where he is reacting against certain specific tendencies. To state this is not to deny Herzl's place in and contribution to the Jewish tradition of Zion. It is merely to say that, within the context of his time, Herzl was both a good Zionist and a good European; indeed, he believed that his being a good Zionist was evidence of his being a good European. His Zionism, as Pauley has said, "was not simply a reaction to antisemitism but was also an integral part of the rise of nationalism in general that was occurring all over Europe" (Pauley, 1992:53–54). Neither Herzl nor his *Jews' State* can be fully understood without placing Herzl firmly and simultaneously within both the Jewish traditions and within the Zeitgeist of late nineteenth-century Europe; we need to put on our bifocals to do him full justice. This section will attempt to place him within this European tradition.

TRADITIONAL RELIGIOUS ANTI-JEWISH FEELING

The nature and context of anti-Jewish feelings—the "clamor against Jews"—and their development in the European and German tradition is a complex story, deeply embedded in the development of the discussion on *Volk*, nation, race, civilization and survival. Traditional European anti-Jewish feeling (antisemitism as a concept was not formulated until 1873 by the German political publicist Wilhelm Marr) had been around since the Middle Ages, but had not occurred in such an wide-ranging political context. In part it had economic roots, but more significantly it was based on Christian religious preoccupations with the myth of the blood libel (see Wistrich, 1995:13–43). It had led to much persecution of Jewish communities by Christian authorities. Founded on commonly held Christian theological positions concerning the Jewish connection with the death of Jesus and the attendant moral-religious guilt imputed to Jews, this type of anti-Jewish feeling made no statements about Jews as foreigners in terms of nationality, race or country. This religious anti-Jewish feeling ebbed and flowed in European consciousness certainly until the advent of the French Revolution, and although it lingered on as the 19th century ran its course, it was gradually subsumed under new secular ideologies that sprang up, only to surface on the odd occasion in the more scurrilous types of Christian religious argument, of which Desmond Stewart (1974:83) and Friedrich Heer (1981:232) cite contemporary examples published in the Catholic journal *La Civiltà Cattolica* in 1881–1882, or, more seriously, as a factor in the pogroms of late Czarist Russia (Kishinev 1903).

VOLK AND NATION

As outlined in the previous section, Jews remember the French Revolution as a catalyst for the civic emancipation of Jews that gradually took effect throughout the countries of Europe. For the Germans of Herzl's time, however, the French Revolution carried other, less favorable, associations—of social disturbance and political upheaval. The advent of Napoleon had brought a period of deep national humiliation to the German people and their lands, culminating in the military defeat the French emperor inflicted on Prussia and Austria in 1806. This defeat sparked off a period of national self-examination across the full spectrum of institutions in German society: what had caused it, what was still truly German, what was still to be valued in German society, what could be still salvaged from the ravages of defeat and humiliation, and how to go about constructing a solid foundation for national self-regeneration. A broad array of social actors at all levels of society became involved in an orgy of national self-examination: government officials, teachers, philosophers, poets, soldiers. They found an appropriate and consoling starting point in the work of Johann Gottfried Herder, who had shown the way in his celebration of the German *Volk*, in his attribution to the German *Volk* of virtues above those of other peoples, and in his insistence that the basis of a new German nation must be the *Volk*. Herder, it must be said, had been saying these things twenty years previously, and, still writing in the full spirit of the Enlightenment, had cautioned that no matter how wonderful the German *Volk*, there were other *Völker*, too. He had warned German scholars against getting carried away with narrow patriotic chauvinism (Herder, 1792; cited in Pross, 1963:86). However, those picking up these ideas after 1806, like the philosopher Johann Gottlieb Fichte, rather tended to made light of Herder's warning. In his *Reden an die Deutsche Nation* [Addresses to the German Nation] (1806) Fichte began telling his Berlin audiences that not only are the Germans a *Volk*, they are indeed the only *Volk*, and that the strength of the German nation that is about to be reborn will lie in the unique qualities of the Germans as *Volk*:

> *nur der Deutsche [hat] wahrhaft ein Volk und [ist] auf eins zu rechnen befugt und . . . nur [er] ist der eigentlichen und vernunftgemäßen Liebe zur seiner Nation fähig (8th Rede, in Fichte, 1846:377–378).*

> Only the German truly has a *Volk* and is entitled to one . . . Only he is capable of real and intelligent love for his *Nation*.

If the Germans were to regenerate themselves as a nation, they would first have to find what was best in their *Volk*, which, of course, begs the question of how to make sense of the concept *Volk* in the first place. It is indeed a difficult concept to come to grips with. In German the word encompasses a wide spectrum of meanings and emotional associations. The English denotation of the word is simply "people," but this rendering is quite inadequate to convey the deep-seated emotional connotations which the word *Volk* carries in German. The German etymologist Friedrich Kluge offers this explanation:

> The change of meaning of the word *Volk* is intimately linked with our [German] political and social development. Its emotional character is dependent on the attitude and mood of its user. The spiritual change of our people at the end of the 18th century was decisive for the meaning of *Volk*, as it taught the people to see in the *Volk* the origin of the noblest spiritual possessions and moral principles; through this the word attained a new dignity, which was strengthened around 1800 through the struggle for liberty and unity, thereby pushing back the foreign word *Nation*. (Kluge cited in Samuel, 1963:143)

As distinct from the man-made, "mechanical" concept of "state," the *Volk* is a unique natural entity, with both biological and spiritual dimensions, growing organically and morally, harboring within it the deepest qualities, longings, and ambitions of a population; it is the repository of the profoundest insights into the nature of life, morality and society; it links the individual with the divine, and is palpable evidence of God working in man. To quote Fichte again:

> *Dies nun ist in höherer, vom Standpunkte der Ansicht einer geistigen Welt überhaupt genommener Bedeutung des Wortes, ein Volk: das Ganze der in Gesellschaft miteinander fortlebenden und sich aus sich selbst immerfort natürlich und geistig erzeugenden Menschen, das insgesamt unter einem gewissen besonderen Gesetze der Entwicklung des Göttlichen aus ihm steht. (Fichte, 1846:381)*

This, then, is the meaning of the word, seen from the more elevated standpoint of a spiritual perspective: a *Volk* as the totality of man living together in society and constantly developing himself naturally and spiritually, wholly subject to a special law through which the Divine develops within him.

The trouble with the contemporary situation, as the experiences of 1806 had shown, was that the Germans as a *Volk* had allowed themselves to become degraded by foreign French influences. Hence the task for the Germans as a *Volk* after 1806 was to rid themselves of these foreign influences, to reconstitute themselves as a *Volk*, to return to their own unique, genuine *Volkserlebnis* [experience of itself as a people]. The *Volk* came to be celebrated as the true foundation of a reborn national life. Friedrich Jahn, a physical education coach, wrote a famous book on *Deutsches Volkstum* [German peoplehood] (1810); the educator Arndt was to say in 1849 that even after the failed 1848 revolution the Germans were "the premier, the greatest *Volk* in world history" (Samuel, 1963:143). The victories over Napoleon in 1813–1815 seemed to confirm the rightness of this chosen path of national regeneration; these victories were ascribed not so much to the military superiority of Napoleon's adversaries, but to the moral and spiritual strength of the German *Volk*, which had overcome the wicked French: *deutsche Treue* against *welsche Tücke*—German troth against French malice. Once on its way, this *Volk* stream of thought grew into a veritable national teutomania, fed by statesmen, thinkers, poets, teachers, the armies. Romantic notions then coming into vogue in literature, music, and art contributed to this growth by linking the regeneration of the *Volk* with a return to the land, to the simple life, to the natural rather than the man-made, to the pious rather than the questing, to the traditional rather than the technological, to *Kultur* rather than *Zivilisation*. They spoke in terms of *Volkslied*, *volkstümlich*, *Volkheit*, *völkisch*, which everyone could identify with, and these concepts came to be endlessly recycled in every possible permutation and combination. As a consequence, the whole spectrum of meanings and associations around *Volk* became part and parcel of social, political, academic and artistic discourse in the German-speaking lands, and its influence remained decisive in Germany certainly until 1945. To be sure, other nations in the nineteenth-century fêted their own people and mission, with their *jingoism*, "white man's burden," or *mission civilisatrice;* what was characteristically German was the peculiar intensity of this teutomania, as well as its persistence well into the present century. *Deutschland über alles*, sang the poet Hoffmann von Fallersleben in 1841; *Am deutschen Wesen wird die Welt genesen* [The German spirit will heal the world] bellowed Kaiser Wilhelm II again and again, misquoting a rather more discreet Emanuel Geibel (*Es mag am deutschen Wesen einmal noch die Welt genesen* [Some time in the future the German spirit may yet heal the world] (*Heroldsrufe*, 1871). Such was the mood that came to prevail.

The *Volk* was not seen simply as the sum of all persons resident within a geopolitical area. From very early times *Volk* became associated with notions of inclusion and exclusion: it was a *selection* from the people living in a country, not the *aggregate*, and it implied the existence of a *Staatsvolk* coexisting more or less uncomfortably with proscribed minorities. Certainly such notions were to gain much currency in Herzl's time in the ethnically polygot regions of the Habsburg Empire. But even as early as 1810 the poets Achim von Arnim, Heinrich von Kleist and Adam Müller, members of the *Christlich-deutsche Tischgesellschaft* [Christian-German Round Table Society] in Berlin were already talking about excluding the Jews from the newly discovered German *Volk* (Pross, 1963:80): the Germans were a Christian *Volk* and "Judaism was not only a lesser revelation than Christianity, but Jews could never share the nation's history, its myths and symbols" (Moss, 1980:73). Ludwig Börne disagreed: he put the view that *all* citizens of Germany have the right to belong to the *Volk* and the nation, and that included the Jews (Börne, 1832 in Pross, 1963:110–112). Heinrich Heine, one of Herzl's literary heroes (Stewart, 1974:43–44), took to exploring the way the German *Volk* might one day exclude all foreigners in the most brutal terms. Seeing deeper than most, he wrote about his "somber vision" (Samuel,

1963:143) of this German *Volk*, this newly strong but still sleeping giant, running berserk one day *(Berserkerwut)* and making the world sit up and take notice (Heine, 1834, *Zur Geschichte der Religion und Philosophie in Deutschland* [The History of Religion and Philosophy in Germany] in Heine/Elster, 1834:IV.294). People like Heine and Börne illustrate that right from the start the ideology of the *Volk* was not without its critics. Yet overwhelmingly we see here the beginning of the German tradition of equating nation and *Volk*, of the *Volk* as a selection of a population, and the attendant German feelings of national superiority and the strength of the *Volk*, directed in the first instance against the French, removed as yet from later racist connotations. It was a tradition with which Herzl was to be very familiar, and which both repelled and attracted him.

The Jew as the Archetypal Non-German

In the generation after Fichte a number of ideologues busily developed these notions (Wistrich, 1995), among them Richard Wagner. Apart from being a composer, Wagner was also a writer and publicist of some note. Having spent a number of unhappy years in Paris in poverty in the 1840s, he took to writing about the inferiority of things French in comparison to things German. In Wagner's case, as was to be expected, the discussion centered around music and art. Whereas he granted the French excellence at *executing* artistic forms such as music, it was the Germans who in addition were truly blessed with the creative genius of *making* new works of art, a level of artistic endeavor which the French lacked. As to the reasons for this inferiority, Wagner argued, it was because the French had allowed Jewish elements to pollute their cultural heritage:

> *Ich hegte einen langverhaltenen Groll gegen diese Judenwirtschaft, und dieser Groll ist meiner Natur so notwendig, wie Galle dem Blute. (Wagner to Liszt, 18 April 1851 in Wagner, n.d., Anmerkungen, 66)*

I carried a hatred against this Jewish business which I have long suppressed, and this hatred is as necessary to me as gall is to blood.

Wagner thought he had some personal experience of this pernicious mixture of Jewish and French influence, as he had been sponsored by Giacomo Meyerbeer (who happened to be Jewish) while in Paris (Wagner to Liszt, 18 April 1851 in Wagner, n.d., Anmerkungen, 66). He wrote:

Der Jude spricht die Sprache der Nation, unter der er von Geschlecht zu Geschlecht lebt, aber er spricht sie immer als Ausländer . . . Eine Sprache . . . ist nicht das Werk einzelner, sondern einer geschichtlichen Gemeinschaft: nur wer unbewußt in dieser Gemeinschaft aufgewachsen ist, nimmt auch an ihren Schöpfungen teil. Der Jude stand aber außerhalb einer solchen Gemeinschaft . . . In dieser Sprache, dieser Kunst kann der Jude nur nachsprechen, nachkünsteln—nicht wirklich redend dichten oder Kunstwerke schaffen. (Wagner, n.d.: IV.71)

The Jew speaks the language of the particular nation in which he lives from generation to generation, but he only speaks it as a foreigner does . . . A language is not the creation of single individuals, but of a historical community; only those who have unselfconsciously grown up in this community, partake of its creations. The Jew, however, stood outside such a community . . . In this language, in this art the Jew can only imitate, he cannot write poetry truly from the heart or create works of art.

Germans had better be careful to avoid going the way of the French lest their own forms of cultural expression suffer this same *Untergang* [demise] (Wagner, n.d., X:44), for as much as the Jew is a pollutor he is a *Herrscher*, a ruler (Wagner, n.d., IV:68). Much of this sort of argument he published, albeit anonymously, in *Das Judentum in der Musik* [Judaism in Music] which had appeared in 1850. Wagner was certainly not the only German intellectual of his generation to play with the idea of the Jew as the agent of cultural pollution and

domination: much the same points had already been made by Bruno
Bauer as early as 1843 in his pamphlet *Die Judenfrage* (for a
discussion see Wistrich, 1995:49ff), and were to be canvassed a little
later even by Karl Marx (Wistrich, 1995:51–53). But unlike Bauer
and Marx, Wagner thought himself to be a creative artist, and the
origins of artistic creativity in the *Volk* were important to him. The
ideas stayed with him for the rest of his life, and by 1869, backed up
by the writings of the likes of Gobineau which had gained ground in
Germany, he published a second edition of *Judentum*, this time under
his own name. The Franco-Prussian War evoked a flood of writings
from him: "I consider the Jewish race the sworn enemy of man and
all that is noble in him. That we Germans in particular will be ruined
by them is beyond dispute . . . I prefer the worst German book to
the best French" (cited in Bracher, 1971:48). He went on to call the
destruction of Paris a symbolic act of deliverance of the world from
evil (Bracher, 1971:48), and warned against grafting a "French-
Jewish democracy" on the newly formed German Empire (Wagner,
n.d.: X.50). What is important about Wagner is that he posits a
causal link between the alleged inferiority of a civilization and its
Jewish connections. This link was not lost on the next generation of
German writers, but with them there came a shift of emphasis: in
their writing, the French connection grew weaker as the Jewish
connection grew stronger in importance. It should be understood
that Wagner, at this stage at least, was still making political and
cultural rather than biological and racial statements (Wagner, n.d.,
IV:66): it is well-known that he characteristically used Jewish
musicians, like the conductor Hermann Levi, in important perfor-
mances of his own works. Even so, Wagner not only maintained the
myth of German national cultural superiority over all comers, but
introduced the new notion of the Jew as a cultural corruptor to
civilization. He and his generation therefore count as an important
bridge between three strands in a tradition which was gradually
taking shape: a claim of German national-cultural superiority,

traditional moral-theological Christian anti-Jewish feeling, and a form of cultural antisemitism.

RACE AS A SOCIO-POLITICAL FACTOR

It was the French Germanophile Arthur de Gobineau who added the concept of race to this potent mix. While working as a French diplomat in Germany from 1853 until 1855, Gobineau wrote his *Essai sur l'inégalité des races humaines* [Essay on the inequality of the human races]. Based on his genealogical research, Gobineau saw all history as dominated by the issue of ethnicity (Gobineau, 1855:I.vi). He maintained that not all ethnic groups were of equal strength and value: there were inferior and superior ethnic groups in his opinion. The most noble of all ethnic groups in history were the Aryans, who were superior in mind and body to all other human groups:

> *Pour la conformation physique, il n'y a pas de doute: c'était la plus belle dont on ait jamais entendu parler. La noblesse de ses traits, la vigueur et la majesté de sa stature élancée, sa force musculaire, nous sont attestées par des témoignages . . . Parmi les couleurs des cheveux et de la barbe, le blond dominait . . . Cette variété humaine, ainsi entourée d'une suprême beauté de corps, n'était pas moins supérieure d'esprit. Elle avait à dépenser une somme inépuisable de vivacité et d'énergie . . . la grandeur intellectuelle de l'espèce. (Gobineau, 1855:I.373–375, II.563)*

With respect to physical build, there is no doubt: it is the most handsome that has ever been reported. The nobility of his bearing, the vigour and majesty of his erect stature, his muscular power, have been attested to by witnesses . . . Among the colours of the hair and beard, blond was predominant . . . This human species, thus surrounded with a supreme beauty of the body, was as superior in spirit. It had an inexhaustible liveliness and energy to contribute . . . to the intellectual grandeur of the species.

The Aryans lived in prehistoric times; their modern heirs are the Germanic tribes (Gobineau, 1855:II.361). It is true that some of the old Aryan gloss has gone from the Germans because they have not kept so well to themselves as the Aryans did, but there is a sufficient residue of the old Aryan qualities left in the Germans of today to make them something special (Gobineau, 1855:II.558). Yet, the warning signals are there: In post-Enlightenment times, since what Gobineau considered the depraved notion of the equality of all human races gained ground, this Aryan superiority of the present Germans was becoming endangered (cf Samuel, 1963:148–150). Gobineau ends his book on a pessimistic note: The march of German decay cannot be stopped; however, the issue is to try and not arrive at the final end in a degraded state (Gobineau, 1855:II.563–564). Gobineau was not well received in France at the time, but in Germany, his ideas spread like wildfire. They helped to locate the reasons for national and ethnic superiority away from the religious, moral, and cultural, and, instead, toward the racial and biological, although it must be said that there was no hint of antisemitism in Gobineau. But, as Schenk (1966:222) has pointed out: "Once Gobineau's assumption was accepted that intermarriage has led to nobler races being tainted by the ignoble, the age-old anti-Jewish bias, which had grown stronger since the emancipation of the Jews, could be transferred to a racial footing." Gobineau and Wagner became friends in 1876, and by 1880, Wagner's cultural nationalism had turned to an ideology of racial superiority of the Germans and hatred of the Jews: If only Germans could rid themselves of the Jews, they might yet hope to become a pure race. By this time, such notions had ceased to cause much of a stir in the German-speaking world: Wagner was only one of a legion of German intellectuals, politicians, and publicists that ran with these ideas in the last third of the nineteenth century. Wilhelm Marr, for instance, in 1873, in his *Der Sieg des Judentums über das Germanentum* [The victory of Judaism over Germanhood], picked up Gobineau's themes, but for good measure added the theme of a national Jewish conspiracy, which had already turned the German world into a "new Palestine" (Marr, 1879:12). In Marr's view this Jewish conspiracy needed to be combatted in the political arena; and for this purpose he specifically founded an *Antisemiten-Liga* [League of Antisemites] (Philippson, 1910:II.11). If this antisemitism were to fail as a political movement in Germany, Marr predicted, Germany and the Germans would face a bleak future of servitude and despair (Marr, 1879:30). Journalists in the popular press, such as Otto Glagau in *Die Gartenlaube* [The Bower] (1876; see Pross, 1960:253) and in Christian newspapers (*Germania*, 10 September 1879—see Stewart, 1974:81), picked up these ideas and gave them a wide circulation among the middle classes in the German-speaking lands. Through the popularity of Gobineau's ideas in Germany, nationalism, xenophobia, and anti-semitism were put on a foundation of racism and racial inequality.

SURVIVAL OF THE FITTEST

The final element in this ideological tradition was added by the popularity of Social Darwinism. Social Darwinism refers to a set of theories about the relationship between societies on the one hand, and between groups within a society on the other. These theories claimed to be based on theories Charles Darwin had suggested in *The Origin of Species* (1859). Darwin's theory in *The Origin of Species* rested on four basic propositions: "new species appear; these new species have evolved from older species; the evolution of species is the result of natural selection; and natural selection depends upon variations and the maintenance of variation in spite of the tendency of natural selection to eliminate 'unfit' variants" (Sills, 1972:XIII.403). But whereas Darwin had been careful to limit the application of his theories to biological phenomena, others, like Herbert Spencer, went further and suggested that these propositions were equally appropriate for the study of history, society and culture.

These social scientists considered society to be a large biological organism, built up from many subsidiary organs and cells dependent on each other, and subject to Darwin's four laws of evolution and natural selection. Historical development, the fates of peoples, nations and cultures, so the argument ran, were subject to the very biological laws Darwin had formulated; that is to say, nations were in a constant fight with one another for survival, only the fittest would survive, fitness was a condition of the racial purity of the *Volk* of the nation, harmful elements must be eliminated, and the eventual triumph of one nation over another would be determined by the quality and progress of the race. Indeed, the famous phrase "the survival of the fittest" is not Darwin's at all, but Herbert Spencer's (Spencer, 1876–1896 in Carneiro, 1974:78).

These theories had currency all over Europe, but they became particularly popular among academics in the German-speaking lands. The historian Karl Dietrich Bracher has written about the impact of Social Darwinism in Germany and Austria in the following terms:

> The underlying idea was that, in the course of a ruthless competition and battle, a "natural" selection takes place which prevents or offsets aberrations and makes for a proper balance between population and available resources. In society, education and penal law serve as the instruments of this process of selection; according to the immutable laws of heredity, the unfit cannot be educated and therefore must be eliminated. (Bracher, 1971:28)

It took well into the 1890s for sociologists like Emile Durkheim to start pointing out the logical fallacy inherent in tackling social sciences by analogy with the biological sciences (Sills, 1972:XIII.404). But in the meantime Darwinian vocabulary permeated the greater part of public discussion not only in biology, but also in politics and the social sciences during the last third of the nineteenth century; it was, in the suggestive term of one recent historian, *Epochenvokabular* [the vocabulary of the times] (Wagner, 1987:165). And "the popularity of Darwinism, in both its biological and social manifestations, stressing the 'struggle for survival' and the 'survival of the fittest,' did not leave the Dual Monarchy unaffected" either (Pauley, 1992:27). It was employed by Jewish as well as mainstream intellectuals. The major work by the Viennese sociologist Ludwig Gumplowicz, *Grundriß der Soziologie* [Introduction to Sociology], which was published in 1875, is full of it. Max Nordau's entire argument on the degeneration of modern culture, as he saw it, rested on notions of the racial degeneration of contemporary bearers of culture (Nordau, *Entartung* [Degeneration], 1892). He also questioned whether the Jewish people were "anthropologically fit for nationhood" (19 November 1895; BT2:280, P1:276), and he was to open the First Zionist Congress with a speech which contained the following extract:

> *Die Mikrobiologie lehrt uns, daß kleine Lebewesen, die harmlos sind, so lange sie in der freien Luft leben, zu furchtbaren Krankheiterregern werden, wenn man ihnen den Sauerstoff entzieht, wenn man sie . . . in anaerobische Wesen verwandelt. Die Regierungen und Völker sollten Bedenken tragen, aus dem Juden ein anaerobisches Wesen zu machen. Sie könnten es schwer mitzubüßen haben . . . um den durch ihre Schuld zum Schädling gewordenen Juden auszurotten. (Barissia, 1911:32)*

> Microbiology teaches us that there are tiny organisms which are perfectly harmless as long as they live in the open air, but which can cause frightful diseases when deprived of oxygen and changed into anaerobic organisms. Let governments and nations take care lest they turn Jews into anaerobic organisms. Their neglect may well put them in the unpleasant position of having to eradicate the Jews who have become a source of harm.

Herzl knew the arguments quite well, and was so impressed by them that he proposed to send a copy of *The Jews' State* to Herbert Spencer for his comments (21 March 1897; BT2:492, P2:527). Equally, a little later he sought out Ludwig Gumplowicz's views about his concept of the *negotiorum gestio* (Zohn, 1987:103). In his diary, Herzl played with the concept of the development of the Jewish people in terms of Darwinian adaptation and survival as follows:

> *Der Antisemitismus, der in der großen Menge etwas Starkes und Unbewußtes ist, wird aber den Juden nicht schaden. Ich halte ihn für eine dem Judencharakter nützliche Bewegung. Er ist die Erziehung einer Gruppe durch die Massen und wird vielleicht zu ihrer Aufsaugung führen. Erzogen wird man nur durch Härten. Es wird die Darwinsche Mimikry eintreten. Die Juden werden sich anpassen. Sie sind wie Seehunde, die der Weltzufall ins Wasser warf. Sie nehmen Gestalt und Eigenschaften von Fischen an, was sie doch nicht sind. Kommen sie nun wieder auf festes Land und dürfen da ein paar Generationen bleiben, so werden sie wieder aus ihren Flossen Füße machen.* (Whitsun 1895, BT2:49–50)

However, antisemitism, which is a strong and unconscious force among the masses, will not harm the Jews. I consider it to be a movement useful to the Jewish character. It represents the education of a group by the masses, and will perhaps lead to it being absorbed. Education is accomplished only through hard knocks. A Darwinian mimicry will set in. The Jews will adapt themselves. They are like the seals, which an act of nature cast into the water. These animals assume the appearance and habits of fish, which they certainly are not. Once they return to dry land again and are allowed to remain there for a few generations, they will turn their fins into feet again. (P1:10)

Striking about this passage is the way Herzl links concepts gleaned from the German racist antisemitic tradition with concepts from the world of Social Darwinism. He was not alone in doing this, and with the benefit of hindsight we now know the ominous consequences to which this contributed. It should however be remembered that, at the time of Herzl's public life, German anti-semitism did not yet show the traits of mass extermination, which were to be the ultimate focus of the great antisemite of the twentieth century. Yet apart from the nightmare of extermination (unforeseen by Herzl, but already darkly suspected by others, like Schnitzler and Freud), the circle of *Volk, Nation, Staat, Rasse* and Social Darwinism was now complete.

EUGEN DÜHRING COMBINES *VOLK, NATION, RASSE, JUDE,* AND SURVIVAL

This complex web of ideological definitions, about *Volk* and *Nation,* about culture and race, about the Jews, about pollution and degeneration, about survival of the fittest, was the subject of the work of Eugen Dühring, professor of philosophy and national economy at Berlin University until his demotion for unprofessional conduct in 1877. Dühring seems to have been one of those individuals who picked a fight with everyone: his university, Marxism, militarism, Bismarck's government, organized religion, and, last but not least, the Jews (*Neue Deutsche Biographie,* 1959:IV.157–158). In 1881, by then a private scholar, he had published his book *Die Judenfrage als Rassen-, Sitten- und Kulturfrage* [The issue of the Jews as an issue of race, mores and culture], which he was to revise and elaborate through four editions under different titles for the rest of his life (Dühring, 1930). The book would hardly have rated a mention here, had not Herzl himself told us that it was through Dühring's work that he became alerted and alarmed about the issue of the Jews in society:

> *Wann ich eigentlich anfing, mich mit der Judenfrage zu beschäftigen? Wahrscheinlich, seit sie aufkam. Sicher, seit ich Dührings Buch gelesen . . . das war, glaube ich, 1881 oder 1882. (Whitsun, 1895; BT2:44)*

When did I actually begin to concern myself with the Jewish Question? Probably ever since it arose; certainly from the time that I read Dühring's book . . . —it was, I believe in 1881 or 1882. (P1:4)

This is what Herzl would have read:

Der allgemeine Weg zu einer nicht halben, sondern ganzen Lösung der Judenfrage ist im vorigen Kapitel gekennzeichnet. Er ist es sowohl in dem, was sein muß, als in dem, was er nicht sein kann. Er kann kein bloß geistiges Prinzip und auch kein Prinzip der Judenbesserung sein. Er muß in Einschränkungen von Ausnahmenatur bestehen, die allein für die Angehörigen des Judenstammes gültig sind. Der banale und kurzsichtige Einwand der Toleranz hat sich auf diesem Wege übel angebracht erwiesen . . . Der letzte Erfolg systematischer Einschränkungsmaßregeln muß notwendig das Zusammenschrumpfen des Judenwesens in Bevölkerungszahl und Reichtum so wie überhaupt in der Teilnahme an Staat und Gesellschaft sein. So viele bessere Nationalitäten haben bereits ihr Schicksal erfüllen müssen, und der übel beschaffene Judenstamm wird ihm nicht entgehen. Er wird aufhören etwas zu sein, sobald die andern Völker dahin gelangt sind, die Plätze in den eigenen Behausungen selber auszunützen und den Juden dort keine Geschäftsbesorgung mehr zu überlassen. Dies wird dann die innere Freiheit der modernen Nationen von der Untermischung mit einer für diese Völker unleidlichen und verderblichen Rasse sein . . . Es wird harte und zähe Arbeit kosten, dem Judenstamm mit seiner aalartigen Schlüpfrigkeit alle Winkel und alle Schleichwege zu verlegen, die er bei den neuen Völkern zu seiner Geltendmachung zu hegen pflegt und auch künftig gegen die verschiedensten Maßegeln ausfindig machen dürfte. Von geringeren Einleitungsmaßregeln wird man zu kräftigeren Mitteln fortzuschreiten haben. Man wird sich erinnern müssen, daß die Juden den Kampf um ihre Ausbreitung und um die zugehörige Vernichtung und Einengung von Elementen der bessern Nationalitäten mit bekannter Skrupellosigkeit und mit allen Mitteln führen, die der schlechten sittlichen Beschaffenheit ihres Stammes entsprechen . . . Es würde also alle Humanität misverstehen heißen, wenn man hier auch nur einen Augenblick Anstand nehmen und sich scheuen wollte, den Kampf gegen die Juden nicht ernsthaft auf eine dauernde Unschädlichmachung einzurichten.

Verjudung der Völker und aller Verhältnisse ist die Tatsache; Entjudung die Aufgabe. Mit einem Male läßt sich diese Aufgabe in ihrem ganzen Umfange nicht lösen; sie muß aber in allen Richtungen sofort in Angriff genommen werden. Die drei hauptsächlichsten Arbeitsgebiete, in denen vorzugehen ist, sind, wie bereits dargetan, das politische, das wirtschaftliche und das gesellschaftliche. (Eugen Dühring, 1886, Die Judenfrage als Frage der Rassenschädlichkeit [The issue of the Jews as an issue of racial harm]. p. 119–120, reprinted in Pross, 1960:257–258)

The aim of the previous chapter has been to present ways toward a complete, rather than a mere partial solution of the issue of the Jews, both from the point of view of what needs to happen as well as what cannot be. It cannot merely be an intellectual principle, nor a principle about the improvement of Jews. It must consist of restrictions of an exceptional nature, which only apply to the members of the Jewish tribe. In this context it is misleading to apply the banal and shortsighted objection of tolerance. . . . The ultimate success of systematic measures of limitation must needs be the contraction of Jewry in terms of its share of the number and wealth of the population, as well as in terms of its participation in state and society. So many superior national groups have already had to meet their destiny, and the evilly-disposed Jewish tribe will not be able to escape its own. It will cease to be of importance, as soon as the other peoples have reached the stage of being able to utilize their own institutions for themselves and not allow any more resources to reach the Jews. This will then lead the modern nations to be free from having to mix with a race so intolerable and decadent to them . . . Given the eel-like slipperyness of the Jewish tribe, it will involve a hard and tough struggle to deprive it of all its hiding places and secret alley-ways, which it tends to cultivate among the newer peoples so as to strengthen its position, and which, moreover, it will use in the future to ward off all manner of measures against it. Smaller, more limited measures taken initially will have to be followed by more forceful means. It will need to be borne in mind that the Jews wage the struggle for their own expansion and for the attendant destruction and limitation of elements in the better nationalities with their well-known lack of scruples and with all the means which are to be expected from the bad moral condition of their tribe. . . . It would be a complete misunderstanding of all humanist philosophy, if even for a moment one objected or shied away from waging the struggle against the Jews seriously and with the full purpose of rendering them harmless forever.

Jewification of all peoples and their conditions—that is the reality; de-Jewification—that is the objective. One single effort will not accomplish this task in all its vastness; it must be tackled immediately from all directions. The three main areas of operation which need to be considered are, as already mentioned: politics, economics and society.

It is evident that in Dühring there is nothing left of the original anti-French bias we noted with writers earlier in the century; the change has been dramatic. The French connection has been dropped, and the Jewish connection has taken over. The ideologies of *Volk* and *Nation*; of race and survival are here integrated into a unified political theory and a call to action. Theological, cultural, national and biological considerations all form part of this theory. It stigmatizes Jews as a degraded race, outside the pale of common humanity, and claims this as the source of what it sees as the pollutive nature of Jewish influence on social life. It identifies the future tasks of the Germans in ridding themselves of this blight on their existence, and recommends measures, even quite forceful ones, against the Jews "from all directions" at the same time. It views these tasks as a challenge in Darwinian terms which the Germans have to take up: just as other peoples have quite properly gone under in the struggle for existence, so it is important that this happens to the Jews as well. It dismisses educative measures to eradicate the impact of ethnic prejudice in the mainstream populations as inappropriate and misplaced, a theme Herzl was to deal with in his *Jews' State*.

The particular harm done by books like Dühring's lies in the fact that they are not merely antisemitic diatribes; rather they deal with antisemitism in a broad context of nationalism, Social Darwinism and racism; in other words, they place it as an integrated component within the common stock of public knowledge at the time. The integrated nature of this literature served to lend it both apparent academic standing and social respectability, both of which even Herzl accords to it. The passage from Dühring, then, is a brilliant illustration of how second and third rate intellectuals in Germany at the time synthesized these notions and popularized them. These ideas are a far cry from the sorts of positions that Herder and even Fichte had put before a defeated German nation less than a century previously. There is no trace left of the Enlightenment tradition of pluralism and tolerance, and the idea of a common humanity is derided as a ridiculous delusion. It was in the form of Dühring that this tradition first impacted on Herzl, and, at one level, *The Jews' State* represents his coming to terms with it.

HERZL AND THIS TRADITION

Herzl's attitude to this tradition is, however, quite complex and not merely reactive. There are four aspects to Herzl's attitude.

Firstly, Herzl sees the issue of the formation of a state for Jews in terms of *Volk, Nation* and *Staat*, precisely the ideological triad that had been developing in German political thinking since Fichte. This view is central to Herzl's development, for once this conception of the Jews as a *Volk* had taken hold of him, it immediately invalidated for him other paradigms of the Jewish existential situation which were part and parcel of Jewish thinking at the time. Conceptions of assimilation, orthodoxy, and reform simply lose their relevance for him (Bunzl, 1994:133). Considerations of philanthropy also do not fit into this conception of the Jewish *Volk*. You cannot deal with a whole people on the basis of charity; people-issues have to be dealt with on the basis of politics (Dethloff, 1986:37). Herzl's play with the concepts of *Volk, Nation* and *Staat* is a typical late-nineteenth-century European game, not a Jewish game, and it is no surprise that Jewish circles of his time picked this up and criticized him for it. His lead-up to the notion of a state for Jews merely confirms this European context. He toyed for quite a while with a Jewish polity under the protection of one of the great European powers (Germany) in the form of a protectorate, an idea he came to reject as his political ideas matured and as he gained experience in dealing with the European powers. When he finally committed himself to the idea of a state for the Jews, his conception of the process of state-formation reads like pure Fichte: the initial regeneration of the Jews as a Volk to be followed by the organization of this regenerated Jewish people into a Nation able to express a political will. The governmental form this nation would ultimately take would result in its *Staat*. Furthermore, what Herzl tells us about his state is not based on Jewish sources, but on classical and European conceptions: Roman law in the case of the *negotiorum gestio*, Montesquieu and the Enlightenment in the case of the aristocratic republic, Cecil Rhodes in the case of the Jewish Company. It is characteristic for Herzl's place in the nationalist tradition, as John Bunzl has pointed out (Bunzl, 1994:133), that he spends so much thought and time on the symbolic trappings and the theatrical ritual of nationality: the seven-star flag and the tail-coats for the First Zionist Congress (see also Beller, 1994:48–57).

Secondly, the basis of Herzl's claim to nationhood and statehood is the assertion that the Jews are a *Volk* (and not just a religious community), and that only in their acceptance of themselves as *Volk* will they find spiritual regeneration and strength. "*Wir sind ein Volk, ein Volk,*" he stresses. As a *Volk* the Jews have a number of defining characteristics, which are not necessarily the same as the characteristics of other peoples:

> So sind und bleiben wir denn, ob wir es wollen oder nicht, eine historische Gruppe von erkennbarer Zusammengehörigkeit . . . wir erkennen unsere historische Zusammengehörigkeit nur am Glauben unserer Väter, weil wir ja längst die Sprachen verschiedener Nationen unverlöschbar in uns

*aufgenommen haben . . . Wir sind ein Volk—der Feind macht uns ohne
unseren Willen dazu, wie das immer in der Geschichte war. In der
Bedrängnis stehen wir zusammen, und da entdecken wir plötzlich unsere
Kraft.*

So we are and will remain, whether we like it or not, an historical group
with recognizable features that stamp us as belonging together . . .
Only in the faith of our fathers can we recognize our common historical
heritage, for we have already indelibly absorbed the languages of various
nations long ago . . . We are a people—the enemy turns us into one
against our wishes—that has been the same throughout history. In
oppression we stand together, and then we suddenly discover our
power.

What defines Jews as a *Volk* is their common historical memory,
their common religion, their common experience. They do not have
a common language, often taken as a defining attribute of a *Volk*. Nor
do they need one, despite what Birnbaum might have advocated
(Birnbaum 1884:15). Nor does Herzl fall into the trap of using the
criterion of race to define the Jewish people: for him simple observation
is sufficient to demonstrate the irrelevance of race as a criterion for
Jewish peoplehood:

*[Zangwill] ist auch für unsere territoriale Selbstständigkeit. Er steht auf
dem Rassenstandpunkt, den ich schon nicht akzeptieren kann, wenn ich
ihn und mich ansehe. Ich meine nur: wir sind eine historische Einheit, eine
Nation mit anthropologischen Verschiedenheiten. Das genügt auch für den
Judenstaat. Keine Nation hat die Einheit der Rasse. (21 November 1895;
BT2:281)*

[Zangwill], too, is in favor of our territorial independence. However,
his point of view is a racial one—which I cannot accept if I so much
as look at him and at myself. All I am saying is: we are a historical
unit, a nation with anthropological diversities. This also suffices for
the Jews' State. No nation has uniformity of race. (P1:276)

Here Herzl and Birnbaum are of like mind: the Jewish people are not defined by race, but by historical, religious and eschatological considerations (Birnbaum, 1893:16).

Thirdly, Herzl maintains that antisemitism is a part of the German nationalist tradition that has to be faced, and nothing much is gained by outright condemnation of antisemites. In a conversation with Ludwig Speidel, the literary editor of the *Neue Freie Presse*, he had this to say about the Jews being foreign bodies within a national context:

> *Ich begreife den Antisemitismus. Wir Juden haben uns, wenn auch nicht durch unsere Schuld, als Fremdkörper inmitten verschiedener Nationen erhalten. Wir haben im Ghetto eine Anzahl gesellschaftswidriger Eigenschaften angenommen. Unser Charakter ist durch den Druck verdorben, und das muß durch einen anderen Druck wieder hergestellt werden. Tatsächlich ist der Antisemitismus die Folge der Judenemanzipation. (Whitsun, 1895; BT2:48)*

> I understand what antisemitism is about. We Jews have maintained ourselves, even if through no fault of our own, as a foreign body among the various nations. In the ghetto we have taken on a number of antisocial qualities. Our character has been corrupted by oppression, and it must be restored through some other kind of pressure. Actually, antisemitism is a consequence of the emancipation of the Jews. (P1:9)

There are certainly the ratbags among the antisemites, but there are also the *anständige* [respectable] ones. You have to pick the "respectable" ones to engage in debate, and *The Jews' State* is part of this debate. Herzl is generous but not alone in according legitimacy to the views of his antisemitic opponents; Birnbaum (1893:7) does much the same thing. This has been seen as a problematical feature of Herzl's ideology; Schnitzler, for example, as we shall see, has been far less generous in this respect and maintained that claiming to be respectable and antisemitic at the same time, as the Viennese mayor

Karl Lueger was to do, was evidence of a moral schizophrenia rather than a maturity of outlook.

Fourthly, in Herzl's view a measure of antisemitism is necessary and useful to his own objectives: it provides the evidence that assimilation of Jews into European society rests on a misreading of the situation, it furnishes the external pressure to keep the Jewish people together as a people, and it keeps attractive the possibility of emigration to a state of their own:

> *Ich sprach schon von unserer "Assimilierung." Ich sage keinen Augenblick, daß ich sie wünsche. Unsere Volkspersönlichkeit ist geschichtlich zu berühmt und trotz aller Erniedrigungen zu hoch, als daß ihr Untergang zu wünschen wäre. Aber vielleicht könnten wir überall in den uns umgebenden Völkern spurlos aufgehen, wenn man uns nur zwei Generationen hindurch in Ruhe ließe. Man wird uns nicht in Ruhe lassen. Nach kurzen Perioden der Duldsamkeit erwacht immer und immer wieder die Feindseligkeit gegen uns. Unser Wohlergehen scheint etwas Aufreizendes zu enthalten, weil die Welt seit vielen Jahrhunderten gewohnt war, in uns die Verächtlichsten unter den Armen zu sehen. Dabei bemerkt man aus Unwissenheit oder Engherzigkeit nicht, daß unser Wohlergehen uns als Juden schwächt und unsere Besonderheiten auslöscht. Nur der Druck preßt uns wieder an den alten Stamm, nur der Haß unserer Umgebung macht uns wieder zu Fremden.*

I have already mentioned our "assimilation." I do not say for a moment that I want it. Our national character is historically too famous and, despite all humiliation, too proud to wish for its demise. But perhaps we could merge without a trace into the peoples around us if we were left in peace for a couple of generations. They will not leave us in peace. After short spells of tolerance the hostility against us awakens anew. There seems to be something in our prosperity that irritates people, because the world has been accustomed to seeing us as the most despised among the poor. At the same time they do not notice, whether from ignorance or narrow-mindedness, that our prosperity weakens us as Jews and dissipates our character. Only

pressure keeps us close to the old tribe, only the hatred that
surrounds us turns us into strangers.

Passages like these in *The Jews' State* also place Herzl in the Social
Darwinist tradition discussed above. They present the hostility to
Jews in mainstream European societies as an occasion for the
struggle for survival of Jewish communities to take place and help
the communities hone their fitness for survival:

> *Wie sehr ich auch die Persönlichkeit verehre, . . . die Gesamtpersönli-*
> *chkeit einer historischen Gruppe von Menschen, die wir Volk nennen, wie*
> *sehr ich auch die Persönlichkeit verehre, beklage ich doch nicht ihren*
> *Untergang. Wer untergehen kann, will und muß, der soll untergehen. Die*
> *Volkspersönlichkeit der Juden kann, will und muß aber nicht untergehen.*
> *Sie kann nicht, weil äußere Feinde sie zusammenhalten. Sie will nicht, das*
> *hat sie in zwei Jahrtausenden unter ungeheuren Leiden bewiesen. Sie muß*
> *nicht, das versuche ich in dieser Schrift nach vielen anderen Juden, welche*
> *die Hoffnung nicht aufgaben, darzutun. Ganze Aöste des Judentums*
> *konnen absterben, abfallen; der Baum lebt.*

However much I venerate the individual, . . . the collective personality of a historical group of human beings which we call *Volk*, I still
do not mourn his destruction. Whoever can, wants to, must
perish—should perish. The collective personality of the Jews as a
people, however, cannot, will not and must not perish. It cannot
perish, because external enemies hold it together. It will not perish;
it has demonstrated that during two millennia under enormous
suffering. It must not perish; that is what I seek to demonstrate in this
publication after many other Jews who never gave up hope. Whole
branches of Jewry may well die away and fall off; the tree lives.

Herzl maintains, therefore, that a certain level of antisemitism is
salutary and necessary in order to make the Jewish communities
uncomfortable enough to emigrate and set up the new state. The
ideas of national superiority and inferiority finally provide him with

a useful tactical measure in his arguments for the support of European powers for his new state: it enables him to present the state of the Jews as a guarantee to Europe against the barbarism and primitivism of the Eastern peoples.

There is no doubt that Herzl is most shaken by the antisemitic tendencies inherent in the tradition, but he is ever at pains to make an effort to see them as an intellectual tradition, uncomfortable but legitimate, rather than as a threat to his or his people's very existence. He "shops around" within the tradition, and uses certain features for his own objectives: the tradition of *Volk* and the nation, the notions of national and personal regeneration, the notions of survival and going under. He is in every way the well-read, well-informed man of his time. But Herzl's struggles with this intellectual stream are not enough to mobilize him into action. This is where his personal experiences from daily life come in, which arouse his interest and anger, and with which he has to come to terms. To these we now turn.

HERZL'S IMMEDIATE SITUATION: THE VIENNA OF LUEGER AND SCHÖNERER

The experiential link that Herzl had with this tradition came through his life in Vienna in the early 1890s with the repeated mayoral campaigns of Karl Lueger and the political activities of Georg von Schönerer. Schönerer had appeared on the Viennese scene as a political agitator in the 1870s in the wake of Austria's defeat by the hands of the Prussians in 1866 and the economic troubles of the next few years. He united within himself a bundle of xenophobic attitudes. He was anti-Slav, seeing the Habsburg Empire as dominated by the non-German groups; he was anti-Catholic, postulating a political nexus between the Vatican and Vienna; and he was antisemitic above all else. He could not cope with the presence of a Jewish minority in Imperial Austria. He "believed that race should be the criterion for all civic rights" (Pauley, 1992:92), summing up his views in his famous dictum *Religion ist einerlei, in der Rasse liegt die Schweinerei* [Religion may be one thing, but race is obscene] (Zweig, 1948:97; also cited in Bracher 1971:64). He had had an early stint in the Austrian Parliament in the 1870s, then was a member again from 1897 until 1907, but his influence on political decision making was marginal. He was a prominent figure in Viennese society in the 1890s, but the extent of his influence on the attitude of the Viennese is difficult to measure (Hertzfeld, 1963:IV.90–91). He was all but forgotten by 1914, although Adolf Hitler later resuscitated his memory in *Mein Kampf*. He was an awful man, a rabble rouser of the streets, an "antisemitic psychopath" (Pawel, 1989:249). The Vienna Society to Combat Antisemitism thought of him in much the same terms as they did of Dühring (Verein, 1894:8); and Herzl deigns to mention him but once in his diaries (16 June 1897; BT2:524, P2:564). A more complicated figure was Karl Lueger. A member of the Vienna City Council since 1875, Lueger was twice elected to the post of Mayor of Vienna on a platform that included a large dose of antisemitism, but the Emperor each time refused to ratify his appointment, so that Lueger could only take the mayoral post after the Emperor relented in the wake of a third election in 1897. He then remained in office until his death in 1910. Whereas Schönerer's antisemitism was squarely based on racial prejudice, Lueger's was a more like a political expedient, a "technique rather than a principle" (Geehr, 1990:173): he indulged in it simply to get the common man to vote for him. Richard Geehr has observed that "considering the bulk of Lueger's surviving papers, antisemitic statements are relatively rare." But he cautions, "because much appears to have been lost, there is no way to determine how much of his writing was devoted to antisemitic topics" (Geehr, 1982:323), and a contemporary Viennese observer cited by Geehr concluded that Lueger's "antisemitism reached only as far as the Fichtegasse, the location of the editorial offices of the *Neue Freie Presse*" (Kielmansegg in Geehr, 1982:321). Joseph Bloch stressed the pragmatic quality of Lueger's antisemitism thus: "Dr Lueger was pious in the same sense as he was antisemitic; it was not of much account, but it was useful" (cited in Geehr, 1990:205). Arthur Schnitzler drew some ethical conclusions about Lueger from this pragmatism: while accepting that Lueger's antisemitism was little more than a political ploy, he pointed out the moral questionability of this person who on the one hand was not above using antisemitic positions in his campaigning, but who on the other hand was completely correct in his personal and official dealings with Jews:

> *Es gab und gibt Leute, die es [Lueger] als Vorzug anrechnen, daß er auch in seiner stärksten Antisemitenzeit persönlich für viele Juden eine gewisse Vorliebe beibehalten und daraus gar kein Hehl gemacht hatte: Mir galt gerade das immer als der stärkste Beweis seiner moralischen Fragwürdigkeit. Oder sind die sogenannten reinlichen Scheidungen zwischen den Forderungen der politischen Parteistellung einerseits und den privat menschlichen Überzeugungen, Erfahrungen und Sympathien auf der anderen Seite wirklich etwas so reinliches, als mit dieser Bezeichnung ausgesagt wird? (Schnitzler, 1968:145–146)*

There used to be, and there still are, people who regard it in a positive light that Lueger, even in his strongest antisemitic period, retained a certain personal preference for many Jews, and never hid this fact. I, however, counted this always as the strongest evidence of his moral questionability. I wonder whether these so-called clear-cut separations between party-political demands on the one hand, and private convictions, experiences, and sympathies on the other hand, are really so clear-cut as is implicit in this view.

Even so, both the contemporary Jewish scholar Josef Redlich and the president of the *Israelitische Kultusgemeine* [Israelite Religious Community] in Vienna at the time wrote glowing obituaries when Lueger died in 1910 (Leser, 1987:51). And Stefan Zweig later characterized Lueger's administration as follows:

*Als seine [Luegers] Bewegung schließlich den Wiener Gemeinderat eroberte
und er—nach zweimaliger Verweigerung der Sanktionierung durch den
Kaiser Franz Joseph, der die antisemitische Tendenz verabscheute—zum
Bürgermeister ernannt wurde, blieb seine Stadtverwaltung tadellos gerecht
und sogar vorbildlich demokratisch; die Juden, die vor diesem Triumph der
antisemitischen Partei gezittert hatten, lebten ebenso gleichberechtigt und
angesehen weiter. Noch war das Haßgift und der Wille zu gegenseitiger
restloser Vernichtung nicht in den Blutkreislauf der Zeit gedrungen. (Zweig,
1948:96–97)*

When at last Lueger's movement conquered the Vienna Municipal
Council, and he was appointed mayor—after being twice knocked
back by the emperor Franz Joseph, who abhorred his antisemitism—
his administration remained utterly correct and even exemplarily
democratic. The Jews, who had lived in fear and trembling of this
triumph of the antisemitic party, continued to live with equal rights
and full honor. The poison of hatred and the will to mutual final
destruction had not yet forced their way into the blood-circulation of
the times.

On the other hand, Hitler was later to praise him extensively in *Mein
Kampf*.

It remains difficult today, in the light of what we now know
happened afterwards, to get a picture of the nature of the antisemitism which stung Herzl into action, which does justice both to
its exact extent and to its awful potential. Marrus reminds us that
"everywhere in pre-Hitler Europe we find spokesmen for the
anti-Jewish obsession, spinning their theories into long, angry books
about the Jewish onslaught on Western civilization," but goes on to
say that "long, angry books" still do not constitute political action or
extermination: indeed these "ideological antisemites were usually
impoverished when it came to practical suggestions" (Marrus,
1982:42). Political leaders at the highest level in the German-
speaking world, like Franz Joseph in Austria and Bismarck in
Germany, stayed clear of any antisemitic political action (Herlitz and

Kirschner, 1927–1930:I.1063–1064). Both Jewish and non-Jewish historians have pointed out that political representation by antisemites in the German and Austrian parliaments was minimal (Bracher, 1971:63, 65; Samuel, 1963:151) and dwindling before the First World War. In Vienna, Lueger may have seen in the Jews a *Bekehrungsobjekt* [an object for conversion] or even a *Beargwöhnungsobjekt* [an object of suspicion]; Schönerer went a step further in seeing Jews as an *Agressionsobjekt* (Leser, 1987:57): The step to view Jews as an *Exterminationsobjekt* still lay some way into the future. Leser (1987:54–55) also warns us against evaluating the antisemitism in Vienna at the turn of the century solely with the benefit of hindsight:

> *So sehr uns heute der Antisemitismus in allen seinen Ausprägungen und Motivationen suspekt und verboten sein muß, so wenig dürfen wir, ohne den historischen Akteuren von damals Unrecht zu tun, verkennen, daß der Antisemitismus für die Menschen von damals und auch in einer historischen Wertung, die von Hitler absieht, bloß ein Spezialfall von vielen Fällen der Minderheitsablehnung war, der allerdings schon damals durch die spezifisch religiöse und theologische Problematik, die im Verhältnis zwischen anderen Minderheiten und Mehrheiten nicht obwaltete, kompliziert und überlagert war. Wer freilich den Antisemitismus von vornherein nur im Hinblick auf Hitler und den Holocaust betrachtet und deutet, befördert—wie schon gesagt wurde—Hitler nicht nur in den Rang der Erfüllung einer historischen Notwendigkeit und der fälligen Konsequenz aus gegebenen Voraussetzungen, der ihm nicht zukommt, sondern verschließt sich den Weg zum Verständnis von Phänomenen, die um ihrer selbst willen und selbständig betrachtet und verstanden werden wollen und nicht von vorneherein mit den unvorhersehbaren und ungewollten Fernwirkungen konfrontiert werden dürfen.*

No matter how much antisemitism, in all its manifestations and motivations, must be suspect and forbidden territory for us in this day and age, we are not entitled to forget—if we are not to do the historical actors of the time an injustice—that antisemitism, in the eyes of the people and in a historical perspective, which leaves Hitler aside for the moment, was merely a special case among the many instances of the rejection of minorities, although admittedly one superimposed with and complicated by specific religious and theological problems that were absent in other mainstream-minority relationships. Whoever considers and interprets antisemitism a priori only with an eye on Hitler and the Holocaust, not only ascribes to Hitler the importance of having drawn the proper conclusions from a set of necessary historical circumstances—a position which he does not deserve—but also denies himself the path to understanding phenomena which must be understood independently and for their own sake, and which should not be confronted with remote effects that could not be foreseen and were not desired.

The great Austrian historian Friedrich Heer (1981:352–353), too, feels the need to make distinctions: he does not see Vienna as traditionally an antisemitic city per se; he locates late 19th century antisemitism specifically in the *mittlere Bürgertum* [lower middle class] rather than in the *gute Gesellschaft* [high society] of the city. Perhaps it is Arthur Schnitzler again who, as poet, participant, and observer of contemporary Viennese cultural life, had the most considered view into the place of antisemitism in Vienna around the turn of the century. Remembering his youth in Vienna, he wrote the following:

In diesen Blättern wird viel von Judentum und Antisemitismus die Rede sein, mehr als manchem geschmackvoll, notwendig und gerecht sein dürfte. Aber zu der Zeit, in der man diese Blätter möglicherweise lesen wird, wird man sich, so hoffe ich wenigstens, kaum mehr einen Begriff zu bilden vermögen, was für eine Bedeutung, seelisch fast noch mehr als politisch und sozial, zur Zeit, da ich diese Zeilen schreibe, der sogenannten Judenfrage zukam. Es war nicht möglich, insbesondere für einen Juden, der in der Öffentlichkeit stand, davon abzusehen, daß er Jude war, da die andern es nicht taten, die Christen nicht und die Juden noch weniger. Man hatte die Wahl, für unempfindlich, zudringlich, frech oder für empfindlich,

*schüchtern, verfolgungswahnsinnig zu gelten. Und auch wenn man seine
innere und äußere Haltung so weit bewahrte, daß man weder das eine
noch das andere zeigte, ganz unberührt zu bleiben war unmöglich, als
etwa ein Mensch gleichgültig bleiben könnte, der sich zwar die Haut
anaesthesieren ließ, aber mit wachen und offenen Augen zusehen muß,
wie unreine Messer sie ritzen, ja schneiden, bis das Blut kommt.*
(Schnitzler, 1968:328–329)

In these pages there will be a lot of talk about antisemitism, more
than one may feel is either necessary, just, or even in good taste.
However, when the time comes that these pages will possibly find a
reader, one will scarcely be able to appreciate the full significance,
spiritual even more than social or political, which was given to the
issue of the Jews at the time that I am writing these lines. At least I
hope so. Especially for a Jew active in public life, it was simply not
possible to disregard that he was a Jew, for other people did not do
so; Christians didn't and Jews even less so. One had the choice of
having a reputation for being insensitive, obtrusive or insolent, or
else for being oversensitive, shy or having a persecution complex.
Even if one managed to maintain one's outer and inner composure
to such an extent that one showed no reaction either way, it was
impossible to remain completely untouched—as though a person
can remain indifferent when his skin is anaesthetized, but sees with
alert and open eyes how dirty knives scratch and cut it till the blood
comes.

Here, Schnitzler gets close to the existential situation of the Jew in
Viennese public life, and how antisemitism was likely to affect him.
Antisemitism in Vienna around the turn of the century was simply
too all-pervasive to leave the Jew in public life untouched. Jews as
well as non-Jews would provide continual reminders of one's
marginal social status as a Jew. In this, Schnitzler brings us close to
the effect of this social climate on Herzl, which eventually galvanized
him into action.

This, then, was the social context of Viennese antisemitism in which some quite specific personal experiences of Herzl's were embedded. But it was not so much his occupation with the academic antisemitism of the likes of Dühring, or his knowledge of the social antisemitism of a Lueger, which set him off: it was his anger with personal snubs, as he tells Rabbi Güdemann (16 June 1895; BT2:135, P1:109) and Baron Hirsch (26 May 1895; BT2:57, P1:19)—that got him going. There was the switch of his student association Albia to a German nationalistic platform which gave him a lot of thought (Bein, 1962:41–42). So did some experiences of name-calling directed against his person, as when somebody yelled the word *Saujude* [Jewish pig] after him as his taxi sped from Baden to Vienna one night (Whitsun, 1895; BT2:50, P1:11). As he pointed out: *"In Österreich und Deutschland muß ich immer befürchten, daß mir hepp-hepp nachgerufen wird* (Whitsun, 1895; BT2:45, P1:5) [In Austria and Germany I must constantly fear that somebody will shout Hep, Hep! after me]," "Hep, Hep!" being the *"neues Schimpf-wort, mit welchem jedem Juden begegnet wurde; Anfangsbuchstaben der Worte: Hierosolyma est perdita, Jerusalem ist verloren* [new curse, which every Jew met everywhere: *Hierosolyma est perdita*, Jerusalem is lost]" (Sondheimer 1906:88). Seen in isolation, and even in the context of what was happening to Jewish communities in Czarist Russia at the time, such incidents do not seem to amount to that much, but they hurt his pride, and helped crystallize his attitudes.

These experiences served to heighten Herzl's sense of being a Jew and of the uncomfortable position of Jews in his contemporary society, and they awakened in him a sense of obligation to try and do something about this, but together they still did not constitute a sufficient condition to set him writing. He himself recalls his bizarre idea of starting a program of mass conversion of Jews to Christianity, whose reception into mainstream society would then be marked by a large-scale procession of Jews to St. Stephan's Cathedral in Vienna, with himself at the head of the crowd, "amidst the pealing of bells" (Whitsun, 1895; BT2:47, P1:7). It was his boss at the *Neue Freie Presse*, Moritz Benedikt, who talked him out of this grotesque intention (Whitsun 1895; BT2:48, P1:8–9). To actually start writing, he seems to have needed to get away from Vienna for a while, to create personal space between the immediate reality of Vienna and his own mental state. This is the importance of his position in Paris as correspondent to the *Neue Freie Presse*. Yet even in Paris it took him some time to begin thinking in terms of a state for Jews, as Chouraqui (1970:66) has observed. But by 1892 he had already submitted an article to his *Neue Freie Presse* about antisemitism in France (31 August 1892, cf. Pawel, 1989:169). By 1895 his stint in Paris had provided enough psychological space between him and Vienna to give Viennese antisemitism his full attention in his writing. This is how he expressed this in his diary:

> *Ich kam auch hier [in Paris] in ein freieres und höheres Verhältnis zum Antisemitismus, von dem ich wenigstens nicht unmittelbar zu leiden hatte. In Österreich oder Deutschland muß ich immer befürchten, daß mir hepp-hepp nachgerufen wird. Hier gehe ich doch 'unerkannt' durch die Menge.*
>
> *In Paris also gewann ich ein freieres Verhältnis zum Antisemitismus, den ich historisch zu verstehen und zu entschuldigen anfing. Vor allem kannte ich die Leere und Nutzlosigkeit der Bestrebungen 'zum Abwehr des Antisemitismus.' Mit Deklamationen auf dem Papier oder in geschlossenen Zirkeln ist da nicht das mindeste getan. (Whitsun 1895, BT2:46)*

Here (in Paris), too, I reached a higher, more disinterested view of antisemitism, from which at least I did not have to suffer directly. In Austria or Germany I must constantly fear that somebody will shout "Hep, Hep!" after me. But here I pass through the crowd unrecognized.

In Paris, then, I gained a freer attitude toward antisemitism, which I now began to understand historically and make allowances for. Above all, I recognized the emptiness and futility of efforts to "combat antisemitism." Declamations made in writing or in closed circles do no good whatever. (P1:5–6)

Herzl's perception of the issue—the social suffering of Jews everywhere—may therefore have been constant; his response to it, however, was triggered off by his personal situation of the moment, and it was immediate, experimental, continually evolving, a matter of trial and error, depending on the here-and-now: the person he was talking to, the situation he was facing, the gathering he was addressing. Wistrich (1989:443) correctly judges that "Der *Juden-staat* should . . . not be attributed to any one cause but rather to a succession of political events in France and Austria during the 1890s and their interaction with Herzl's complex personality." Klaus Dethloff's comment (Dethloff, 1986:29) in this context is particularly telling: he sees Herzl not so much as a writer at all, but rather as an actor, who records his actions minutely and allows them slowly to change his ideas—a *protokollierender Akteur*. Through his actions and experiences Herzl gradually grows into his ideas, so to speak. Herzl acts to be able to write, then writes to be able to act (Dethloff, 1986:29). Once the issue of the Jews had dawned on him, he took to constantly juggling his ideas, discussing them with others, reformulating them in the light of criticisms and suggestions. From considering mass conversion to writing a newspaper article or a political treatise, from persuading wealthy Jews to preparing a Zionist Congress, from starting a newspaper to visiting the world's rich and famous: they were all different actions and experiences which he used to tackle the issue of the Jews, but each of these experiences also shaped his ideas, opening new doors (Weizmann, 1966:45), closing others. As a result, with Herzl we are in a unique and particularly fortunate position of seeing ideas in the process of *becoming*, and in an important sense the whole *Jews' State* is a stage in this developmental process which did not stop until he died. Ideas in process, however, pose unique problems of interpretation, in that many positions expressed in *The Jews' State* represent interim positions he takes on a subject, not final ones, as Herzl himself readily acknowledged on more than one occasion:

Tout d'abord il ne faut pas prendre mon livre sur "l'État Juif" comme la forme définitive du projet. Je suis le premier à reconnaître qu'il y avait là dedans beaucoup d'idéologie. J'avais lancé, simple écrivain, cette idée, sans savoir comment elle serait reçue par le peuple juif. La meilleure preuve en est que j'avais proposé de nous établir soit en Argentine—soit en Palestine. (Letter to Sidney Whitman, 20 May 1897; BT2:513; also letter no 989 in BT4:269)

First of all, my book on the Jews' State should not be taken as the definitive form of the project; I am the first to admit that there is a lot of ideology in it. A simple writer, I launched the idea without knowing how it would be received by the Jewish people. The best proof is that I had suggested that we establish ourselves either in Argentina or in Palestine. (P2:550)

Both in his defense as well in hostility toward him, critics have dealt with *The Jews' State* as if it were his last word on the subject, but no interpretation which treats *The Jews' State* as product rather than as link in a process is likely to do justice to it. The audiences he had with the rich and famous, at which he often had to face hostility and inertia, necessitated a rethink, a remake of the program bringing it into ever sharper focus, and they helped Herzl to consider the matter of audience. In the words of David Vital:

Each experience, each failure, impelled him marginally to revise his views and, in the end, radically to recast the form in which he presented them—and, once he had overcome his disappointment, to fortify himself for the stage that was to follow. (Vital, 1975:248)

Thus what he planned to tell the Kaiser in 1897 is far more precise than anything he ever said in *The Jews' State*:

In den letzten drei Tagen des August d. J. versammelten sich 204 Vertreter des jüdischen Volkes aus allen Ländern in Basel. Dieser Kongreß der Juden, der mich zum Präsidenten wählte, formulierte das Programm des

Zionismus: Schaffung einer öffentlich-rechtlich gesicherten Heimstätte für diejenigen Juden, die sich an ihrer jetzigen Wohnorten nicht assimilieren können oder wollen. (Letter to Kaiser Wilhelm II, 22 October 1897; BT2:550–551, also in BT4:365 letter no 1170)

On the last three days of this past August, 204 representatives of the Jewish people from all countries assembled at Basel. This Congress of Jews, which elected me President, formulated the program of Zionism: the creation of a publicly and legally safeguarded home for those Jews who cannot or will not assimilate in their present places of residence. (P2:595)

How Herzl described this program in detail in *The Jews' State* will be analyzed in the next section.

The Work

HERZL'S AIMS

The purpose of the previous two sections of this commentary has been to show that the sources of Herzl's thinking in *The Jews' State* lie in his understanding of the Jewish tradition on the one hand, and the general ideological and political conditions of his time on the other. He has examined the tradition of Zion and the Jewish emancipation movement with its checkered assimilation history during his century. He has come to the conclusion that the results of this movement for Jews in Europe were patchy and ultimately illusory: civil emancipation had not reached the bulk of European Jewish communities—those in Czarist Russia—as the pogroms testified. Even where, as in Austria, Jews enjoyed full equality as citizens, there were still forces in society at work which made assimilated Jewish existence in these countries problematical and precarious. Running essay competitions for students on topics like "*Wie groß ist die gesammte materielle Steuerleistung aller in den im Reichsrate vertretenen Ländern und speziell in Wien wohnhaften Bekenner des israelitischen Glaubens* [How substantial is the total amount contributed to taxation revenue by the adherents of the Israelite faith living in all the provinces represented in the Reichsrat but especially in Vienna]," as the Society to Combat Antisemitism proposed to do in 1894 (Verein, 1894:10), was hardly going to make a difference. Herzl knew as much from personal experience, and the very recent election campaign of Karl Lueger for the Vienna mayoralty merely served to confirm this. In addition, in true Darwinian spirit, Herzl was convinced that the continued salience of these hostile conditions were having their degenerative effect on the Jewish character: he spoke of the "*Schwächung unseres Selbstbewußtseins* [lowering of our self-esteem]"; he saw Jews becoming ever more afraid, intimidated, cowardly, unwilling to stand up for themselves in the public arena; and the worst feature of this development was that, precisely because of their willingness to please at all times, be quiet and not complain, they merely fanned the attitudes of the antisemites, which this very quietism was supposed to lessen. As he said in *The Jews' State*:

> *Wir sind durch unsere geschichtlichen Leiden so gedrückt und mutlos geworden . . .*

> Through our historical sufferings we have become so oppressed and discouraged . . .

Coming to terms with this vicious circle is basic to Herzl's thinking, and he tried to work it out both in his diary and in *The Jews' State*. There is a moving passage in the diary, describing the effects of one of Karl Lueger's victories on some of his Jewish friends. It gives an insight into both the timorous nature of the assimilated Jews and of Herzl's exasperation with it (8 June 1895; BT2:81):

> *Abends bei Schiff's diniert. Ihre Schwägersleute aus Wien waren da. Wohlhabende, gebildete gedrückte Menschen. Sie stöhnten leise über den Antisemitismus, auf den ich fortwährend das Gespräch brachte.*
> *Der Mann erwartet eine neue Bartholomäusnacht. Die Frau meint, daß es nicht mehr schlechter gehen könne. Sie stritten ob es gut oder schlecht*

sei, daß Lueger's Wahl zum Bürgermeister von Wien nicht bestätigt wurde.
Sie haben mich mit ihrer Mattigkeit ganz verzagt gemacht. Sie ahnen es
nicht, aber sie sind Gettonaturen, stille, brave, furchtsame.
    So sind die meisten. Werden Sie den Ruf zur Freiheit und Menschen-
werdung verstehen?

In the evening I dined with the Schiffs. Their in-laws from Vienna
were visiting them. Well-to-do, educated, depressed people. They
moaned softly about antisemitism, to which I continually steered the
conversation.
    The husband expects a new St. Bartholomew's Night. The wife
believes that conditions could hardly get any worse. They argued
about whether it was good or bad that Lueger's election as mayor of
Vienna had not been ratified.
    Their faintheartedness completely dismayed me. They do not
suspect it, but they are ghetto types, quiet, decent, timorous. Most of
our people are like that. Will they understand the call to be free and
become human beings? (P1:46)

Emancipation or no emancipation, it was clear to Herzl that life in
a non-Jewish environment merely adds to the degradation of Jewish
persons, both psychologically and spiritually; they end up as "ghetto
types." Herzl was to build up an extended picture of this degrading
existence in his description of the family of David Littwak in
Altneuland; yet there are already enough indications in *The Jews'
State*. "*Wir sind, wozu man uns in den Ghetti gemacht hat* [We are
what they have made us to be in the ghettoes]," speaking "*verküm-
merte und verdrückte Jargons* [stunted and oppressed jargons],"
"*Ghettosprachen*," in fact, "*die nur Sinn und Entschuldigung als ver-
stohlene Sprache von Häftlingen hatten* [which had sense and justification only as the stealthy tongue of prisoners]" (7 June 1895;
BT2:75, P1:40), and which "*werden wir uns abgewöhnen* [which we
will accustom ourselves to drop]." This degradation is simply
inescapable as long as its causes are not addressed.
    Herzl is not alone in his time to comment on how the constant

experience of this antisemitism degrades the Jewish character. Even prominent non-Jews had noticed this and commented. Bismarck (Pawel, 1989:237), negotiating at the Congress of Berlin in 1878, had spoken in these terms:

> Fürst Gortschakov, am 28. Juni 1878 . . . [bat] die Berliner, Pariser, Londoner und Wiener Juden, denen man sicherlich kein politisches und bürgerliches Recht verweigern würde, nicht zu verwechseln mit den Juden Serbiens, Rumäniens und der russischen Provinzen, die seiner Ansicht nach eine Plage für die einheimische Bevölkerung seien. Darauf gab Bismarck als Präsident des Kongresses die für seine ganze Stellung zum Judentum bedeutsame Antwort, 'daß der bedauerliche Zustand der Israeliten vielleicht gerade auf die Beschränkung in den politischen und bürgerlichen Rechten zurückzuführen sei.' (Herlitz und Kirschner, 1927–1930:I.901)

> On 28 June 1878 . . . Prince Gortchakov requested not to confuse the Jews from Berlin, Paris, London and Vienna from whom nobody would dream of withholding civil rights, with the Jews of Serbia, Rumania and the Russian provinces, who in his view were "a pest to the local people." To which Bismarck, in his function as president of the Congress, gave the following significant reply which shows his attitude to Judaism: "The regrettable nature of the Israelites must in all probability be attributed to precisely this limitation of their political and civil rights."

This was the social-psychological condition of contemporary Jewry which Herzl saw and which he wished to address. That is why he wrote *The Jews' State*. Establishing a state, a political entity for Jews, was the way to do it. But even more important, it would seem, was to create a new type of Jew, a Jew who was no ghetto-type, who had not been degraded by the Darwinian mimicry he had noticed (Whitsun 1895; BT2:49; P1:10). The new type of Jew which he wanted to create was going to be an independent being, a free and unfettered political agent, who took his place in the brotherhood of

man as a free and equal agent to everyone else. The political state
was, in the final analysis, merely to be the instrument towards
creating this transformed Jew. He writes in his diary (16 June 1895;
BT2:131):

> *Niemand dachte daran, das gelobte Land dort zu suchen, wo es ist—und*
> *doch liegt es so nahe. Da ist es: in uns selbst! . . . Das gelobte Land ist*
> *dort, wohin wir es tragen!*

No one ever thought of looking for the Promised Land where it
actually is—and yet it lies so near. This is where it is: within
ourselves! . . . The Promised Land is where we carry it! (P1:105)

This passage finds its way into *The Jews' State* almost literally:

> *Jeder trägt ein Stück von Gelobten Land hinüber: der in seinem Kopf, und*
> *der in seinen Armen, und jener in seinem erworbenen Gut.*

Everyone carries a piece of the Promised Land in his luggage: one
person in his head, the next in his arms, the next in the wealth he has
acquired.

There is a play on the word *Land* here, just as Herzl plays on the
word *Staat*: the two words are used alternatively as denoting a
political entity and a psychological phenomenon. The promised
land, the Jews' state, is as much as anything else a spiritual and
psychological phenomenon, potentially present in every Jew of
Herzl's time, but only to come to full blossoming within the context
of a new political state specifically for Jews. There needs to be an
"*Umdenken und Umlernen* [re-thinking and re-learning]" among the
Jews. The establishment of the state will eliminate the "*schlechten*
äußeren Bedingungen, unter denen mancher Charakter verdorben ist
[bad external conditions, which have caused many a character to go
astray]." "*Unser Volk wird seine Tüchtigkeit wiederfinden im Siebenstun-*

denlande [Our people will regain its moral fiber in the land of the
seven-hour working day]." A new, better generation will be born,
and the new state will introduce "*ein hoher Stolz und das Glück der
innerlichen Freiheit in ihr Dasein* [a great pride, an inner freedom and
joy into their lives]." Jews will become a people of David and Miriam
Littwaks, as in *Altneuland*, who "epitomize a new kind of Jew"
(Wistrich, 1989:455). That is not political utopia, that is spiritual
rebirth; in short, moral regeneration is to be the aim; statehood is to
be the instrument.

The early Zionists picked up this relationship of basic moral
generation through the instrument of statehood very clearly. And not all
of them were quite as crude as Max Nordau, who looked forward to the
creation of a *Muskeljudentum* (muscle Jews) (Nordau, 1923:424).
Zionism has "*den Juden Rückgrat verliehen, die Judenehre und der
Judenstolz wieder aufgerichtet* [given Jews a spine, resurrected the
Jews' honor and pride]" (*Jüdische Zeitung*, 16 August 1912); it
renders it "*selbstverständlich, daß jedermann, wenn ihm zugerufen wird:
'Du bist ein Jude!,' sich nicht ängstlich krümmt und duckt, sondern stolz
und selbstbewußt aufrichtet* [self-evident, that someone who is confronted with the cry 'You are a Jew' does not stoop and cringe in fear,
but stands up proudly and confidently]" (*Österreichische Wochenschrift*, 12 February 1909). Herzl's precise purpose in outlining the
sorry history of antisemitism and persecution was to show that for
historical, religious and socio-psychological reasons it was impossible to achieve this spiritual and psychological aim in the political
constellation of the 1890s, consisting as it did of a series of
nation-states, in which Jews were invariably a minority. Thus in
accordance with the spirit of the times, the only way out of this
dilemma was to form their own national state, hence a state for the
Jews. But after all was said and done, the state was to be no more than
an instrument in the realization of his more fundamental objective,
the psycho-social regeneration of Jews on the level of person and
community. Herzl's state is as much personal-psychological allegory
as political reality: "The longing for a Jewish state can then be seen

as the attainment of the 'inner freedom' that would turn the Jews into real *Menschen*" (Bunzl, 1994a:66). It is in the articulation of this clear vision of the new Jew that Herzl's greatness resides:

> One aspect of Zionism, hardly assimilated by any assimilated Jew, but seen very clearly by Herzl, was that Zionism was not just a nationalist movement like any other. It did hold out to the Jewish millions the hope of a free life in their own country, but over and above it also held the promise of the rise of a new and different type of Jew, different from the insecure assimilants and different from the ghetto-created perversions of Jewry. The Jews who killed themselves rather than surrender at Massada, the warrier Jews described by Flavius Josephus, or more recently in history, the Jews of Spain before Ferdinand and Isabella, and those of Italy, France and Germany before the Crusades and persecution began, were proud men and women, different from the downtrodden, cringing ghetto-Jews. The return of a whole people to its true nature, that was the ultimate aim of Herzl's Zionism, that was and is the true greatness of his vision. (Clare, 1982:91)

Or in the eloquent words of Ernst Pawel:

> The most powerful message of *Der Judenstaat* was one of pride and defiance: Stop trying to be other than what you are; be proud to be a Jew, just as the German is proud to be a German. Simple to the point of banality, but for many Jews it radically changed the way they saw themselves. (Pawel, 1989:267)

This seems to have been felt keenly at the time, but in the subsequent political activities attending the organization of the state, it seems to have been rather lost sight of. Yet once this hierarchy of priorities is clearly understood, it is much easier to understand Herzl's experimental attitude to such issues as the location of his state and the structure of its future government.

Herzl is above all concerned that his plan of state formation is a

practical one, not merely a pie-in-the-sky, and he takes pains to
distance himself from other plans of colony and state formation
which were at that time before the public, such as that discussed in
great detail in his colleague Theodor Hertzka's book *Freiland*. He sees
four stages in the establishment of the new state for the Jews, which
interact with each other although they are conceptually distinct: the
preparation of Jewish communities and the national governments of
the countries in which they live at present for the emigration of Jews
to the new state; the occupation of the new land; the legal and social
organization of the new society; and the organization of the economy
of the Jews' State.

PREPARATION

As with everything that has to do with the new Jews' state, the
preparation for the emigration of Jews has to do both with the
preparation of Jewish communities themselves and with the preparation of the outside world. Both receive Herzl's full attention. As far
as the Jewish communities are concerned, they are to be persuaded
that emigration is worthwhile, and Herzl goes into considerable
detail about how to reach the Jewish people with his proposals, how
to get the wealthy Jewish financiers on his side, how to organize
local emigration groups, how to book travel accommodation and the
like. At every stage of these preparations he anticipates quite a level
of opposition, and he takes great pains to meet objections through
reasoned argument: and he expects those who are convinced to be
committed to the cause. Preparation of the Jews encompasses
spiritual and psychological preparation as well as organizing the fair
and equitable transfer of Jewish community resources, and canvassing the support of the government authorities from the departing
countries. He shows an equal concern for the legitimate worries of
the governments of departing countries: The exodus he is planning
may be large, but it must occur with minimum disruption and social

upheaval. This concern for orderly evacuation, as much as for Jewish community needs, lies behind his recommendation for the establishment of Jewish community authorities who provide the guarantees.

CHOICE OF TERRITORY

Herzl's thoughts about the state had much more to do with the preparation of the Jews and gentile communities for the changes the state would bring than with a choice of a territory where the state might be located. Herzl never made up his mind about the location of a suitable territory for the state. Nor was he alone in this; Max Nordau, too, was flexible about the location of the territory Jews were to have as their state (Nordau, 1897:2) Herzl, in fact, even proposes that a territory is neither a necessary nor a sufficient condition for statehood: "*nicht die Landesstrecken sind der Staat, sondern die durch eine Souveränität zusammengefaßten Menschen sind es* [But a state is not constituted of pieces of land; rather a group of people gathered under a sovereignty make up a state]." Even before writing *The Jews' State*, Herzl had taken to exploring a number of territorial options, without any great commitment to any of them. The very first mention of any suitable territory is in the diary entry of 9 June 1895, where Palestine is taken under consideration, albeit without great enthusiasm:

> *Gegen Palästina spricht die Nähe Rußlands und Europas, Mangel an Ausbreitung, sowie Klima, dessen wir schon entwöhnt. Dafür die mächtige Legende.* (BT2:90)

> In Palestine's disfavor is its proximity to Russia and Europe, its lack of room for expansion as well as its climate, which we are no longer accustomed to. In its favor is the mighty legend. (P1:56)

On 11 June 1895 he feels somewhere in South America looks promising (BT2:101, P1:69), but two days later he thinks either

Palestine or Argentina would be suitable without expressing a preference (13 June 1895; BT2:156, P1:133). This is the position which he takes in *The Jews' State*. Apart from getting "*die Souveränität eines für unsere gerechten Volksbedürfnisse genügenden Stückes der Erdoberfläche* [sovereignty over a piece of the earth's surface sufficient for the legitimate needs of our people]," he has no further requirements in the matter. If he were in a position to choose, the choice would be between Argentina and Palestine. Each of these choices has its advantages and drawbacks. Argentina is to be preferred on a number of criteria: its natural wealth, its moderate climate, its sparse population, its vast spaces. Palestine, however, is "*unsere unvergeßliche historische Heimat* [our unforgettable historical home]," and it would serve as a rallying-cry in Jewish communities. Moreover, there would be advantages both for the European powers and for the Sultan in a Jewish national presence in Palestine. Europe would be served by the fact that a Jewish Palestine would be a barrier against the wild hordes of Asia: the Jews' state would guarantee a "*Vorpostendienst der Kultur gegen die Barbarei* [outpost of civilisation against barbarism]." The Sultan would gain in that the Jews would put the finances of his empire into order. But beggars cannot be choosers: "*Die Society wird nehmen, was man ihr gibt und wofür sich die öffentliche Meinung des Judenvolkes erklärt* [The Society will accept what it is given and what has the support of public opinion among the Jews as a people]." That there might come to be a discrepancy between the two criteria he mentions here does not enter his mind. In subsequent months and years a variety of options engendered by a variety of encounters and situations are canvassed: Southern Arabia ("absurd," 3 August 1896; BT2:428, P2:448), Cyprus (1 July 1898; BT2:593, P2:644), "from the Brook of Egypt to the Euphrates" (15 October 1898; BT2:650, P2:711), Mesopotamia, Syria, Anatolia (17 February 1902; BT3:350, P3:1222), the Sinai peninsula (5 July 1902; BT3:408, P4:1294 and 23 October 1902; BT3:465, P4:1363), Uganda (24 April 1903; BT3:551, P4:1473). Privately he went on exploring these other options right until he died, and in this he seems to have started something of a trend. In the contemporary German-Jewish press one encounters the occasional territorial speculation, for example Alaska, where the immigrating Jews would have to cope with merely a handful of *verkommene* [dilapidated] Indians and Eskimos (*Jüdisches Volksblatt*, 22 April 1910), or even Western Australia, with whose premier Israel Zangwill discussed the immigration of 100,000 Jews, and which was characterized as a "*Land voll Sünde, Sonne, Schweiß, Sand, Salz, Sorge und—schlimmer Augen* [land full of sin, sun, sweat, sand, salt, worry, and bad eyesight] (*Jüdisches Volksblatt*, 2 September 1910). Successive Zionist Congresses were increasingly exasperated by these explorations, in which they refused to follow Herzl. It was only the seventh Zionist Congress, held in 1905, the year after Herzl's death, which finally rejected all territorial options other than Palestine (Israel Pocket Library, 1973:243). Indeed most of Herzl's diplomatic activity between the publication of *The Jews' State* and his death was devoted to finding a suitable location for the state, and as such the effort involved must be rated a failure. The scenario that might have ensued had Herzl's diplomatic efforts been successful has been explored, tongue-in-cheek, by one critic:

> *Herzl starb an der Ungeduld des Herzens, weil er in acht kurzen Jahren nicht die zweitausendjährige Judenfrage lösen konnte. Es ist ein ironischer Gedanke, was wohl geschehen wäre, hätten seine diplomatischen Initiativen Erfolg gehabt. Was hätte ein jüdischer Vassallenstaat unter dem halb verrückten und ganz bankrotten türkischen Sultan Abdul Hamid bedeutet? Er ging in die Geschichte ein als ein Schlächter der Armenier. Oder als deutsches Protektorat unter Wilhelm II.? Hätten die Zionisten zum britischen Angebot von Uganda, das ja gar nicht Uganda, sondern Kenya war, ja gesagt, dann hätten die Juden die blutrünstigen Mau-Mau an Stelle der PLO zu bekämpfen gehabt. (Weiser-Varon in Leser, 1987:185–186)*

Herzl died of impatience of the heart, because he could not solve in eight short years the issue of the Jews which was two thousand years old. It is ironic to think what would have happened if his diplomatic achievements had been successful. What would a vassal state under the half-mad and completely bankrupt Sultan Abdul Hamid have looked like? He has gone into history as a butcher of the Armenians. Or perhaps a German protectorate under Wilhelm II? If the Zionists had agreed to the British offer of Uganda—which was not Uganda at all but rather Kenya—the Jews would have had to fight the blood-thirsty Mau-Mau instead of the PLO.

RELATIONSHIP WITH NATIVE POPULATION

Herzl concedes that the choice of territory for the Jews' state brings into focus issues of the relationship between the emigrated Jews and the native population of the land chosen as the location for the Jews' state. This distinguishes him from those Zionists such as Israel Zangwill (1903 in Simon, 1937:80), who at various stages presented the location of the Jews' state as a *terra nullius*. Indeed for Herzl one of the attractions of Argentina as the chosen site is that the impact of this population issue would be minimized, as Argentina provides a happy combination of "*riesigem Fläheninhalt* [enormous size]" with "*schwacher Bevölkerung* [sparse population]," the implication being that even here the issue of a local population would have to be coped with. The most extensive discussion of how Jews might relate to the native population of the chosen land occurs in the following diary entries (12 June 1895; BT2:117–118 and BT2:126):

> Bei der Landnahme bringen wir dem Aufnahmestaate gleich Wohlfahrt zu. Den Privatbesitz der angewiesenen Ländereien müssen wir sachte expropriieren.
>
> Die arme Bevölkerung trachten wir unbemerkt über die Grenze zu schaffen, indem wir ihr in den Durchzugsländern Arbeit verschaffen, aber in unserem eigenen Lande jederlei Arbeit verweigern.
>
> Die besitzende Bevölkerung wird zu uns übergehen. Das Expropriationswerk muß ebenso wie die Fortschaffung der Armen, mit Zartheit und Behutsamkeit erfolgen.

Die Immobilienbesitzer sollen glauben, uns zu prellen, uns über dem Wert zu verkaufen.

Aber zurückverkauft wird ihnen nichts.

Selbstverständlich werden wir die Andersgläubigen achtungsvoll dulden, ihr Eigentum, ihre Ehre und Freiheit mit den härtesten Zwangsmitteln schützen. Auch darin werden wir der ganzen alten Welt ein wunderbares Beispiel geben.

Anfangs wird man uns übrigens meiden. Wir stehen in schlechtem Geruch.

Bis der Umschwung in der Welt zu unsern Gunsten sich vollzogen haben wird, werden wir schon fest in unserem Land sitzen, Zuzüge Fremder nicht mehr fürchten, und unsere Gäste mit edlem Wohlwollen, mit stolzer Liebenswürdigkeit aufnehmen.

Die gutwillige Expropriation wird durch unseren geheimen Agenten gemacht. Die Gesellschaft würde zu teuer kaufen.

Wir verkaufen dann nur an Juden, und alle Liegenschaften bleiben nur im Commerzium der Juden . . .

Ziehen wir in eine Gegend, wo es für die Juden ungewöhnliche wilde Tiere gibt—große Schlangen etc.—so benütze ich die Eingeborenen, bevor ich sie in den Durchzugsländern beschäftige, dazu, diese Tiere auszurotten. Hohe Prämien für Schlangenhäute etc. und für die Brut.

When we occupy the land, we shall bring immediate benefits to the state that receives us. We must expropriate gently the private property on the estates assigned to us.

We shall try to spirit the penniless population across the border by procuring employment for it in transit countries, while denying it any employment in our own country.

The property owners will come over to our side. Both the process of expropriation and the removal of the poor must be carried out discreetly and circumspectly.

Let the owners of immovable property believe that they are cheating us, selling us things for more than they are worth.

But we are not going to sell them anything back.

It goes without saying that we shall respectfully tolerate persons of other faiths and protect their property, their honor and their freedom with the harshest means of coercion. This is another area in which we shall set the entire old world a wonderful example.

At first, incidentally, people will avoid us. We are in bad odor.

By the time the reshaping of world opinion in our favor has been completed, we shall be firmly established in our country, no longer fearing the influx of foreigners, and receiving our visitors with aristocratic benevolence and proud amiability.

The voluntary expropriation will be accomplished through our secret agents. The Company would pay excessive prices.

We shall then sell only to Jews, and all real estate will be traded only among Jews . . .

If we move into a region where there are wild animals to which the Jews are not accustomed—big snakes, etc.—I shall use the natives, prior to giving them employment in the transit countries, for the extermination of these animals. High premiums for snake skins, etc., as well as their spawn. (P1:88–89 and 98)

In his diary entries about his only trip to Palestine there are also a number of reflections about Palestine and its people. On board ship Herzl acknowledges the emotions Palestine engenders in the passengers, including the Arabs who have been on board since Constantinople (27 October 1898; BT2:674, P2:739). In fact, Arabs are mentioned five times altogether in the diary. There is a reference to "Arab beggars" waiting in a crowd to meet the Kaiser in Palestine (29 October 1898; BT2:678, P2:743), as well as the following record of a discussion in Jerusalem (27 October 1898; BT2:676):

Zum Schluß sprach ich mit dem Arzt der Kolonie Dr. Mazié. Der schenkte mir reinen Wein ein. Fieber! Die Kolonisten leiden alle am Fieber. Nur durch großartige Drainagen, Entsumpfungen ließe sich das Land bewohnbar machen. Das ist auch meine Ansicht u. Absicht. Das wird Milliarden kosten u. Milliarden neuer Werte schaffen! Als Arbeiter wären solche Araber zu verwenden, die gegen das Fieber immun sind.

Finally I spoke to the physician of the colony, Dr. Mazié. He gave it to me straight. Fever! All the colonies suffer from fever. Only large-scale drainage operations and the elimination of swamps, he said, could make the country habitable. This is also my view and intention. It will cost billions, but create billions of new wealth! Such Arabs as are immune to the fever might be used for the work. (P2:740–741)

These passages present a stark and uncompromising view of the relationship between the state-seeking Jews and the native populations who are going to have to cope with them. Ernst Pawel draws up the following balance sheet:

Not once does he refer to the natives in his notes, nor do they ever seem to figure in his later reflections. In overlooking, in refusing to acknowledge their presence—and hence their humanity—he both followed and reinforced a trend that was to have tragic consequences for Jews and Arabs alike. (Pawel, 1989:382)

That may be so, but that was said from the vantage point of 1989. It needs to be borne in mind that these passages are neither better nor worse than similar ideologies propagated by colonizers and state-builders at the time, whether in the German-speaking world or elsewhere. Herzl knew of and admired Cecil Rhodes and his methods—a "visionary politician" and a "practical visionary"—and even begged for his support in the establishment of the Jews' state (11 January 1902; BT3:327–329, P3:1193–1195 and 1 March 1899; BT2:718, P2:793). The above passages in Herzl have, for rather obvious reasons, not received much of an airing and public discussion in the critical literature sympathetic to him. There is no reference to them in Bein's biography. David Vital, in his monumental history on Zionism, is silent on the matter. Brude-Firnau (1976), in her edited version of the diary skirts around any problems by the simple device of omitting them from her selection, and then she takes Nahum Goldmann (Goldmann, 1975:72) to task in her postscript for the latter's view that Herzl might with profit have spent as much energy on thinking of Arab–Jewish relations as he did on meeting the Kaiser and other politicians (Brude-Firnau, 1976:295). The Arab critic James Zogby, on the other hand, has a field day with these passages and maintains that the entire troublesome history of Arab–Jewish relations started with Herzl's diary entries (Zogby, 1991:121–142). What can be said about such claims?

Firstly, these entries occur only in the diary, and there is an argument to be made that Herzl would not be prepared to represent such ideas to the public. There is something in this; however, that argument needs to be balanced with Herzl's own assertion that he is writing the diary so that posterity will see how his ideas develop: it is to be a document for a public audience—*"ein Denkmal für die Menschen* [a monument for humanity]" (Whitsun 1895, BT2:43, P1:3), which he senses always to be looking over his shoulder as he is writing (30 November 1900, BT3:160, P3:996). So in a real sense Herzl intends his diary to be more than a candid record of his own development—*"Ehrlichkeit dieser Aufschreibung—die völlig wertlos wäre, wenn ich mir etwas vorheuchelte* [the honesty of this diary, which would be utterly worthless if I were hypocritical with myself]" (Whitsun, 1895; BT2:44, P1:4). Even so, Herzl must have thought better of including this matter in *The Jews' State*. There the issue only surfaces implicitly and occasionally. Echoing the then current imperialist-colonial ethos, Herzl maintains that there is an advantage to the civilized world in having a Jews' state in Palestine; such a state would form a first barrier protecting (*Vorpostendienst*) Europe against the *Barbarei* of those who live beyond. Furthermore, in true Darwinian spirit, Herzl quite accepts as proper that there will be some peoples who cannot stand up for themselves in the international arena and are ready to go under, it being understood that the Jewish people are not such a group. Indeed, echoing his thoughts that you need antisemites in order to bring out the full Jewishness in persons, you need an enemy in order to call forth the *höchste Anstrengung der Persönlichkeit* [the highest exertions of personality], and *die allgemeine Verbrüderung ist nicht einmal ein schöner Traum* [the general brotherhood of man is not even a beautiful dream]. In the Jews' state itself, the workforce will not admit any *nichtjüdische Arbeitssklaven* [non-Jewish slave laborers], but only persons committed to the seven-hour working day—but Herzl does not make clear whether only Jews, or foreigners in the Jews' state as well, will be the beneficiaries of the seven-hour working day. At any rate, based on his experience of Jewish-gentile relations *in manchen Ländern* [in many countries], Herzl does not anticipate extensive contact between the Jews and other groups in the population.

Secondly, it must also be considered that in his later years of public activity, as he refines his ideas of the Jews' state and presents them in different forums, Herzl also calls into question these original simplistic notions of evacuating the local population. This process starts in *The Jews' State* itself (72):

Jeder ist in seinem Bekenntnis oder in seinem Unglauben so frei und unbeschränkt wie in seiner Nationalität. Und fügt es sich, daß auch andersgläubige, Andersnationale unter uns wohnen, so werden wir ihnen einen ehrvollen Schutz und die Rechtsgleichheit gewähren. Wir haben die Toleranz in Europa gelernt.

Everybody is as free and unfettered in practicing his belief or unbelief as he is in his nationality. And should it come to pass that persons of other faiths or nationalities live among us, then we will accord them honorable protection and equality before the law. Tolerance we have learnt in Europe . . .

In his *Testament für das jüdische Volk* he writes to his Jewish people: *Macht euren Staat so, daß sich der Fremde bei euch wohl fühlt* [Make your state in such a way that the stranger feels good in your company] (6 August 1899; BT3:43, P3:856). Discussing the Cyprus option with Minister Chamberlain in London in October 1902, "*so sei die Sache so, daß dort Griechen und Mohammedaner leben, und die könne er neuen Einwandern zuliebe nicht verdrängen* [the reality of the

situation is that there are Greek and Mohammedan inhabitants, and
they cannot really be pushed out in favor of the new immigrants],"
yet he still expects that they can be bought over with a Jewish
"*Goldregen* [shower of gold]" (23 October 1902; BT3:464–465,
P4:1361–1362). And in *Altneuland*, which with some justification
can be regarded as Herzl's final thoughts on the Jews' state, he gives
a sympathetic portrayal of the Arab Rashid Bey, who, as a resident of
the Old New Land, leads a fully free political and economic
existence in the new Jews' state. We are again, in this instance, seeing
Herzl's ideas as process rather than product, and it would be unfair
to take what he said in his diary in 1895 as his final say on the
matter.

LEGAL AND SOCIAL FRAMEWORK

Having addressed the issues of the mass emigration of Jews,
canvassed a number of possible locations for his new Jews' state, and
given thought to the relationships Jews may need to establish with
the already existent population in the new location, Herzl now turns
his attention to the issue of what is involved in developing a Jews'
Staat on the basis of the Jewish *Volk*. He sees this process as involving
two steps. As a first step it is necessary to reconstitute the Jewish *Volk*
as the Jewish *Nation*. Early on in *The Jews' State*, Herzl has already
stressed a number of times that Jews constitute a *Volk*, that is, a
group of people feeling a sense of identity on the basis of a common
tradition consisting of a religion, a sense of otherness, and a history
of persecution. This recognition, however, is not by itself a sufficient
condition for the solution of the general sense of alienation and
persecution of the Jewish people. To bring this about necessitates
dealing with the issue of Jews as a national issue; in other words, the
Jewish *Volk* has to become a Jewish *Nation*: that is a group which, on
the basis of being this group, is able to make political claims
internally (of its members) and externally (of other nations), and can

make such claims stick. That is the first step. The second step in the establishment of statehood for Jews is to build the state on this sense of nationhood, in other words, how to devise the governmental and administrative arrangements which are most suited to a nation, building on a Jewish sense of identity.

Herzl addresses these issues with his recommendation to establish the Society of Jews. His starting point is that although the Jewish people are a *Volk*, and a unified *Volk*, they are a people living in a variety of countries under a variety of political and social conditions, unable to act as a nation, without a clearly identifiable leadership which could be a believable player in the rough and tumble of the international negotiations that are going to be necessary to establish the state. Trying to get the majority of the *Volk* to agree on anything under these conditions is a sure recipe for inertia and failure. So Herzl canvasses a number of political theories to see whether they offer anything of use. He has a look at Rousseau's *Du contrat social*, but decides that, given the present dispersed situation of the Jews, Rousseau with his theory of the social contract is hardly going to be much use for state-building, for there are simply no contracting parties able to speak in the interests of the Jews (7 June 1895; BT2:76, P1:41 and 11 June 1895; BT2:111, P1:80). He then alludes to the theory of divine right of kings, to a patriarchal set-up, to the then so popular theory of Heinrich von Treitschke that the state is power—all of these are dismissed as inappropriate. As his way out of this impasse Herzl now remembers his studies of Roman law, and recalls some passages from the *Imperatoris Iustiniani Institutionum* (Moyle, 1896), the *Institutes*—a summary of the law of the Roman Empire which the Byzantine emperor Justinian had drawn up in 533. Herzl calls on the *Institutes* to engender an authority for the Jews that will set the formation of the state into motion. He begins by offering some thoughts on the question of a mandate as a way of tackling the issue of emerging statehood, based on title 26 of the *Institutes* (Moyle, 1896:454–460; see also Kaser, 1971:I.577–580). The designated territory for the Jews could be mandated to a great power, at least temporarily, so as to assist the Jews in getting their act together (cf. Berger, 1953:574). The basis of the mandating would then be the belief that the territory in question was inhabited by "peoples not yet able to stand by themselves under the strenuous conditions of the modern world," so that the act of governing them should "be entrusted to advanced nations" (Article 22, Covenant, League of Nations, cited in Patai, 1971:749). This, of course, was in fact done with respect to Palestine by the League of Nations in 1922. Herzl is disinclined to go along this road for the obvious reason that a mandating power will be of a different group than the mandated people; hence, under such circumstances the Jewish people would surrender control over their own nation building. So he dismisses this as "impractical," and "nowhere sanctioned by law" (24 December 1898; BT2:709, P2:779). In the light of the later Mandate his suspicions may have been well-founded. Herzl finally considers the best way of solving the problem is for himself to simply assume a sort of power of attorney over Jewish community affairs. He simply asks both Jew and gentile to accept that in the first instance at least he himself is the person who can legitimately represent the Jews, empowered to do so by the simple device of saying he is that person (9 June 1895; BT2:93, P1:59 and 11 June 1895; BT2:110–111, P1:80).

> . . . *ich will mich in den Dienst aller Juden stellen.*
>
> *Jedermann, besonders jeder Jude, ist ja berechtigt, sich der bedrohten Sache der Juden anzunehmen; vorausgesetzt, daß er es als redlicher Mann nach bestem Willen und Gewissen tut. Die Zukunft wird ihm dann entweder die Gutheißung seiner Handlungen, oder die Verurteilung wegen angerichteten Schadens bringen.* (13 June 1895; BT2:154)

> . . . I want to place myself at the service of all Jews.
>
> After all, every person, and most of all every Jew, is entitled to take an interest in the jeopardized Jewish cause, provided that he does it as an honest man with the best intentions and conscience. The future

will then bring him either approval of his actions or condemnation
for the harm he may have done. (P1:131)

He calls this representative person, recalling the *Institutes*, the
gestor, in this case himself. And in the picturesque words of *The Jews'
State*: "*Darum setzt der Gestor einfach den Hut auf und geht voran* [So
the *gestor* simply puts on the hat and leads the way]." It is this
gestor who assumes two kinds of powers with respect to his
community: firstly, the power to conduct negotiations on behalf of
the community—the *negotiorum gestio*, and secondly, the power to
direct the internal development of his community. *The Jews' State* is
full of examples of how both these powers work in practice. The
functions of the *gestor*, in effect, give the *Volk* the capacity to express
a communal will; it turns the *Volk* into a *Nation*. Herzl knew of no
such function or procedure in international law, so he adapted Title
27 of the *Institutes*, which actually dealt with issues of *negotiorum
gestio* in Roman *commercial* law, to suit his objective of creating a
political entity (Moyle, 1896:461–464), and he argues his case by
analogy. The Jewish *Volk*, in whose name the decisions concerning
the states are going to be made, is simply regarded as the *dominus*,
the principal. Not being able in its present situation to act properly
as a principal, the Jewish *Volk* simply accepts the actions by a *gestor*
on its behalf, and is bound by the decisions of the *gestor* as if a
contract existed between it and the *gestor* (*quasi ex contractu*). The
actions of the *gestor* are legitimate, so long as "*die allgemeine Sache in
Gefahr und der Dominus durch Willensunfähigkeit oder auf andere Art
verhindert ist, sich selbst zu helfen* [if generally the cause is in danger
and the *dominus* is incapable of helping itself through lack of
willpower or whatever]." What makes the *gestor* different to the
mandator is the fact that, unlike the mandator, the *gestor* is a
member of the group for which he acts, and this accords him the
credibility and the legitimacy which the mandator lacks (cf. the
discussion in Berger, 1953:593–594; also Kaser, 1971:I.586–590).
Herzl repeatedly stresses that his own adoption of this role was to be

a temporary device, simply to set the ball rolling, although he later was to have difficulty in letting the reins go (letter from Herzl to Zadoc Kahn, 26 July 1896; BT2:419, P2:439; also as letter no. 797, BT4:122; and 24 August 1897; BT2:537, P2:579). This function should pass at the earliest opportunity from himself as a person to a properly consituted legal *persona* (the German word *Person* has the meaning of both "person" and "persona"); a body accepted as such by both Jews and non-Jews. This was the body that was to be called the Society of Jews. In *The Jews' State*, Herzl is still quite vague about how this transfer of *gestor* functions from himself to the Society was to occur, how the Society was to be called into being, and who should be its members. Typically, it took subsequent developments to fully clarify these matters in his mind, and Herzl was later to claim with considerable justification that it was the Zionist Congress, when meeting as a congress, which truly functioned as the *gestor* for the Jewish nation:

Nordau schickt mir einen ganz unglaublichen Aufsatz, den er für den "Achiasof"-Kalender geschrieben zum Abdruck in der "Welt." Darin wird der Standpunkt verfochten, die Gespräche der Führer mit Staatsmännern etc. über den Zionismus hätten nicht mehr Bedeutung als Unterhaltungen über das neueste Lustspiel oder das letzte Derbyrennen, solange die Zionisten nicht überall in strammen Vereinen organisiert seien, in deren Namen die Führer sprächen.

Das ist prinzipiell unrichtig, weil wir nur im Wege der negotiorum gestio u. der ratihabitio, nicht aber im unpraktischen u. wohl nirgends von den Gesetzen ermöglichten des Mandates vorgehen können. Es kommt hinzu, daß heute der—allerdings im vorigen Juni geschriebene—Aufsatz geradezu gegen meine Unterredungen mit dem Kaiser aufgefaßt werden kann.

Ich antwortete ihm, daß ich, wenn ich als Präsident des Kongresses u. als von sämmtlichen Zionisten anerkannter Führer—ohne Schmockerei— mit Staatsmännern spreche, nicht als Privatmann, der über Salonstoffe plaudert, angesehen werden kann. Auch könne es nicht als Leichtsinn oder Verbrechen angesehen werden, wenn ich im Namen des jüdischen Volkes

spreche—ich könne mich auf ihn selbst als Kronzeugen berufen, da er mir
nach dem ersten Kongresse geschrieben: Betrachten Sie sich als Regierung!
(24 December 1898; BT2:709–710)

Nordau sent me an utterly incredible essay, which he wrote for the
"Achiasaf" calender, for publication in the *Welt*. In it he propounds
the view that the conversations about Zionism between its leaders
and statesmen, etc., had no more significance than discussions about
the latest comedy or the last Derby race—as long as the Zionists were
not everywhere bound together in tight organizations in whose name
the leaders spoke. This is basically incorrect, because we can proceed
only by the method of *negotiorum gestio* and *ratihabitio* [consent by
the *dominus* of the gestor's activities], and not by the impractical
method of the mandate, which presumably is nowhere sanctioned by
law. Added to this is the fact that today this article—which was
written last June, to be sure—could almost be taken as being against
my conversations with the Kaiser. I answered him that if I, as
president of the Congress and the leader recognized by all Zionists—
without bragging—speak with statesmen, I cannot be considered a
private person chatting about the subjects of the salons. Also, it
cannot be regarded as levity or a crime if I speak in the name of the
Jewish people—I can refer to Nordau himself as my chief witness,
because after the First Congress he wrote me: Consider yourself as
the government! (P2:779)

Ultimately, the *gestor* became the government of the state of Israel.

With the formation of the Society of Jews, which was to act as the
gestor, Herzl had solved the ideological and legal problems involved
in the reconstitution of the Jewish people as a nation. He then
turned his attention to the second step toward statehood, that is the
decisions the *gestor* must make about the form of the state and the
type of governmental and institutional framework of the state. In his
own words:

Die Juden, welche sich zu unserer Staatsidee bekennen, sammeln sich um
die Society of Jews. Diese erhält dadurch den Regierungen gegenüber die

Autorität, im Namen der Juden sprechen und verhandeln zu dürfen. Die Society wird, um es in einer völkerrechtlichen Analogie zu sagen, als staatbildende Macht anerkannt. Und damit wäre der Staat auch schon gebildet.

Those Jews who commit themselves to our idea of the state will gather around the Society of Jews. In this way the latter will gain the authority to have dealings with governments in the name of all Jews. To use an analogy from international law, the Society will be recognized as the power behind the formation of the state, which would be tantamount to the actual establishment of the state.

The Society was to have ultimate responsibility for the political and social organization of the state. In an attempt to supply an outline of this organization, Herzl now turns to the political writings of Montesquieu, and his discussion of the form of state virtually reads like a summary of Montesquieu's arguments in the second and third books of *L'esprit des lois* [The spirit of laws] (Montesquieu, 1950:35–67). Montesquieu is interested in the phenomenon of government, and he suggests that all government is characterized by a nature and a principle. The nature of the government refers to what this government is like—to the person or the group in whom power is vested. The principle is the attitude or orientation that must inform the person in power to act so that the government functions at optimum capacity (Montesquieu, 1950:55). Montesquieu sometimes refers to this principle as a *ressort*—spring of a clock (Montesquieu, 1950:56)—that sets the nature of government into motion. The legislator is viewed as the exceptional person called upon by the society to give it its laws—this is obviously Herzl's *gestor*. Having made these points about the defining characteristics of all government, Montesquieu now suggests that there are three types of government, each with a nature and a principle: republics, monarchies and despotisms (Montesquieu, 1950:35). As far as the nature of these three types of government is concerned, a republic is that form of government in which the people (or a number of important families) hold power. In a monarchy it is the prince who rules, but whose rule is channelled to the people through the aristocracy and the clergy, and mediated through established laws. A despotism is rule by a single person without such mediating classes or procedures (Montesquieu, 1950:35). With respect to the principle attaching to each type, the animating principle which drives a republic is virtue (Montesquieu, 1950:56); that which drives a monarchy is honor (Montesquieu, 1950:63), the one for despotism is fear (Montesquieu, 1950:65). When considering republics, Montesquieu further subdivides them into democratic and aristocratic republics: in a democracy, the guiding orientation is general public virtue and modesty in claims and demands; in an aristocracy, this modesty in claims and demands is confined to the upper classes (Montesquieu, 1950:55; Sills, 1972:IX–X.469–471; Shklar, 1987:74–78). It is these ideas from Montesquieu which inform the discussion on the constitution which Herzl offers towards the end of *The Jews' State*. A despotic government for the new state is dismissed out of hand. Herzl considers a monarchy for the new state to be inappropriate in view of the long-interrupted political history of the Jews; it would simply be ridiculous. He has his doubts about a democratic republic as his new state, as he is not sure whether the Jews as a people will be able to adopt a general attitude of political virtue, and, after all, here he cites Montesquieu, the spring which animates a democracy is virtue. So he opts for an aristocratic republic, in the manner of the old Venetian Republic.

The Jewish Company, the second organization Herzl recommended in *The Jews' State*, was to have a function different from that of the Society of Jews. Its aim was to be the organization of the orderly migration of the Jewish communities, and the development of an economic base for the new state. The functions and scope of the Jewish Company are worked out in considerable detail in *The Jews' State*. The size of its founding capital, how this capital was to be raised, the organization of subscriptions, the development of industrial plants and housing, the conditions of labor—all these are discussed extensively. Whereas Herzl was almost apologetic about his theoretical discussion of the Society of Jews, his imagination really takes wing when he is considering the work of the Jewish Company in all its scope and detail. After the publication of *The Jews' State*, Herzl was to devote a great deal of his time and energy to the development of the Jewish Company, and he regarded the establishment in London of the Jewish Colonial Trust on 20 March 1899 as the realization of this aim (20 March 1899; BT2:731, P2:805). Just as he had foretold in *The Jews' State*, he was unable to interest any of the wealthy Jewish bankers in subscribing to the venture, so the Jewish Colonial Trust was developed from subscriptions among the Jewish people.

In 1902 the Trust established a subsidiary, the Anglo-Palestine Company, which in 1955 became the National Bank of Israel (*Bank Leumi l'Yisrael*) (Patai, 1971:620).

On the Day of Atonement in 1897, Herzl described the importance of the two institutions on which he had spent so much time and energy, with his customary clarity, in these terms:

Ich nehme jetzt die Jewish Company in Angriff. Der Basler Kongress bedeutete die Bildung der Society of Jews gemäß Judenstaat, wenn auch mit opportunistischen Modifikationen u. in schwacher Ausführung. Die Arbeit des nächsten Jahres ist die Herstellung der Jewish Company, vorläufig Jüdische Kolonialbank genannt. (6 October 1897; BT2:549)

I am now tackling *The Jewish Company*. The Basel Congress meant the creation of the *Society of Jews* looking forward to the Jewish State, although with opportunistic modifications and weakly executed. The work of the coming year will be the establishment of *The Jewish Company*, provisionally named the Jewish Colonial Bank. (P2:593)

THE STATE IN PRACTICE

On the basis of the legal arrangements which Herzl discusses, and tempered by economic implications of the transitional emigration period, Herzl makes many practical suggestions about the shape of the institutional framework of the new state. The detail of some of these thoughts and recommendations were important to him, for they served to confirm his claim that he is not interested in devising another utopian dreamworld, of which there were already plenty in circulation. To the modern reader the practical suggestions place Herzl as a man in his times, a man concerned with the legality and the practicality of the takeover of the new land as state, a man worried about the good name and reputation of his new state, a man worried about the increasing popularity of the revolutionary socialist parties which were becoming such an issue (*Umstürzler*), a man aware of the social and economic conditions of work, of the necessity for universal education, universal suffrage, the place of the army in the new society, the organization of religion within the state as well as of the leisure activities of the people. He has much to say about the legal and informational context of the new society. He discusses in some detail how the new emigrants will continue to be subject to the laws of the old country until new arrangements are in place. He explores the question of the language of the new state, and concludes that the new state will be a multilingual entity. He has his say on the role of the media in the new state, how the national interest and freedom of expression are going to be balanced. Much of his attention to detail focuses on the organization of labor in the new state, a field in which he shows himself at the forefront of contemporary thinking. Pride of place goes to his conception of the seven-hour working day; an innovation so important to him that he even wants to include it pictorially into the flag for the new state. It will make the "Seven Hour Land" the "*Musterland für soziale Versuche* [the model country for social experiments]" (16 June 1895; BT2:132,

P1:105), and it will be used in an international publicity campaign (7 June 1895; BT2:75, P:140). He has his thoughts on the labor of women and children, even foreshadowing maternity leave for mothers. He has recommendations for the alleviation of unemployment, and the operation of state relief systems (*assistance par le travail*). He turns his attention to worker's accommodation. He explores what he calls the "truck system" of labor: the situation where the laborer is paid in kind rather than in money. Where some of this detailed discussion now strikes us as anachronistic, it still demonstrates his detailed concern for his people and their new state.

Reception
and Impact

MAINSTREAM REACTIONS

Chaim Weizmann asserts that *The Jews' State* "came like a bolt from the blue" (Weizmann, 1966:43).

Well, hardly. Much as one would like to agree with Weizmann, with the best will in the world it could not be said that the world shook when the 3,000 copies of the first edition of *The Jews' State* hit the bookshops in February 1896. Mainstream Austrian society passed over the event in silence: *totschweigen* (silencing to death) is Pawel's apt description (Pawel, 1989:267). The press in Austria gave it scant attention. The newspaper which employed Herzl, the *Neue Freie Presse*, boycotted the publication. The *Wiener Allgemeine Zeitung*, although ever ready to comment on antisemitic happenings and Jewish protests in Vienna, took until 1 March 1896 to take the new Zionists to task: "*Die Maccabäer der Flucht* [The Maccabaeans of Flight]," as it mockingly called them. It poured scorn on the idea of Jews as a people, and predicted that if the Jews ever got together into the one state, they would hack one another to pieces ("*zerfleischen*") (*Wiener Allgemeine Zeitung*, 1 March 1896, p. 3). The political leaders of the day hardly knew about the work, and those that did seem to have given it no more than cursory comment. The German

foreign minister Bernhard von Bülow in his autobiography devoted
a paragraph to Herzl, the "*Wiener Publizist*," without even mentioning *The Jews' State* by name (Bülow, 1930:254). None of the other
important political interlocutors Herzl was to meet in his remaining
years seems to have read the little work: the Sultan, the Pope, the
Kaiser, the Italian king, the British colonial secretary Chamberlain,
the Russian minister of the Interior Plehve; and with each of them
he had to start from scratch to reformulate its chief message, as the
diary amply shows. The only non-Jewish person of any substance
who seems to have been enthused by the publication was William
Hechler, chaplain at the British Embassy in Vienna, who saw in
Herzl's ideas the restoration of the biblical state of Israel. Herzl
subsequently was to find the enthusiastic Hechler a useful instrument in establishing contacts with the mainstream political world in
Germany through the latter's connections with the Grand Duke of
Baden, by whose good offices he ultimately met with the Kaiser. But
otherwise he viewed Hechler with a mixture of bemusement and
disdain, and certainly did not enter into any messianic notions of the
rebirth of the biblical state with him. Apart from Hechler, the
reaction of mainstream intellectual and political Europe of the day
seems to have been precisely nil. In the words of David Vital
(1975:267):

> The general, non-Jewish public and the great figures of state whom
> Herzl had hoped to arouse on the grounds that the Jewish problem
> was *their* problem as much as anybody's virtually ignored *Der
> Judenstaat.*

JEWISH REACTIONS

Yet the first run of *Der Judenstaat* sold out so rapidly that three more
editions came off the presses during 1896; the fifth edition, the last
to be published during Herzl's lifetime, appeared in 1903. Transla-

tions quickly followed: a Russian one in 1896 (twice) and 1898, a Rumanian one in 1896, a French one in 1897. Sylvie d'Avigdor published her English translation of the work in April 1896—in revisions by Jacob de Haas (1904, 1917), Israel Cohen (1934, 1936, 1943, 1946, 1972), and I. M. Lask (1954, 1956), it has remained the standard English version during the century since the work was published. Harry Zohn offered an alternative English translation in 1970. In all, during Herzl's lifetime, seventeen editions of the work were published (Vital, 1975: 260, note 43).

Not surprisingly, Jewish reaction was extremely varied. Herzl had to absorb a lot of criticism and scorn from his colleagues at the *Neue Freie Presse*. Moritz Benedikt made it clear to him even before the publication of *The Jews' State* that his paper was not going to mention Herzl's developing Zionist activities and his forthcoming book in any shape or form; doing so, in his view, would merely serve to confirm the prejudices of the Viennese antisemites, who suspected the *Neue Freie Presse* was no more than a *Judenblatt*—an ascription which Benedikt was at pains to avoid at all costs (20 October 1895; BT2:254–255, P1:246). The subject was again touched upon by Benedikt, evidently with some heat, early in February 1896, just before the book hit the market:

> *Kampfunterredung mit Benedikt. Er sagte: (1) dürfe kein einzelner die ungeheure moralische Verantwortung auf sich nehmen, diese Lawine ins Rollen zu bringen, so viele Interessen zu gefährden. (2) Wir werden das jetzige Vaterland nicht mehr und den Judenstaat noch nicht haben. (3) Die Broschüre ist unreif für die Veröffentlichung.(4 February 1896; BT2:294–295)*

> Showdown discussion with Benedikt. He said: (1) No individual has the right to take upon himself the tremendous moral responsibility of setting this avalanche in motion and endangering so many interests. (2) We shall no longer have our present fatherland and not yet have the Jews' state. (3) The pamphlet is not yet ripe for publication. (P1:292)

This was the characteristic worry of the assimilated Jew, further confirmed by the remark made to him by a colleague: "*Sie verbrennen die Schiffe hinter sich* [You are burning your bridges behind you]" (4 February 1896; BT2:294, P1:291). This opposition to Herzl remained, and may indeed have been strengthened by certain antisemitic developments in Viennese public life in the year following the publication of *The Jews' State:*

> *Ich traf heute Benedikt auf der Gasse bevor ich ins Bureau ging u. er begleitete mich eine Stunde durch die Stadt. Ich fragte ihn, ob er heute schon dem Zionismus näher gekommen sei durch alles was sich in Öestreich seit einem Jahr abgespielt hat—Lueger beim Kaiser, Badenis Aussöhnung mit den Antisemiten etc? Er beharrte darauf, daß die N Fr Pr auf dem deutschliberalen Standpunkt bleiben müsse. Die jüdisch-nationale Bewegung sei ein Unglück etc. (5 October 1896, BT2:450)*

> Today I met Benedikt on the street before I went to the office, and he walked along with me through the city for an hour. I asked him whether he had not been brought closer to Zionism by all that had happened in Austria within a year—Lueger with the Emperor, Badenis's reconciliation with the antisemites, etc. He insisted that the N. Fr. Pr. had to keep up the German-Liberal standpoint. The Jewish-nationalist movement was a misfortune, etc. (P2:474)

In their lighter moments, the boys at the office continued to have a whale of a time:

> *Man sprach in der Redaktion vom Mars. Bacher sagte überlegen zu mir: "Den Judenstaat können sie vielleicht auf dem Mars errichten." Gelächter der Corona. (28 January 1897; BT2:479)*

> At the office they were discussing Mars. Bacher said to me in a superior tone: "Maybe you can set up your Jewish State on Mars." Laughter among the smart boys. (P2:512)

The Berlin Zionist Convention of July 1896 also expressed "violent opposition" to him (1 August 1896; BT2:426, P2:447). Two days later Herzl's publisher Breitenstein asked him for his attitude to him publishing a "cute answer to my pamphlet" by a Dr. Ludwig Ernst (Ernst, 1896), "author of a book about secret remedies for venereal diseases" (3 August 1896; BT2:428, P2:448), an obtuse assimilationist piece that carried the motto "Striking a blow is the best defense!" A further week or so later the book had come to the notice of a Dr. Singer Coblenz, who in the *Allgemeine Israelitische Wochenschrift* made a "venomous attack" on him (12 August 1896; BT2:432, P2:454). And in Jewish circles in Budapest, the rumor began to circulate that "for the publication of *The Jewish State* I had received a large honorarium from an English land company that wants to do some business in Palestine" (1 December 1896; BT2:469, P2:500). Benedikt's worries apart, most of the above reaction seems simply to have been at the level of ad hominem attack.

The same could not be said about the reaction of the famous sociologist Ludwig Gumplowicz, whom Herzl had written to ask why serious thinkers had taken so little notice of *The Jews' State* and Zionism, and in particular why nobody had taken up his suggestion of the *negotiorum gestio* (letter of Herzl to Gumplowicz, 11 December 1899, BT5:267–268, letter no. 2161). Gumplowicz's answer may have been dismissive, but he at least explained his attitude in terms of scholarly argument. Zionism, in his view, is basically nonsense, but it might result in some salutary self-examination of the Jewish people about their situation. Herzl is simply naive to believe that he can form a state with the help of "*diese zwei fetten Fleischklumpen* [those two greasy lumps of meat]," the Kaiser and the Sultan. Nevertheless, Zionism might be a useful tool for the Jewish community to strengthen itself against the ever-increasing influence of antisemitism (letter of Gumplowicz to Herzl, 12 December 1899; BT5:601–2). Arthur Schnitzler, who knew Herzl personally and had a long-standing professional relationship with him, was very wary

about endorsing Herzl's ideas, but later obliquely paid Herzl the
great compliment of discussing the whole assimilation-nationalism
issue in his novel *Der Weg ins Freie* (1898). Karl Kraus, in his
pamphlet *Eine Krone für Zion*, ridiculed the idea in his own
inimitable style, but on the basis that the Jews are at most a religious,
not a national community (Kraus, 1979:289–314).

The reaction of Moritz Güdemann, chief rabbi of Vienna, is of
great interest. Herzl had sought him out as early as August 1895 to
get his views on a state for the Jews, and he even submitted some
manuscript material for his perusal. Initially the chief rabbi had been
full of enthusiasm, and had gone so far as to call him the new Moses
(18 August 1895; BT2:242; P1:233). He soon began to have
reservations about the state for the Jews, however, and in April 1897
he expressed them in his pamphlet *Nationaljudentum*, published by
Herzl's publisher Breitenstein, of all people. Güdemann put his
difficulties in terms of identity by putting the question, "Who was
more assimilated, the nationalist Jew who ignored the Sabbath or the
practising Jew who felt himself a German?" (Stewart, 1974:247). The
problem with *The Jews' State* was a religious one, and had to do with
Herzl's basic objective, the spiritual reformation of the new Jew by
means of the development of the state. For Güdemann, the
development of the state was neither here nor there, but it was not
within Herzl's province to link the salvation of the Jewish personality
with national ambition: if there was to be a new Jew, he was to be
defined in religious terms, and his development was to be seen in
religious contexts only. Neatly turning Herzl's own arguments on
himself, Güdemann wrote that defining Judaism as a national issue
was actually a kind of antisemitic label that reduced everything to
race and nationalism:

> *Wenn man denjenigen Juden, welchen in ihrer bisherigen Heimat der
> Kampf ums Dasein allzusehr erschwert wird, Gelegenheit bietet, sich
> anderwärts anzusiedeln, so ist dies in hohem Grade löblich und verdienst-
> lich. Man kann nur wünschen und hoffen, daß die jüdischen Kolonien, wo*

immer solche bereits bestehen oder künftig angelegt werden, sei es nun im
heiligen Lande, oder anderwärts, ihr gedeihliches Fortkommen finden,
aber es ist durchaus verkehrt, und streitet wider den Geist des Judentums
und seiner Geschichte, wenn diese an sich der höchsten Anerkennung
würdige Kolonisationstätigkeit mit nationalen Bestrebungen verquickt und
als die Einlösung prophetischer Verheißung hingestellt wird. Nein, das ist
sie nie und nimmer. (Güdemann, 1897:39)

If someone offers the opportunity to settle somewhere else to those
Jews whose struggle for existence in their present home country gets
simply beyond them, then this is a highly praiseworthy and merito-
rious act. One can only wish and hope that Jewish settlements,
whether already existing at present or projected in the future, be it in
the Holy Land or somewhere else, face a prosperous future. But it is
totally wrong, and it goes against the spirit and history of Judaism
when this otherwise highly praiseworthy settlement activity is mixed
with national aspirations and is represented as the fulfillment of the
promises of the prophets. No, it can never be that.

Rabbi Güdemann's concerns were the concerns of other rabbis.
The *Geschäftführender Vorstand des Rabbinervorstandes in Deutschland*
[Executive of the Society of Rabbis in Germany] had similar
concerns about Herzl's claims that through the state he would
engender the new Jew:

Die Bestrebungen sogenannter Zionisten, in Palästina einen jüdisch-
nationalen Staat zu gründen, widersprechen den messianischen Ver-
heißungen des Judentums, wie sie in der heiligen Schrift und den späteren
Religionsquellen erhalten sind. Das Judentum verpflichtet seine Bekenner,
dem Vaterlande, dem sie angehören, mit aller Hingebung zu dienen und
dessen nationale Interessen mit ganzen Herzen und mit allen Kräften zu
fördern (cited in Herzl, 1897b)

The aims of so-called Zionists to establish a national Jewish state in
Palestine contradict the messianic promises of Judaism as contained
in the Holy Scriptures and later religious sources. Judaism places an

obligation on its members to serve the fatherland to which they belong with complete dedication, and to promote its national interests wholeheartedly and with all their energies.

Herzl was evidently shaken by Güdemann's pamphlet:

> *Von Dr. Güdemann ist eine tückische Gegenbroschüre unter dem Titel "Nationaljudentum" erschienen. Offenbar auf Wunsch der hiesigen Upper Jews. Er hält sich in vagen, feigen Unbestimmtheiten, hat aber die ersichtliche Absicht, Munition für kühnere Streiter zu liefern. Ich antworte ihm. Und zwar, nach dem Machiavellischen Rezept, vernichtend. Der Verleger Breitenstein, der natürlich alles nimmt u. nur sein Geschäft verfolgt, sagt mir, Rothschild habe gleich nach dem Erscheinen der Güdemann'schen Schrift dreißig Exemplare holen lassen. (17 April 1897; BT2:501)*

> Dr. Güdemann has published a malicious counter-pamphlet entitled *Nationaljudentum [Jewish Nationalism]*, evidently at the behest of the local "upper Jews." He confines himself to vague, cowardly generalities, but with the obvious intention of providing ammunition for bolder warriors. I shall answer him—and, following the Machiavellian precept, it will be devastating. The publisher Breitenstein, who naturally accepts anything and has only business in view, tells me that as soon as Güdemann's tract appeared, Rothschild sent for thirty copies. (P2:536–537)

He replied to Güdemann with an article in Josef Bloch's *Österreichische Wochenschrift* (23 April 1897) entitled *Das Nationaljudentum von Dr. Güdemann* [Dr. Güdemann's National Judaism], in which he repeats his injunction of *The Jews' State* that the new Zionism allows all to get to heaven in their own way and that Güdemann should stick to his religious duties (Herzl, 1897a:346). Just to make sure that his points were driven home, Max Nordau contributed to the dispute with his article in *Die Welt* entitled *Ein Tempelstreit* [A dispute in the temple] (Nordau, 1897).

Outside Vienna the situation was much the same. The initial reactions of the Berlin Zionists, and the scurrilous rumors circulating in Budapest have already been mentioned. In Paris, Baron Edmond de Rothschild rejected Herzl's plan and carried most of the European Hovevei Zion with him (Patai, 1971:492).

With the indifference of the mainstream world, and then the hostility of much of the Jewish world to contend with, Herzl reached a low point late in 1896:

> *Ich muß es mir offen gestehen: ich bin demoralisiert. Von keiner Seite Hilfe, von allen Seiten Angriffe. Nordau schreibt mir aus Paris, daß sich dort niemand mehr rührt. Die Maccabaeans in London sind immer mehr Pickwickier, wenn ich den Berichten meines getreuen de Haas glauben darf. In Deutschland habe ich nur Gegner. Die Russen sehen teilnehmend zu, wie ich mich abrackere, aber keiner hilft mit. In Öestreich, besonders in Wien, habe ich ein paar Anhänger. Hievon sind die Uninteressierten völlig untätig, die Anderen, die Tätigen wollen durch den Redacteur der N Fr Pr vorwärtskommen.*
>
> *Hinzu kommt die Verleumdungscampagne, deren Leiter der brave Scheid zu sein scheint.*
>
> *Die Juden, denen es gut geht, sind alle meine Gegner. So daß ich anfange das Recht zu haben, der größte aller Antisemiten zu sein.*
>
> *Oft denke ich an Levysohns Wort: 'Die, denen sie helfen wollen, werden sie zunächst recht empfindlich ans Kreuz schlagen'.* (13 October 1896; BT2:456)

I must frankly admit it to myself: I am demoralized. From no side help, from all sides attacks. Nordau writes me from Paris that nobody stirs there any longer. The Maccabeans in London are more and more Pickwickian, if I may believe the reports of my faithful de Haas. In Germany I have only opponents. The Russians look on sympathetically while I wear myself out, but none of them lends a hand.

In Austria, particularly Vienna, I have a few adherents. Of these, the disinterested ones are completely inactive; the others, the active ones, want to advance their careers through an editor of the *N. Fr. Pr.*

Added to this is the slander campaign, whose leader appears to be

the worthy Scheid. All the Jews who are well off are my opponents.
   So that I am beginning to have the right to be the biggest of all
antisemites. I often think of Levysohn's words: "Those whom you
want to help will start by nailing you rather painfully to the cross."
(P2:481–482)

It was indeed because of all this hostility that Herzl decided to
found his own *Judenblatt, Die Welt*, and explore the possibility of
continuing his mission with groups other than the high and mighty
of the Jewish community, just as he had anticipated in *The Jews'
State*.

He could not have undertaken such a task without at least some
support. Even before the publication of *The Jews' State*, the Vienna
Kadimah had got wind of Herzl's ideas through an advance notice by
Herzl, placed in the London *Jewish Chronicle*. They sent a deputation
to Herzl on 7 February 1896 to invite him to address their meeting
in the *Jüdische Akademische Lese- und Redehalle* [Jewish Academic
Reading and Conference Room]. His address was so impressive that
they invited him back on the 20 February for another seminar. A
number of students visited him in the ensuing weeks, and on 7
March they suggested that a propaganda drive be launched in
Vienna. By June 1896 Vienna boasted a Zionist Association. On 15
September there was a debate about the future of the Zionist
movement in the Vienna Café Louvre, and a month later Herzl was
guest of honor at a gala gathering of the *Kadimah* (21 October). On
6 and 7 March 1897 the *Kadimah* organized a meeting of Zionists in
Vienna, which adopted Herzl's suggestion to convene a general
Zionist Congress later in the year. It was the members of the *Kadimah*
who shouldered the task of preparing the Congress. Preliminary
steps included the first public meeting of Zionists in Vienna on 16
March, chaired by Leon Kellner and attended by almost a thousand
persons. A Zionist Executive was elected at a meeting on 20 May. On
11 May the decision was taken to found a Zionist newspaper, to be
termed *Die Welt*; its first issue appeared on 2 June 1897 (the above

is based on Patai, 1971:91–94). The Congress was held at Basel from 29 to 31 August 1897. "Nothing comes closer to the miraculous," Ernst Pawel comments, "than the speed with which the literary editor of the *Neue Freie Presse* established himself within a matter of months as the leader, spokesman, and standard-bearer of secular Jewish nationalism" (Pawel, 1989:268). At its golden jubilee in 1933, the *Kadimah* summed up its activities in those crucial months in these terms:

> *Hätte es im Jahre 1896, als Herzl, tief verstimmt von der Absage der reichen Juden, auf seinen Judenstaat resignierte, keine "Kadimah" gegeben, alte Herren und junge Studenten, wer weiß, ob wir heute einen politischen Zionismus hätten.* (Kadimah, 1933:35-36)

If in the year 1896 there had not been a *Kadimah* of old boys and young students, when Herzl, deeply disturbed by the apathy of the wealthy Jews, had given up on his *Judenstaat*, who knows if today we would have a political Zionism at all.

Once the *Kadimah* had shown the way, the Zionist Congresses carried the responsibility of continuing the movement.

Although the *Kadimah* were the most important, there were other encouraging voices. Max Nordau, the famous sociologist and academic of international repute, let himself be converted and put his not inconsiderable reputation in the service of the Zionists. The publisher Max Bodenheimer in Cologne became one of Herzl's most enthusiastic supporters. Through him he was introduced to David Wolfssohn. The support of Wolfssohn was particularly valued by Herzl, for not only did he bring vast experience in industrial management and banking into the the budding Zionist movement, but, being of Lithuanian extraction, he provided the movement with a profound knowledge of the situation of Russian Jewry (Vital, 1975:270–271). *The Jews' State* even seems to have carried Herzl's reputation to Palestine itself, and Herzl was particularly gratified by his contact with a Dr. D'Arbela, for this Dr. D'Arbela was the director of the Rothschild hospitals in Jerusalem, and, as such, was on the spot in the future *Judenstaat*, so to speak:

> *Gestern war Dr. D'Arbela aus Jerusalem bei mir. Er ist Direktor der Rothschildschen Spitäler . . . Er erzählte mir wunderbare Dinge aus Palästina . . . Von unserem Nationalplan spricht ganz Palästina. Wir sind ja doch die angestammten Herren des Landes. Die türkische Besatzung Jerusalems ist derzeit schwach—etwa 600 Mann. Schon jetzt bilden die Juden die Mehrheit der Einwohnerschaft in Jerusalem, wenn ich D'Arbela recht verstanden habe. Wir sprachen so schnell u. von allen Dingen, daß ich den Punkt gar nicht tiefer angriff. Das Klima ist vortrefflich, der Boden nicht verkarstet, nur die Humusschicht ist von den Bergen wo einst die Terrassen der Fruchtbarkeit waren, in Schlünde geschwemmt. Jetzt blühen in Palästina die Orangen. Alles ist zu machen in diesem Lande. Diesen prächtigen Menschen wollen wir uns merken für kommende Aufgaben. (20 February 1897; BT2:483–84)*

Yesterday Dr. D'Arbela from Jerusalem came to see me. He is the director of the Rothschild hospitals . . . He told me wonderful things about Palestine . . . All Palestine talks about our nationalist plan. After all, we are the hereditary lords of the land. The Turkish occupation forces of Jerusalem are weak at present—about 600 men. Even now the Jews constitute the majority of Jerusalem's inhabitants, if I understood D'Arbela aright. We spoke so quickly and about so many things that I did not even go more closely into this point. The climate is excellent, the soil not barren, only the humus layer has been washed into gorges from mountains where once there were terraces of fruitfulness. Now oranges are blooming in Palestine. Everything can be done in that country. We shall make a note of this splendid man for future assignments. (P2:516–517)

By the time Herzl's life had drawn to a close, some eight years after the publication of his *Jews' State*, his reputation, the reputation of his little book, and the reputation of the movement he had set in motion had become immortal. In Robert Wistrich's assessment, "*Der Juden-*

staat placed Zionism on the map of international politics" (Wistrich, 1989:445). Israel Zangwill, who had known Herzl, wrote, deeply moved by Herzl's recent death, with flourish:

This morning he was buried. Buried at the age of forty-four, in the prime of his princely manhood! But is there one of us who cannot see him upon this platform? He has not broken his word. He is with us, speaking to every heart; he will never leave us again. *Nicht gestorben weil unsterblich*—not dead because undying. Of Moses we are told that no man knew the place of his sepulchre. And who can say where Herzl will lie buried, since his living influence is everywhere? It could easily be traced . . . My friends, you cannot bury a great man. If you cannot bury a great man, still less can you bury a great cause . . . Of Zionism, too, it can be said, *Nicht gestorben weil unsterblich*. Herzl had from the first provided against the event we mourn tonight, just as he provided in his will that his body should some day be borne with us to Palestine. He knew too well that he might only gaze upon the Promised Land, and he has laid his hands upon the head of more than one Joshua, and filled them with the spirit of his wisdom to carry on his work. And though there will never arise one like unto him, though there is no one with his fiery energy, his magnificent dash, his inspired impatience, yet our cause, our cause is too great to rest upon an individual. And so he leaves behind him not only his disciples but a Constitution. If some of the machinery he has bequeathed to us, constructed in the early stages of our movement, will be unworkable without him, the loss of him forces us more than ever to reorganize our institutions and to try to make up in system for what we have lost in genius. But the Congress will always remain a lasting creation of Herzl. *Nicht gestorben weil unsterblich*. Our Congress supplies a Jewish parliament, and our Jewish parliament will one day supply a Jewish state. (Zangwill, July 1904, in Simon, 1937:131–132)

The Jews' State

An Attempt at a Modern Solution to the Issue of the Jews

by Theodor Herzl
Doctor of Laws

Preamble

The concept with which I am dealing in this paper is very old. It is the establishment* of the Jews' State.

The world resounds with clamor against Jews, and that arouses this concept out of its sleep.

At every stage of my argument, it should be kept clearly in mind that I am not making anything up. I am making up neither the situation of the Jews,* which has developed historically, nor the means of overcoming it. The material components of the building, which I am designing, are available in real life; they can be seized with both hands; everyone can convince himself of this. If this attempt to solve the issue of the Jews is to be characterized in one word, then it should not be called a "fantasy," at most it may be called a "project."

First of all, I must defend my plan against the charge of being utopian. Strictly speaking, in doing so I am merely protecting superficial critics from committing an absurdity. For it would hardly be a shame to write a humane utopia. I could also give myself an easier literary success if to the reader, keen to be entertained, I brought this plan couched in the irresponsible form of a novel. But

---

*See glossary for explanations of marked terms.

this is no charming utopian scheme, such as has been produced so often before and after Thomas More.* I believe the situation of Jews in various countries is so bad as to render introductory trifles superfluous.

To throw some light on the difference between my construct and a utopian scheme, I choose an interesting book, recently published, *Freeland* by Dr. Theodor Hertzka.* Conceived by a thoroughly modern scholar, trained in the area of national economics, this is a talented piece of fantasy, as far from real life as the Equator-Mountain, where this dreamland is situated. *Freeland* is a complicated machine with many cogs and wheels which even slot into each other, but nothing convinces me that it can be made to work. Even if I were to see the establishment of "Freeland-Societies," I would still regard them as a joke.

By contrast, the present plan is concerned with the application of a driving force which is present in real life. In all modesty, and being well aware of my inadequacy, I content myself with merely pointing out the cogs and wheels of the machine, trusting that there will be better practical mechanics than I am, who can build it.

The important point is the driving force. And what is this force? The plight of the Jews.

Who dares deny that this force exists? We will deal with it in the chapter about the basis of antisemitism.

We know the power of steam, developing in the teapot as the water heats, and lifting the lid. The Zionist experiments and the many other forms of associations "to ward off antisemitism": they are this phenomenon of the teapot.

Now I say that this force, properly applied, is powerful enough to drive a large machine, to profit people and things. It will not matter what this machine will look like.

I am convinced to the very depths of my being that I am right; I do not know whether I shall be proved correct during my lifetime. The first men who will start this movement will probably not see its glorious culmination. But even just by starting it, a great pride, an inner freedom, and joy will enter their lives.

I shall also be sparing in filling in the picture with picturesque details, so as to guard my plan against the suspicion of being utopian. In any case, I suspect that some will thoughtlessly try to mock and caricature what I have designed so as to rob everything of its power. An otherwise quite intelligent Jew, with whom I discussed the issue, thought that "potential detail portrayed as real is a characteristic of utopian" description. That is wrong. Every finance minister prepares his budget with future estimates—not merely with figures calculated from the averages of past years or derived from documents from other countries, but also with projected data that have no precedent, for example, when introducing a new tax. If you do not know that, you can never have studied a budget. Would you consider a financial bill utopian, even if you knew that the projections could never be precisely achieved?

But I put even more difficult challenges to my readers. From the educated persons whom I address, I demand that they rethink and relearn many old notions. I specifically challenge the best Jews who are involved in a practical way with solving the issue of the Jews to regard their attempts so far as failed and impractical.

In presenting the idea I have to be careful of a danger. If I practice discretion when I say all these things which lie in the future, then it could seem as if I do not believe they are possible. If, on the contrary, I announce their realization without reserve, then everything could look far-fetched.

So I say clearly and firmly: I believe it is possible to bring the idea to reality, even though I do not pretend to have found it in its final form. The world needs the Jews' State; consequently it will come about.

If pursued by a single individual, this idea would be insane, but if many Jews get involved at the same time, it is completely rational, and bringing it to fruition poses no difficulties to speak of. The idea merely depends on how many people support it. Perhaps our ambitious young people, to whom all avenues have been blocked and to whom the Jews' State offers the prospect of honor, freedom and happiness, perhaps they will take on the task of spreading the idea about.

Personally, I think that my task is completed with the publication of this paper. I will only speak to it if attacked by opponents of note, or if needed to counter unforeseen objections or to put aside errors.

Is what I say not yet appropriate for the present time? Am I ahead of my time? Are the sufferings of the Jews not yet great enough? We shall see.

At any rate, it depends on the Jews themselves whether for the time being this paper represents political fact or political fiction. If the present generation is still too apathetic, then another, higher, better one will come. Those Jews who want it will have their state, and they will deserve it.

Introduction

What practical men, standing in the midst of life, understand of economics is often startlingly little. This explains why even Jews faithfully repeat the slogan of the antisemites that we live off "host" populations, and that we would starve to death if we did not have a "host" population around us. Here is an instance that shows how unjust accusations can lower our self-esteem. So what is the real truth about the concept of "host" populations? Assuming the concept does not rest on old physiocratic* limitations, it is based on the naive misconception that economic life rests on the constant recirculation of the same wealth. Now unlike Rip van Winkle,* we do not need to wake up out of a long sleep to realize that it is the constant production of new wealth which changes the world. In our wonderful times replete with technical progress even the most benighted person with his eyes shut can see the emerging new wealth. It has been created by the spirit of enterprise.

Labor without enterprise is old and stationary; the typical example is agriculture, which is standing still at the point reached by its precursors a thousand years ago. All material progress has come through entrepreneurs. You almost feel ashamed to write down such an obvious triviality. Even if we were all entrepreneurs, which is a foolish exaggeration, we would still not need a "host" population.

We do not depend on the constant recirculation of the same wealth, because we create new wealth.

In machines we possess slaves of enormous power, which have made their entry into the civilized world as deadly competitors for manual workers. Admittedly, you also need workers to operate the machines, but for this purpose we have more than enough people. Only those who are not familiar with the situation of Jews in the various regions of Eastern Europe would be so bold as to maintain that Jews are not suited to manual labor or are unwilling to perform it.

However, I really do not want to use this paper to defend the Jews. That would be useless. All that is reasonable and charitable has already been said about this subject. It is not enough to find the appropriate arguments to change intellect and attitudes; if your audience does not have the capacity to understand, you are a voice crying in the wilderness. If, however, your audience has a capacity for understanding, then the whole sermon is superfluous. I believe that humanity progresses to ever higher levels of morality, even though I consider this progress to be desperately slow. If we had to wait until the man in the street learns the tolerance shown by Lessing when he wrote *Nathan the Wise,** then we would be waiting a long time, as would our children, grandchildren and great-grandchildren. The spirit of the times assists us from another angle.

By virtue of its technical achievements, the present century has offered us a precious renaissance. Unfortunately, this fabulous progress has not yet affected our humanity. The earth has been conquered in all its vastness, yet we still suffer the pains of our own narrowness. We now speed in enormous steamships over formerly unknown seas without danger. Trains now lead us safely into the mountains, which we used to fear on foot. What happens in countries which were not even thought of when Europe already confined Jews to ghettos is now known within the hour. That is why the plight of the Jews is an anachronism—not because we had the Enlightenment a century ago, which in fact merely affected the greatest scholars.

In my opinion electricity was not discovered so that a few snobs could light up their ostentatious rooms, but rather so that we could solve the great questions of humanity by its light. The issue of the Jews is one of these, and not even the most insignificant one. In devising a solution, we do not only act for ourselves, but also for many others who are burdened and bothered.

The issue of the Jews does exist. It would be foolish to deny it. It is a worn-out relic from the Middle Ages, which the community of civilized nations still cannot leave behind with the best will in the world. They did show their generous disposition when they emancipated us. The issue of the Jews exists in all those places where Jews live in appreciable numbers. Where it does not exist, it is brought in by Jews that go to live there. Obviously, we go where they do not persecute us; but as soon as we appear, persecution sets in. That is true and will always be true, as long as the issue of the Jews is not solved on a political level. Even in highly developed countries: France provides the evidence. At this very moment the poor Jews carry antisemitism into England, they have already introduced it into America.

I believe I understand antisemitism, which is a highly complicated movement. I view this movement from the standpoint of a Jew, but without hatred or fear. I believe I can recognize those aspects of antisemitism which are a coarse joke, common jealousy, inherited prejudice, religious intolerance; but also those aspects born out of alleged self-defense. I consider the issue of the Jews neither in social nor religious terms, even though these things do come into it. It is a national issue, and if we are to find a solution, we must make it into a political question for the whole world, to be tackled in counsel with all civilized peoples.

We are a people, *one* people.

We have tried everywhere in all honesty to assimilate into the communities around us, while preserving the faith of our fathers. We are not allowed to. We are faithful and often even over-enthusiastic patriots—in vain. We make the same sacrifices in life and limb as our countrymen—in vain. We do our utmost to further the reputation of our home countries in the fields of arts and science—in vain. We toil to increase the wealth of our lands with our commerce and trade—in vain. In our home countries, where we have been living for centuries, we are decried as foreign, often by those whose forebears were not even living there when our forebears were already being persecuted. It is the majority which decides who is an alien in the land; it is a question of power, like all relations between peoples. By saying this as a single individual without a mandate I do not put any of our acquired rights on the line. Given the present state of the world, might will have precedence over right in the foreseeable future. Therefore we are good patriots everywhere in vain, just like the Huguenots,* who were forced to go elsewhere. If they only left us in peace . . .

But I believe they will not leave us in peace.

Pressure and persecution will not eradicate us. No people in history has coped with such struggles and suffering as we have. Jew baiting has only ever persuaded our weak members to fall away. Strong Jews return defiantly back to their tribe once persecution breaks out. That became clear during the period immediately after the emancipation of the Jews. The more highly educated and wealthier Jews completely lost their feeling of solidarity. Given some lasting political well-being we assimilate everywhere; I do not believe that to be dishonorable. The statesman keen to have a touch of the Jewish race in his nation would have to look after our political well-being in the long run. And even a Bismarck could not manage that.

For deep down within the feelings of peoples there are old prejudices anchored against us. If you want evidence, you only need to listen where the people express themselves simply and truthfully: folktales and proverbs are antisemitic. Everywhere the common people is like a big child to be educated, but at best this education would take so much time that we can solve our problems far more quickly in other ways, as I have already said.

Assimilation—which I take to be not just external assimilation in dress, ways of living, customs and language, but rather becoming equal in mind and kind—such assimilation of Jews could only be achieved through mixed marriage. This, however, should be experienced by the majority as a need; it is not enough to simply permit mixed marriage in terms of the law. The liberals in Hungary,* who have recently done this, are curiously mistaken. They illustrated this officially sanctioned mixed marriage by an early example of a baptized Jew marrying a Jewish woman. The difficulties with the present law on marriage in Hungary have widened in many cases the divisions between Christians and Jews and harmed rather than promoted the mixing of the races. There is only one way if you want to see the decline of Jews through mixed marriage. Jews would first have to attain such a degree of economic power that the old social prejudice against them is conquered. The classic example is the aristocracy, in which most mixed marriages take place. The old aristocracy guilds itself with the money of Jews, and Jewish families are absorbed into it. But how would this phenomenon work with the middle-classes, where the issue of the Jews is most pertinent, in view of the fact that Jews are a middle-class people? In this context the prior need for Jews to attain status would be synonymous with Jews attaining a monopoly of economic power, which some think they have already, albeit wrongly. If the power the Jews hold at present already gives rise to the angry and distressed bleatings of the antisemites, how much worse would such outbreaks be if this Jewish power grew even bigger? Such a first stage of absorption is unattainable, for it would imply the subjugation of the majority by a minority, disdained until recently and not in possession of the instruments of war and administration. That is why I believe the absorption of Jews on the basis of their prosperity to be improbable. Jewish residents of present antisemitic countries would agree with me. My compatriots in those other countries, where Jews are doing well at present, will probably disagree violently with my opinion. They will only believe me when next confronted with Jew baiting. The longer antisemitism is kept at bay, the more furious it will be when it does break out. The infiltration of emigrating Jews, attracted by the seemingly secure conditions, coupled with the rising class movement of the local Jews, will then form a mighty movement and force a revolution. Nothing is more simple than this conclusion.

Because I fearlessly draw conclusions which are founded in truth, I anticipate in advance that there will be objections and hostility from those Jews living in better conditions. Insofar as these represent private interests of people who feel threatened by their own stupidity and cowardice, they can be brushed aside with a disdainful smile. For the cause of the poor and oppressed is more important. Even so, I would not want to give the wrong impression that well-off Jews would lose their property if this plan were ever realized. That is why I will provide detailed explanations of what will legally happen to property. If the whole concept remains on paper, then nothing will ever change.

A more serious objection would be that by calling Jews a people, or rather one people, I am giving a boost to the antisemites; that I am hindering the assimilation of Jews where it is about to occur, or that I am endangering in retrospect the position of those Jews already assimilated—as if one solitary writer is in a position to seriously hinder or endanger anything at all.

This objection is likely to come in the first instance from France. I also expect it from other places, but I will answer the French Jews in anticipation, because they provide the most striking example.

However much I venerate the individual, be it the unique, strong individual personality of the statesman, the discoverer, the artist, the philosopher or the general, or the collective personality of a historical group of human beings which we call *Volk*, I still do not mourn his destruction. Whoever can, wants to, must perish— should perish. The collective personality of the Jews as a people, however, cannot, will not, and must not perish. It cannot perish, because external enemies hold it together. It will not perish; it has demonstrated that during two millennia under enormous suffering.

It must not perish; that is what I seek to demonstrate in this publication after many other Jews who never gave up hope. Whole branches of Jewry may well die away and fall off; the tree lives.

My answer to all or some of the French Jews who may object to my plan because they are already "assimilated" is simple: the entire issue is of no concern to them. They are Israelite Frenchmen, excellent! This, however, is an internal concern of Jews.

Of course, the movement toward statehood which I am proposing would harm neither Israelite Frenchmen nor "assimilated" Jews of other countries. On the contrary, it would be of great benefit to them. For, to use Darwin's expression, they would no longer be disturbed in their "chromatic function."* They could go on assimilating in peace, for the antisemitism of today would stop for ever. Indeed, as persons assimilated to the innermost depths of their soul, their credibility would be enhanced if they stay where they now live after the new state for Jews, with its better institutions, has become a fact of life.

Getting rid of the Jews who remain true to their group would be even more advantageous to assimilated Jews than to Christian citizens, for assimilated Jews would no longer have to cope with the worrisome, inevitable, incalculable competition of the Jewish proletariat, thrown about from place to place and country to country by political pressure and economic distress. This floating proletariat would become tied to one place. At present, many Christian citizens—commonly known as antisemites—are in a position to protest against the immigration of foreign Jews. The Israelite citizens cannot do so, even though they are the more heavily affected, because they are in competition with their own economic kind, who, apart from everything else, are responsible for importing antisemitism from abroad or even for increasing local antisemitism. This is the lament of assimilated Jews, to which they then give expression in "philanthropic" projects. They establish emigration societies for immigrating Jews. This phenomenon is a paradox, which might even be funny, were it not that suffering human beings are involved. In offering assistance, some of these societies do not work for but rather against persecuted Jews. The poorest among these must be taken away, very quickly and very far. Indeed when you go into it carefully you realize that many a would-be friend of the Jews is no more than an antisemite of Jewish background in disguise.

Yet even the colonizing efforts of really well-meaning individuals have thus far not taken root, even though they have been interesting as experiments. I do not really believe that they regarded these experiments of uprooting poor Jews as a sport in much the same way as horse racing. The issue is simply too serious and sad. These experiments were interesting insofar as they represent in a limited sense precursors of the idea of the Jews' State. And even the mistakes that were made have their use, for we now know what to avoid when the real thing takes place. Unfortunately, these experiments have also done some harm. That as the inevitable consequence of such artificial infiltration, antisemitism has been transplanted to new regions, I would regard as the least of the disadvantages. It is more serious that the unsatisfactory experiences have led the Jews themselves to cast doubt on the quality of Jewish human resources. Intelligent persons having this doubt may be answered quite simply as follows: what is impracticable or appropriate at a micro level, need not be so at a macro level. A small business may well experience losses under the same conditions that a large business makes a profit. You might not be able to float a rowing boat on a brook, yet the river into which it flows can carry stately iron ships.

No one person has sufficient strength or wealth to transplant a whole people from one domicile to another. Only an idea is powerful enough to do that. The idea of the state has such power. For the whole night of their history Jews have not stopped dreaming the royal dream. "Next year in Jerusalem" is our ancient watchword. The question now is to demonstrate that the dream can be turned into an idea as bright as day.

To achieve this, we must wipe our souls clean of all the old, superseded, confused, narrow-minded ideas. Some dull spirits may at first feel that wandering away from civilization must necessarily lead into the desert. Not true! Our emigration will take place in the midst of civilization. You do not go back to a lower stage, but advance to a higher stage of civilization. You do not occupy clay huts, but you build yourselves beautiful modern houses where you can live without fear. You do not lose your hard-earned wealth, but put it to good use. You only exchange your present rights for better rights. You do not give up the ways which have become dear to you, but you find them again. You do not leave the old house before the new one is ready. The only ones among us to leave are those who are certain to improve their situation by doing so. First the desperate among us, then the poor, then the well-off, then the wealthy. Those who leave first will be raised to the next social level as the inevitable consequence of such artificial infiltration, until people at this new level start sending their representatives. Apart from anything else, this emigration is an ascending class movement.

The emigration of the Jews will not lead to any economic disturbances, crises or persecutions, but will introduce a period of prosperity in the countries Jews leave behind. There will be a movement internally by Christian citizens into the positions the Jews leave vacant. The transformation will be gradual, free from trauma, and its intinial stages will mark the end of antisemitism. The Jews will be leaving as valued friends, and should some isolated individuals subsequently return, they will be received back in the civilized countries with kindness and treated like other foreign nationals. This emigration is not a flight, but an orderly transfer supported by public opinion. The movement must be based solely within a framework of law; indeed it can only be accomplished with the friendly cooperation of the participating governments, which themselves stand to gain substantially from it.

To guarantee the integrity of the idea and the power of putting it into practice, guarantees will be necessary which can only be found in so-called "moral" and "juridical" entities. I would like to keep these two categories, which in legal language are often bundled together, quite separate. As moral entity, which incorporates legal status outside the sphere of private property, I establish the Society of Jews. Beside it stands the juridical entity of the Jewish Company, whose purpose is to handle resources.

Any individual who thinks he could undertake this gigantic task on his own could only be a crook or a madman. The integrity of the moral entity is guaranteed by the good character of all its members. Whether the juridical entity has sufficient power is measured by the resources at its disposal.

With the above introductory remarks I have aimed to deflect the swarm of objections which the very term "Jews' State" is likely to evoke. We will now go on in a somewhat more leisurely fashion to explain things; we will tackle other objections and we will develop more fully many of the things which we have only hinted at so far. In the interest of this publication, which should take flight, we will try to stay clear of complicated matter and language as far as we possibly can. Short pithy chapters will be most suited to this objective.

If I want to build a new building on the site of an old one, I must first demolish before constructing. So I will stick to this sensible sequence. Initially, in the general part I will define ideas, clear away old concepts that have become meaningless, indicate the political and economic conditions, and develop the concept.

In the particular part, which is divided into three chapters, the practical issues will be presented. These three chapters are: Jewish Company, Local Groups and Society of Jews. The Society will be established first, the Company last of all; but they are best discussed the other way round, because the financial feasibility presents the most difficulties, which therefore have to be addressed first.

In the conclusion I will introduce those possible objections which we have not hitherto met. I hope my Jewish readers will follow me patiently to the end. Many readers will think of objections in a different order than I tackle them. If, however, your reservations have been intelligently dealt with, then you should commit yourself to the cause.

Though I try to be purely rational, I know very well that reason alone is not enough. Old prisoners find it difficult to leave the dungeon. We shall see whether our young people, whom we need, have the capacity to follow our lead—our youth, who will sweep the old along with them, carry them in their powerful arms, and who will transform our intellectual reasons into enthusiasm.

General Part

THE ISSUE OF THE JEWS

Nobody will deny the perilous situation of the Jews. They are persecuted in all countries where they live in significant numbers, more so in some, less so in others. To their disadvantage, social and legal equality has indeed been abandoned in practice nearly everywhere, even where it still exists in law. Even middle-ranking positions in the army, in public and private life, are not accessible to them. Attempts are being made to force them out of the business world: "Don't buy from Jews."*

Day by day, attacks on Jews increase in the parliaments, at meetings, in the press, on the pulpit, in the street; when they travel, they are denied entry into hotels or places of amusement. The character of these persecutions varies, depending on country or social circle. In Russia they plunder Jewish villages, in Rumania they beat a few people to death, in Germany Jews are on the receiving end of a good thrashing now and again, in Austria public life is terrorized by antisemites, in Algeria there are preachers roaming the countryside extolling hatred, in Paris high society closes ranks and shuts itself off against Jews. The variety is endless. However, this is not an attempt to provide a melancholy list of all Jewish hardships. We will not worry about details, however painful.

It is not my intention to create an atmosphere sympathetic to us. All that would be useless, in vain, and unworthy of us. For me it is sufficient to ask the Jews: is it not a fact that in countries where we live in significant numbers, the position of Jewish lawyers, doctors, technicians, teachers and all types of public servants is becoming increasingly unbearable? Is it not a fact that our whole Jewish middle class is under serious threat? Is it not a fact that all the passions of the lower classes are being marshalled against our wealthy people? Is it not a fact that the poor among us suffer much more than the rest of the proletariat?

I believe this pressure to be around everywhere. In the highest economic circles among Jews it evokes unease. In middle-class circles the feeling is one of heavy anxiety. In lower-class circles it is sheer naked despair.

The fact is that it amounts to the same thing everywhere, and it can be summarized in the classic slogan of the Berliners: Away with the Jews!*

I will now express the issue of the Jews in its most concise form: if we must be away, then where to?

Or can we still stay put? And for how long?

Let us first tackle the question of staying put. Can we hope for better times, can we be patient, put our faith in God and wait until the rulers and peoples of the world get into a more benign mood towards us? I say we cannot expect a turnaround in the general trend. Why not? Kings and emperors cannot protect us, even if they wished to treat us equally. They would only inflame hatred against the Jews if they showed the Jews too much sympathy. And this "too much sympathy" would at any rate still amount to less than what is normally due to every normal citizen or social group.

The peoples with whom Jews live are all antisemites, without exception, discreetly or brazenly.

Common people have no understanding of history, and are incapable of any. They do not know that the sins of the Middle Ages are only now coming to haunt the peoples of Europe. We are what they have made us to be in the ghettoes. Without a doubt we have attained superiority in financial matters because we were thrown into it during the Middle Ages. Now a similar process is repeating itself. We are again forced into the business of finance, now referred to as the stock exchange, while being barred at the same time from all other branches of economic activity. We are now established at the stock exchange, and that in itself has become a new source for contempt. In addition we produce an endless stream of middle-range intellectuals who are not being siphoned off into jobs and who thus present a danger to society just as great as our accumulating wealth. Of such educated Jews, those who have no assets are now drifting away into socialism. We will have to fight the social revolution lying on our backs, because both in the capitalist as well as the socialist camp we find ourselves in the most exposed positions.

ATTEMPTS AT SOLUTIONS UP UNTIL THE PRESENT TIME

The artificial means employed thus far to overcome the distress of the Jews have been either too small in scale, like the attempts at colonization; or wrongly conceived, like the attempts to turn Jews into farmers in their present home countries.

What use is it to shift a few thousand Jews into a different region? Either they prosper, and then their developing wealth will lead to antisemitism, or they perish on the spot. We have already dealt with the attempts thus far to make Jews emigrate to other countries. At any rate emigration is insufficient and aimless, if not counterproductive. It only causes the solution to be put off, dragged out or perhaps even made more difficult.

Whoever wants to turn Jews into agricultural producers is really making a strange mistake. Peasants are a historical category, which is easily recognized by their dress, which in most countries is hundreds of years old, as well as their tools, which are still as they were in

ancient times. Their plough is still the same; they still carry the seed
in their aprons; they use the historical scythe to do their mowing,
and the flail to do their threshing. But we know that we now have
machines to do all this. The agrarian question is therefore no more
than a question of machines. America must be victorious over
Europe, just as large landownership will destroy small landownership. As a phenomenon the peasant is dying out. Artificially preserving the peasant is only done to serve specific political interests.
To create new peasants using the old recipe would be an impossible
and foolish undertaking. Nobody is strong or wealthy enough to
forcibly turn civilization backward. Even the mere task of hanging
on to superseded cultural conditions is an enormous task which can
scarcely be accomplished with all the means of power at the disposal
of even an autocratic state.

Would you require of a Jew, who is intelligent, to become a
peasant of the old type? That would be the same as telling the Jew:
"Here is a crossbow; go to war." What, with a crossbow, when the
others have small-caliber rifles and Krupp canons? Those Jews you
want to turn into peasants are perfectly right not to move under such
conditions from their present place of abode. The crossbow is a
beautiful weapon, and I can get sentimental about it when I have
nothing else to do, but it belongs in a museum.

Now there are indeed regions where desperate Jews go into the
fields or at least would like to go into the fields. Now it seems that
precisely these spots—like the Hessen* enclave in Germany and a
few provinces in Russia— become the main haunts of antisemitism.

The do-gooders who want to send the Jews out into fields forget
one important individual who rather has an interest in all this. That
is the peasant himself. And the peasant is completely right. His life
has already become embittered enough with land-tax, the uncer-
tainty of the harvest, pressure of the big land-owners, and especially
the competition from America. You cannot go on endlessly increasing import duties on wheat. You certainly cannot let the factory

workers starve; indeed, you are bound to consider their interests, because their political influence is growing.

All these difficulties are well-known, so I merely mention them in passing. I simply wanted to indicate how worthless the attempts up to now have been to find a solution, even though they have been, in most cases, well thought out and sympathetic. Artificially diverting or depressing the intellectual level of our proletariat will not help. The miracle drug of assimilation I have already discussed.

We cannot make an impression on antisemitism. It cannot be got rid of, as long as its causes are not got rid of. However, is it possible to get rid of these?

CAUSES OF ANTISEMITISM

We are no longer talking about psychological causes, old prejudices and narrow-mindedness, but rather about political and economic causes. Present-day antisemitism cannot be put in the same league as the religious hatred of the Jews of times past, even though today the hatred of the Jews in various countries is still tinged with religious connotations. In its main tendencies today's hostile movement toward Jews is different. In the main countries where antisemitism is rife, the movement is a result of the emancipation of the Jews. When the civilized peoples realized the inhumanity of our special legal status and set us free, this liberation came too late. In our traditional regions we were no longer capable of being emancipated. In a peculiar way we had made ourselves into a middle-class people in the ghetto, and we were coming out as a fear-inspiring competitor for the middle class. So after emancipation we suddenly stood in the ranks of the bourgeoisie, and we now have to withstand a double pressure: from the inside and from the outside. The Christian bourgeoisie would not mind throwing us as a sacrifice into the arms of the socialists; but that would not solve the problem.

Even so, the juridical equality of Jews can no longer be abolished, wherever it may exist. Not only because this would be against modern consciousness, but also because all Jews, whether poor or rich, would immediately be driven into the camp of the revolutionary parties. They can really do nothing effective against us. In the past they took away the jewels from the Jews. How can they get hold of the fluid wealth of Jews today? It is contained within printed documents which probably are inaccessible, locked up in Christian institutions. It is of course possible to slap taxes on the actions and priorities of the railways, the banks, industrial enterprises of all kinds: through progressive income tax you can get access to the whole spectrum of fluid wealth. But all those types of measures cannot be just directed against Jews; if it were to be tried anywhere, it would lead immediately to deep economic crises which would not stay confined to just the Jews who were hit first. The impossibility of getting at Jews only embitters and increases the hatred against them. Antisemitism among the various peoples is growing day by day, hour by hour, and it must continue to grow, because its causes remain and cannot be eradicated.

The remote cause of antisemitism is the loss of our assimilability, which began in the Middle Ages; the immediate cause is our overproduction of a middle-range intelligentsia, which cannot flow on into appropriate jobs and cannot rise socially. There is no healthy economic flow-on or social advancement. We are being pushed down and turned into proletarian revolutionaries; we are the under-officers of all the revolutionary parties while at the same time our frightening economic power keeps growing.

EFFECTS OF ANTISEMITISM

The pressure exerted upon us does not make us any better. We are no different from other human beings. It is quite true that we do not love our enemies. But only those able to overcome their own natures can make such reproaches to us. Pressure naturally evokes in us hostility against our oppressors; and then our hostility in turn increases the pressure. It is impossible to break the vicious circle.

"Nevertheless," so the gentle daydreamers will say, "nevertheless, it is possible by working patiently to draw out what is good in people."

Do I really still have to demonstrate that this is just sentimental twaddle? If you wanted to improve your situation by relying on the good will of people, you would certainly be writing a utopian romance.

I have already mentioned our "assimilation." I do not say for a moment that I want it. Our national character is historically too famous and, despite all humiliation, too proud to wish for its demise. But perhaps we could merge without a trace into the peoples around us if we were left in peace for a couple of generations. They will not leave us in peace. After short spells of tolerance the hostility against us awakens anew. There seems to be something in our prosperity that irritates people, because the world has been accustomed to seeing us as the most despised among the poor. At the same time they do not notice, whether from ignorance or narrow-mindedness, that our prosperity weakens us as Jews and dissipates our character. Only pressure keeps us close to the old tribe, only the hatred that surrounds us turns us into strangers.

So we are and will remain, whether we like it or not, a historical group with recognizable features that stamp us as belonging together.

We are a people—the enemy turns us into one against our wishes—that has been the same throughout history. In oppression we stand together, and then we suddenly discover our power. Yes, we have the power to create a state, even a state that would stand as a model for all. We possess all the necessary human and material means.

This would already be the right place to speak of "human resources," to use a rather coarse expression. But first, the main elements of the plan on which everything depends need to be mentioned.

THE PLAN

In its basic form the whole plan is infinitely simple: it just has to be if it is to be understood by everyone.

We should be given sovereignty over a piece of the earth's surface sufficient for the legitimate needs of our people. We will look after everything else.

Establishing a new sovereignty is neither ridiculous nor impossible. In our own times we have experienced it in the case of people who are not middle-class people like us, but who are poor, uneducated, and therefore weaker than ourselves. The governments of those countries affected by antisemitism have a lively interest in providing us with this sovereignty.

To get this concept off the ground, so easy in principle but so difficult in practice, we will establish two large organizations: the Society of Jews and the Jewish Company.

The Jewish Company will apply in practice what the Society of Jews has prepared intellectually and politically.

The Jewish Company has the task of liquidating all assets of the Jews who emigrate and of organizing the economic spade-work in the new land.

As I have already said, the departure of the Jews should not be seen as a sudden phenomenon. It will occur gradually and will take decades. First the poorest Jews will go and make the land arable. In accordance with a previously developed concept they will build the streets, bridges and railways, they will construct the telegraph system, they will regulate the rivers and build homes for themselves. Their work will lead to business, business will bring markets, markets will entice new immigrants to come. Everyone will come of their own free will, and bear their own costs and risks. The work which we sink into the earth will increase the value of the land. Jews will not take long to realize that a new and lasting target has been opened up for their spirit of enterprise, for which hitherto they have been hated and despised.

If you want to establish a country in this day and age, you cannot do so in the only way that might have been appropriate a thousand years ago. It is foolish to want to hark back to old concepts of culture, as many Zionists are keen to do. If, for instance, we were ever in a position to have to clear a country of wild animals, then we would not go about that in a way Europeans might have used in the fifth century. We would not go out to kill bears with spear and lance, but we would organize a merry hunt, drive the animals into a corner and throw a melinite bomb among them.

If we want to construct buildings, we will not put up helpless pole-houses by the seaside, but we will build in the way it is done today. We will build more boldly and beautifully than has ever been done before, because we have means which have not been available throughout history.

Our most lowly economic classes will be followed gradually by the next in line. Those who are really desperate go first. They will be guided by our middle-range intelligentsia, which we over-produce and which is persecuted everywhere.

This publication will put the question of emigration of Jews on the general agenda. Yet that does not mean that we will have a referendum, as then the matter would be a lost cause from the start. If you do not want to join us, you can stay put. The objections of a few do not matter.

If you want to join us, then stand behind our flag and fight for it in thought, word and deed.

Those Jews who commit themselves to our idea of the state will gather around the Society of Jews. In this way the latter will gain the authority to have dealings with governments in the name of all Jews. To use an analogy from international law, the Society will be recognized as the power behind the formation of the state, which would be tantamount to the actual establishment of the state.

If the Great Powers are prepared to grant the Jews as a people sovereignty over a neutral land, then the Society will enter into negotiations about the land which is to be selected. Two regions will be considered: Palestine and Argentina. Significant colonizing projects have already been attempted in these two regions, albeit under the mistaken principle of gradual infiltration by Jews. Infiltration always ends badly, as without fail the moment will arrive that the government stops the further flow of Jews because the resident population feels threatened. Consequently, emigration is only sensible if it is based on our secured sovereignty.

If the relevant governments of our day support this concept, then the Society of Jews, under the protection of the European Powers, will negotiate with them. We can offer the present government enormous advantages: we take over a part of its national debt, we can build roads which, in any case, we need ourselves, as well as many other things. Even the very establishment of the Jews' State represents a gain to the neighboring countries, because in small and big ways the civilization of a region increases the value of the surrounding lands.

PALESTINE OR ARGENTINA

Is Palestine or Argentina to be preferred? The Society will accept what it is given and what has the support of public opinion among the Jews as a people. Both will be determined by the Society.

In terms of natural resources Argentina is one of the wealthiest countries in the world, enormous in size, sparsely populated, and with a moderate climate. It would be in the interest of the Argentinian republic to cede us a piece of territory. Unfortunately, the present infiltration of Jews has created ill feeling there; we would have to explain to Argentina the fundamental difference of the new Jewish migration.

Palestine is our unforgettable historical home. This very name would already be an enormously powerful rallying cry for our people. If His Majesty the Sultan were to give us Palestine, we could undertake the responsibility of putting the finances of Turkey completely in order. To Europe we would represent a part of the barrier against Asia; we would serve as the outpost of civilization against barbarism. As a neutral state we would remain allied to all of Europe, which in turn would have to guarantee our existence. An internationally acceptable arrangement would be found to guarantee the extra-territorial status of the holy places of Christendom. We would form the guard of honor around the holy places, and guarantee the execution of this duty with our very existence. This guard of honor would be the great symbol of the solution of the issue of the Jews after eighteen centuries of agony.

NEED, ORGANIZATION, BUSINESS

Two chapters ago I said: "In the new country it is the Jewish Company which will organize economic activity."

I believe I should add a few explanations here. The basis of a concept like the present one is in danger if "practical" people object to it. Now as a rule, practical people are little more than hacks, incapable of stepping out of the narrow circle of old ideas. Yet their objections are important insofar as they can greatly harm a new idea, at least as long as the new idea is not strong enough by itself to topple the practical people with their worn-out concepts.

When the era of the railways came to Europe, there were practical people who declared that the construction of certain lines was simply foolish, "because not even the post coaches on those routes get enough passengers." At that time they could not yet know the fact, which now seems childishly simple, that travellers do not beget a railway, but a railway begets travellers, although admittedly there must be a potential need beforehand.

You are faced with a similar type of such pre-railway, "practical" objections when people today cannot imagine how the economic activity of immigrants is to be conceptualized in a new country that is not yet cultivated or does not yet exist. A practical man may well speak rather dismissively in the following terms:

If we concede that the present situation of Jews in many places is untenable and worsening all the time, if we concede that the desire for emigration is alive and well, even if we concede that Jews will emigrate to the new country: how will they make their living and what will they earn? How will they live? You simply cannot establish many people in business artificially from one day to the next.

My answer to this is as follows: I am not talking about artificially establishing anyone in business, and even less am I saying that this will happen from one day to the next. If you cannot establish a person in business, you can at least provide a stimulus. How? By suggesting a need. The need will be recognized, an organization will be created based on it, and business will come automatically.

If the need of Jews to improve their situation is true and deep, if the Jewish Company, as the organization to give expression to this need, has sufficient power, then a wealth of business will come to the new land. To be sure, that is still a thing of the future, just like the development of the railway system used to be for the people of the 1830s. Yet the railways were built. Fortunately, we have got over the reservations of the practical supporters of the post coaches.

The
Jewish Company

BASIC CHARACTERISTICS

The Jewish Company is partly conceived after the example of the large colonization companies*—a Jewish Chartered Company, if you like, with the proviso that it has no governing rights, and that its functions are not confined to the colonial sphere.

The Jewish Company will be established as a limited company in the English legal sense, under the laws and protection of England. Its main office is in London. I cannot be clear at the present time about the size of the company's capital. Our countless financial wizards will work that out. But to avoid vague estimates, I shall assume one billion marks. It may need to be more, it may need to be less. The way the money is raised, which still has to be looked at below, will determine how large a proportion of this vast sum has to be available in practice at the beginning of the project.

The Jewish Company is a transitory institution. It is a purely commercial enterprise, which will always be carefully kept separate from the Society of Jews.

Initially it will be the task of the Jewish Company to liquidate the assets of the Jews who are emigrating. It will be done in such a way to avoid crises, to ensure that the process is fair, and to enable the inner emigration of Christian citizens to take place, which has already been mentioned.

Transferring Assets

The assets in question are houses, rural properties, and business goodwill. In the initial stages the Jewish Company will go no further than play a facilitating role in the sale of these assets. For early on the sales by Jews will not be subject to controls and greatly falling prices. The branches of the Company in each town will become the centers of sale for Jewish property. In return each branch will charge a commission no larger than what is needed to ensure the continuation of the branch.

A side effect to this movement is likely to be that the value of the assets falls sharply, or even that it becomes impossible to sell them. If that happens, the Company branches out into new fields. The Company takes on the administration of the assets left behind and waits for an appropriate time to realize them. It imposes an administration charge, leases out landed properties, and, exercising due caution, appoints managers, if possible with contracts of lease. In all cases the objective of the Company will be to facilitate the transfer of full ownership to these Christian managers. It will gradually introduce Christian officials and independent agents (lawyers, etc.) into its ranks; these must on no account be stigmatized as merely servile to the Jews. As free controlling agents with Christian associations they are in a position to guarantee that everything is above board, that transactions are effected reasonably and in good faith, and that there is no intention to break down the general standard of living.

At the same time, the Company will act as a sales office, or rather, as an office of exchange. It will exchange a house "there" for a house "here," a property "there" for a property "here." As far as possible everything is to be transplanted in the same way as it was "here."

This opens up a source of large and legitimate profits for the Company. It will be in a position to offer more attractive, modern, comfortably appointed houses and better rural properties "over there," which are nevertheless much cheaper, as the land was bought much more cheaply in the first place.

Purchasing the Land

The land guaranteed to the Society of Jews by international law is, of course, available for purchase as private property.

Each person's individual arrangements for his emigration do not lie within the scope of the present discussion. However, the Company needs large tracts of land for its own needs and for our needs. It will ensure the availability of the necessary land through centralized purchase. In the main this will mean purchasing state land belonging to the present government authorities. The objective is to acquire property rights on land "over there" without driving the price of the land to speculative heights, and at the same time to sell "here" without depressing the price. We will stay clear of wild speculation, because the land will only gain in value well after the Company has purchased it, and starts to settle it, with the consent of the Society of Jews, which has a supervisory function. As well, the latter will see to it that the enterprise does not end up like Panama, but more like Suez.*

The Company will make available building allotments to its officials under cheap conditions, will grant them loans to build their beautiful homes, and will deduct payments from their salaries or bill them separately in installments. It will be not only an honor for them, which they might have expected, but also a kind of reward for faithful service.

The vast profits from the land speculation will flow in their entirety into Company coffers, because it has a right to unlimited profits like every free entrepreneur. Wherever there are attendant risks to an enterprise, profits from the enterprise should be equally generous. But only in cases of risk can large profits be tolerated. The correlation of risk and profit forms the basis of financial morality.

Buildings

So the Company will exchange houses and properties. In the final analysis, the Company must come out on top—and it will. So much is clear to everyone who at some time in some place has observed how land increases in value once real estate has been built on it. You see that most clearly where built-up and rural areas are in close proximity. Rural tracts increase in value because of the wreath of civilization that is established around them. A simple but quite ingenious land speculation occurred in Paris, where the city's developers did not build their new houses immediately next to exisiting houses at the edge of town, but bought building allotments further out in the country, and started to build from the very outer edge back towards the older built-up areas. By turning the building procedure inside out in this way, the value of the building allotments increased extremely quickly. Instead of always having to build on the edge of town, they built, after the outer ring had been completed, only towards the center of town, that is, on sites that had become more valuable.

Will the Company itself build or will it commission independent architects? It can and will do both. It has, as will be demonstrated shortly, a huge reservoir of workers, which need not be exploited, but which have been introduced to happy and cheerful life circumstances and yet are not expensive. The supply of building materials was looked after by our geologists, when they were selecting the building allotments for our towns.

What principles will our building be based on?

Housing for Laborers

Housing for laborers, which includes housing for all skilled laborers, should be provided under their own management. I am not thinking of the sad barracks for workers found in European cities, nor of the rows of wretched huts around factories. It is true the Company can only build cheaply if it manufactures the building materials in great quantities, so our laborer housing must also have a uniform look about it; but these single houses with their little gardens will everywhere be incorporated into a beautiful overall concept. The attractiveness of the natural surroundings will inspire the happy genius of our young architects, as yet not burdened down by routine; and even if the people fail to understand the total concept, they will still feel well in this gentle environment. The temple will be visible from all directions, because, after all, it is only the old faith that has held us together. Light will stream into our friendly, healthy schools, complete with all modern teaching materials. There will be technical continuation schools enabling simple workers to acquire high-level technical skills and acquainting them with machine technology. There will be amusement centers for the people, directed by the Society of Jews to promote public morality.

In any case, here I am only talking about the buildings, not about what is going to happen in them.

I am saying the Company will build cheaply, not only because all building materials will be available in bulk, not only because the Company owns the land, but also because it does not have to pay the workers.

Farmers in America have developed a system of mutual self-help in building one another's houses. This system is as naive and good-natured as the clumsy log cabins which it engenders, but it can be much refined.

The Unskilled Laborers

Our unskilled laborers, who initially will come out of the large Russian and Rumanian reservoir, also have to help one another build their houses. In the beginning we will not have our own iron, and we will have to build in wood. That will change later on, and the minimal temporary structures of the intitial stages will then be replaced by better ones.

Our unskilled laborers will be told before they leave that they will have to build their own accommodation. By their labor they will gain the right to own their houses—not immediately to be sure, but only if they give evidence of good behavior for a period of three years. In this way we will develop a diligent people who can be readily employed. A man with the discipline of three years' work behind him is ready for life.

I said before that there is no need for the Company to pay the unskilled laborers. So how will they live?

In general terms I am against the truck system,* but it will have to be applied in the case of these first settlers. The Company looks after them in many respects, including feeding and housing them. At any rate, the truck system will only be applied in the first few years, and it will be to the advantage of the workers, because it prevents their exploitation by small traders, innkeepers, etc. In this way the Company prevents right from the start that our little folk over there will fall back into the sort of door-to-door selling which historical circumstances have forced upon them up to now. The Company will keep a tight rein on the drunk and disorderly. So will there be no wages for laborers in the initial stages after settlement?

Of course there will be: overtime.

The Seven-Hour Day

The normal working day is the seven-hour day!

That does not mean that every day there are only seven hours of cutting trees, digging earth, carting stones or a hundred other jobs. No, there will be fourteen hours of work. But the gangs of workers will be relieved after three and a half hours. This will be organized along strict military lines, with charges, promotion and retirement. I will discuss later where retirement pensions will come from.

A healthy man is capable of giving a great deal of concentrated labor in three and a half hours. After a break of three and a half hours, which he devotes to his rest, his family or his further education, he is quite refreshed. Such laborers can work miracles.

The seven-hour day. It makes possible fourteen working hours; more does not fit in a day.

Besides, I am convinced that the seven-hour day is completely practicable. We know of the experiments in Belgium and England.* A few socially progressive politicians even maintain that the five-hour day would be quite sufficient. The Society of Jews and the Jewish Company will gather valuable new experiences in this field, which will also be of advantage to the other peoples of the world. When it is clear that the seven-hour day is a practical possibility, our future state will introduce it legally as the normal working day.

Only the Company will guarantee the seven-hour working day to its people from the start. It will always be in a position to do this.

We will use the seven-hour day as a rallying-cry for our people throughout the world, who, of course, are free to come. It must really be the Promised Land . . .

Whoever works longer than seven hours will receive payment for overtime in cash. As all his needs have been covered, and as all his dependents unable to work are looked after by the centralized social service system which has been transferred over there, he will be able to save. We want to encourage the saving habit which our people have in any case, because it facilitates the entry of individuals into the higher levels of society and enables us to prepare an enormous reservoir of capital for future loans.

Overtime for the seven-hour working day should be no more than three hours, and then only after a medical examination. Our people will be keen to do as much work as possible, and it will be for all the world to see what kind of a diligent people we are.

To avoid confusion I will not now discuss how we should organize the truck system for the settlers (coupons, etc.), as well as the countless other details. Women will not be allowed to do any heavy work at all, and will not be able to do overtime. Pregnant women are relieved from any work and will be fed copiously through the truck system, because we need strong children for the future.

Right from the start we will bring up the children as we want them. I will not go into this at the moment.

What I have just said about unskilled laborers, their workers' houses, and their way of life is not utopian, just as everything else is not. All this is already present in the real world, but it is terribly small-scale, unnoticed and misunderstood. For the solution of the issue of the Jews the *assistance par le travail*, which I got to know and understand in Paris, was of great use to me.

Workers' Assistance

Workers' Assistance, as it exists today in Paris and a number of other cities in France, as well as in England, in Switzerland and in America, is something pitifully small, but it can be transformed into something gigantic.

What is the principle of *Assistance par le travail*?

The principle is to give everybody in need unskilled labor, consisting of light work for which no skills are necessary, for example, wood chipping, manufacturing the bundles of kindling with which each Parisian family lights the fire. It is a kind of prison labor *before* the crime; that is to say, it does not involve loss of reputation. Nobody willing to work needs to succumb to a life of crime anymore. There is no need to kill yourself because you are hungry. These are, in any case, among the worst stigmas of a civilization, where the rich drop their dogs dainty morsels from their table.

Hence Workers' Assistance provides work for everyone. But can it sell its products? No. At least, not all. This is where the present organization falls short. This Assistance always runs at a loss. It is of course meant to lose money, for it is a charitable organization. The cost involved is the difference between cost of production and the selling price. Instead of giving the beggar two pennies, the Assistance gives him work that will in effect cost it two pennies. Our shabby beggar, however, who has been transformed into a noble worker, earns one franc fifty centimes. A hundred and fifty centimes in exchange for ten; that's tantamount to increasing a good deed fifteen fold, for which you need feel no embarrassment. That means making fifteen billion out of one billion!

It is true that the Assistance does lose the ten centimes. The Jewish Company will not lose the billion, but it will reap huge profits.

There is a moral aspect to all this. By means of this small assistance as it exists at present, you achieve a moral uplift through work, until the unemployed person finally finds a new position or a new occupation which is commensurate to his capabilities. Each day he has a few hours free to look for work; on top of that the Assistance provides a range of services.

The limitation of the present small organization is that it may not enter into competition with established wood dealers. Wood dealers are voters; they would make a noise, and they would have a point. Equally, it is not sensible to compete with the prison industry; the state has a responsibility to look after its criminals and keep them busy.

In an established society it will be difficult to make room for the *assistance par le travail.*

But in our new order!

Above all else we need huge quantities of unskilled labor for our initial programs of land settlement, construction of roads, afforestation, excavation, rail and telegraph construction, and so on. All this will be guided by an all-encompassing master plan, determined beforehand.

MARKET EXCHANGE

At the same time as we are transferring our labor into the new country, we will bring in markets and business. Initially, of course, only a market for the basic necessities of life: cattle, cereals, workers' clothing, tools, weapons, just to name a few. At first we will buy these in neighboring countries or in Europe; soon we will be making them ourselves. Jewish entrepreneurs will soon realize the opportunities that will open up.

Gradually the army of Company officials will articulate more specific and refined requirements. (I count among these officials also the officers of the defense forces, which should always be at least a tenth of the total number of male immigrants. That will be sufficient to deal with mutinies among bad people; most immigrants will be peace-loving).

The more specific requirements of well-situated officials will in turn engender more specific niche markets, which will grow steadily. Married people will invite their families to come, single persons will invite their parents and brothers and sisters, as soon as they have a home over there. Indeed, we are seeing this movement among the Jews who are at present emigrating to the United States. The moment they have bread to eat, they send for their relatives to come. For family ties are so strong in Jewish civilization. The Society of Jews and the Jewish Company will cooperate in strengthening and fostering the family even further. Here I do not mean in a moral sense—that goes without saying—but in a material sense. The officials will get special marriage bonuses and child endowment. We need people: all of those already there, and all of those who are to follow.

OTHER CATEGORIES OF HOMES

I now leave the main train of argument about the building of workers' houses under their own management. I now return to other categories of homes. The Company will also commission architects to build houses for the lower middle classes, and either exchange or sell them. The Company's architects will design and produce about a hundred different models of houses. These delightful model homes will serve at the same time as part of our propaganda. The price of each house is fixed, its quality and appointments are guaranteed by the Company, which operates the venture without a profit. Where will these houses be situated? That will have to be decided by the local authorities.

As the Company only intends to make a profit by selling its building allotments and not by building the houses, it is desirable that many architects take on private commissions. That increases the value of real estate, that introduces luxury into the country. We need luxury for a number of reasons, especially for artistic activity, for industrial development and, at a later stage, as a means of breaking up large accumulations of capital.

Yes, those wealthy Jews, who at the present time have to anxiously hide their treasures, and who are ill at ease when they give their parties behind drawn curtains, will be able to enjoy life freely over there. If the emigration gets off the ground with their assistance, then in turn we will free up their wealth over there; it will show its usefulness in exemplary fashion. When the wealthiest Jews begin to build their castles over there, which cause so much jealousy here in Europe, it will soon become the done thing among them to settle there themselves in magnificent houses.

SOME TYPES OF LIQUIDATION

The Jewish Company is conceived of as the agency to take over and manage the assets of Jews.

These functions are easily arranged where houses and land are concerned. But what is to be done where a business is involved?

There are likely to be various forms of management. They cannot easily be predicted beforehand. Yet there should not be undue difficulties. In each individual case the proprietor of the business, who has freely decided to emigrate, will agree upon the most favorable form of liquidation with the branch of the Company in his district.

The transfer of assets will be most easily effected in the case of the smallest businesses, where the personal input of the proprietor is the most important factor and the small amount of stock and plant is of subsiduary importance. The Company creates a secure area of operation for the personal activity of the emigrant, and his small amount of stock can be replaced on the other side with an allotment of land supplemented by a credit for new plant. Our people, being flexible, will soon learn new spheres of activity. It is well-known that Jews are very smart at adapting to any new economic activity. In this way we can turn many traders into small agricultural processors. In taking over the non-movable assets of the very poor, the Company can even carry so-called losses, because in this way it promotes the free cultivation of land, which in turn will cause the value of the remaining lots to rise.

In the case of medium-sized businesses, that is those in which the organization of assets is of equal value or even more important than the personal input of the proprietor, and where his personal credit is a decisive but unknown factor, various types of liquidation are possible. This is one of the main areas where the inner emigration of Christians can take effect. The Jew who is emigrating does not lose his personal credit rating, but takes it with him, and will be able to use it when establishing himself on the other side. The Jewish Company opens a giro account* for him. He can also either sell the business he had up to now on the free market, or leave it in the hands of managers supervised by a branch of the Company. The manager can be a lessee, or he can be encouraged to gradually buy the business through a series of part-payments. Through its supervisors and lawyers the Company sees to it that the business which has been left behind is run in an orderly fashion, and that the payments come in on time. Here the Company acts as the curator for the absentee-owner. Where a Jew cannot sell his business, where he does not trust a manager with it or does not want to give it up, he just stays put where he now lives. The situation of those staying behind will not grow worse; they have got rid of the competition of those who have emigrated, and antisemitism with its "Don't buy from Jews" will be a thing of the past.

Should the emigrating businessman wish to continue in the same branch of business over there, then he can plan for that from the very start. Let us give an example. Firm X has a large fashion house. The owner wishes to emigrate. At first he establishes in his future place of living a branch of the firm, which he supplies with samples. The initial poor emigrants over there are his clientele. Gradually people will emigrate who have more advanced fashion needs. X now sends more modern articles, and finally the most modern ones. The branch itself is becoming a money spinner, while the main business is still in existence. Finally X has two businesses. He sells the old one, or leases it to his Christian representative to carry on; he himself moves to the other side into his new business.

A more substantial example: Y and Son have an extensive business in coal with mines and factories. How can such a gigantic complex be liquidated? Firstly, the coal mines with everything associated with them could be bought by the state. Secondly, the Jewish Company could procure them and pay the purchase price partly in terms of agricultural lands over there, partly in cash. A third possibility would be establishing his own limited company, "Y and Son." A fourth way would be to carry on as before, except that the proprietors who emigrated, even when returning on occasion to inspect the business, would be foreigners, and as such would be entitled to full legal protection given to all foreigners by civilized states. You see this every day in public life. I shall merely indicate a fifth possibility, particularly fruitful and magnificent, of which there are already a few examples, albeit rather weak ones, even though our modern consciousness is well aware of it. Y and Son can transfer their entire business to the full complement of their workers for a suitable compensation. The workers form a company with limited liability, and can, perhaps assisted by the state treasury—which is not interested in making huge profits—pay the transfer sum to Y and Son. The workers then pay off the loan which they had received from either the state treasury or from the Jewish Company, or even from Y and Son themselves.

The Jewish Company liquidates the smallest as readily as the largest companies. And while the Jews are emigrating in peace and are establishing their new home country, the Company is the large juridical entity which directs the emigration process, which protects the assets left behind, and which, with its own visible concrete assets, provides lasting guarantees for the orderly transfer of property for those who have already left.

GUARANTEES BY THE COMPANY

In what ways will the Company be able to guarantee that there will not be economic crises in the exit countries?

It has already been said that decent antisemites will be involved in the operations as controlling agents of the people as it were. Their independence, which we value so greatly, will be respected.

But the state, too, has fiscal interests which are liable to be hurt. It stands to lose a class of taxpayers which may be numerically small, but which is financially most valuable. It is necessary to offer it compensation for this. When we allow Christian citizens to advance into the positions which we have vacated, thus enabling a uniquely peaceful advance of the masses to prosperity, we indirectly transfer the fruit of our Jewish perspicacity and of our Jewish diligence— our businesses—to the state. The French Revolution witnessed a similar process on a small scale; but blood had to flow under the guillotine in all the French provinces and, indeed, on all the battlefields of Europe. Inherited and acquired rights had to be broken. And only those with the cunning to buy up the national wealth were the eventual winners.

In addition, the activities of the Jewish Company will bring individual states direct advantages. Governments everywhere can be assured of acquiring the property of Jews, which is to be left behind on favorable terms. Governments in turn can then use this large-scale expropriation of wealth to improve social conditions.

The Jewish Company will be in a position to assist the governments and parliaments, which want to encourage the inner emigration of their Christian citizens.

The Jewish Company will also pay substantial transfer fees.

The central office will be located in London, because for matters of private law the Company needs to stand under the legal protection of a great power which at present is not antisemitic. But the Company will be able to deliver a broad tax base in all those countries where it receives either official or unofficial assistance. The Company will establish taxable daughter-organizations and branches everywhere. In addition, it will yield double taxation, as property has to be legally transferred twice. Even in those places where the Company functions solely as property agency, it will act as a temporary buyer. Even though it does not want to be a proprietor, it will, for the purposes of the registration, momentarily appear as such in the property register.

Now these are, of course, purely matters of economics. How far the Company can enter this field without endangering its existence is an issue which can only be raised and determined on a case-by-case basis. It will negotiate these matters as a free agent with the ministers of finance. The latter will be able to judge our good intentions for themselves, and they will grant the facilities everywhere, which are so patently necessary to bring the large undertaking to a successful conclusion.

A further direct application is in the transport of goods and persons. This is immediately obvious where the railways are state-owned. In the case of privately-owned railway companies, the

Company will negotiate discounts, like every large transport agent. Of course it must ensure that our people travel and move as cheaply as possible, for each person is responsible for his own costs. The middle-classes can avail themselves of the Cook system,* and the poor classes will use personal tickets. The Company would be in a position to make large profits from the retail of personal and freight transport, but, as always, the principle here must be to merely cover costs.

In many localities travel is in the hands of Jews. The first type of business needed by the Company will be traveling agencies, and they will be the first liquidated by it. The present owners of these agencies will either enter the service of the Company or establish themselves over there independently. The country of arrival is in need of travel agencies specializing in the reception of people, and as this is a superb business capable of yielding earnings right from the start, there will not be a lack of enterprising people. It is unnecessary to expand on the business details of this mass-travel enterprise. They should be developed from sensible objectives, and many bright minds will have to work out how best to do this.

SOME ACTIVITIES OF THE COMPANY

A great number of activities will be integrated. Here is but one example: gradually the Company will begin to organize industrial production in the initially primitive settlements: clothing, linen, shoes, etc.—at first for our own poor emigrants. In the European dispatch centers our people will receive new clothing. This will not be in the nature of a gift, for we do not wish to humiliate them. Their old clothes will simply be exchanged for new ones. If the Company incurs losses on this deal, these will simply be written off as business losses. Those people without any money will incur a debt to the Company for their clothing, to paid off over there with their labor, from which they will be exempted for exemplary behavior.

At any rate, in this respect the existing emigration societies have an opportunity to offer assistance. Everything they have done up to the present time for Jews emigrating, they should continue to do in the future for the colonists of the Jewish Company. Appropriate forms of such cooperation should not be difficult to find.

In addition, providing the poor emigrants with new clothes should be seen as a symbolic act: you are now starting a new life. The Society of Jews will see to it that a festive but serious atmosphere prevails among the emigrants before and during their journey: it will organize prayers, popular lectures, and discussions on the significance of the enterprise, standards of hygiene for the new towns, suggestions for future work. For the Promised Land is the Land of Labor. On arrival the emigrants will be solemnly received by the top officials of our administration. Without foolish festivities, for the Promised Land has yet to be conquered. But right from the start the poor people have to be made aware that they are at home.

The Company's clothing industry for poor emigrants will not work without a plan. The Jewish Company will receive timely information from the Society of Jews about the numbers, the day of arrival, and the specific needs of the emigrants. This will enable it to plan ahead in detail.

INDUSTRIAL INITIATIVES

The tasks of the Jewish Company and the Society of Jews cannot be strictly separated in the present publication. In fact, these two large organizations will have to work together constantly. The Company will be dependent on the moral authority and support of the Society for some time to come, while the Society will not be able to do without the material support of the Company. In planning the direction of the clothing industry, for example, a start will be made with attempts to prevent crises in production. This will be the procedure in all areas where the Company functions as an industrial entity.

On no account may it use its superior industrial power to stifle free enterprise. We will only act collectively where required by the enormous difficulties of the task. For the rest we wish to protect and foster the individual and his rights. Private property, the economic basis of independence, will be developed in our society freely and respected by all. Indeed, we even permit our unskilled laborers to advance immediately into ownership of private property.

The spirit of enterprise will be encouraged in every way possible. The establishment of industries will be favored by an intelligent policy on tariffs, by the use of cheap raw materials and by establishing an office for industrial statistics, which will publish material regularly.

The spirit of enterprise will need to be stimulated in every healthy way. Speculative development without proper planning will be avoided. The establishment of new industries will be given publicity well beforehand, so that entrepreneurs who come to think six months later of developing this industry do not build themselves into a crisis and into misery. As the objectives of a new establishment must be lodged with the society, the industrial conditions prevailing will be known to everyone at all times.

In addition, entrepreneurs can fall back on the centralized distribution of laborers. The entrepreneur contacts the central labor exchange, which will charge him a small fee just to cover costs. The entrepreneur sends a telegram: By tomorrow I will need five hundred unskilled laborers for three days, or three weeks, or three months. The next day the five hundred in question, which the central exchange has drawn from its own resources, report at the agricultural or industrial enterprise. The rough-and-ready system that already exists in Saxony of recruiting seasonal laborers from Poland for the sugar beet harvest* will be refined into an instrument organized sensibly on military lines. It goes without saying that there will be no slave laborers delivered, only free workers on seven-hour contracts, who even when changing jobs maintain their labor organization, their entitlements, their promotion rights and their pensions. The free entrepreneur may also get his laborers from other sources, if he so wishes. But he would find this difficult. The Society will prevent the immigration of non-Jewish slave laborers by boycotting recalcitrant industrialists, by putting obstacles in the way of business, and the like. So they will have to accept laborers on seven-hour contracts. In this way we will approach the normal seven-hour working day virtually without compulsion.

THE SETTLEMENT OF SKILLED WORKERS

It is clear that whatever applies to unskilled laborers is even easier in the case of skilled laborers. The same rules can be applied to part-time workers in factories. The central labor exchange provides them.

As far as independent and small-scale master craftsmen are concerned, these independent workers will also be searched out and found by the central exchange of the Society. We wish to cultivate these workers in particular, in the light of future technological progress. Even where they are no longer young, we still wish to educate them in technical skills, and we wish to give them access to the horsepower that streams provide, and to the light that comes along electric wires. The local branch contacts the central exchange: We want so-and-so many carpenters, locksmiths, glaziers, etc. The central exchange publishes this. People apply. They move with their families to the town where they are needed, and settle down there, unaffected by damaging competition. A lasting, a good place to live has opened up to them.

MONEY SUPPLY

I suggested a vast amount of money as working capital of the Jewish Company. The actual amount of working capital needed will have to be determined by the financial experts, but it will in any case need to be a gigantic sum. How is it to be raised? There are three ways, which the Society will take into consideration. The Society, this great moral entity, the *gestor** of the Jews, consists of our best and purest men, who cannot and may not draw a profit from this project. Although initially the Society can have no more than a moral authority, this in itself will be sufficient to guarantee the credibility of the Jewish Company to the Jews as a people. The Jewish Company will have real prospects of commercial success only if it has been given the stamp of approval, so to speak, by the Society. Not every conceivable group of financiers thrown together can call itself the Jewish Company. The Society will examine, hold elections, and determine and secure all the necessary guarantees for the approval of the conscientious execution of the plan. Experiments backed by insufficient assets will not be permitted, for enterprises must be successful at the first attempt. Lack of success would prejudice the whole project for decades to come, and perhaps even make it impossible forever.

The three forms for raising working capital are: (1) through the central bank, (2) through the trading banks, (3) through popular subscription.

The quickest, easiest, and safest way to found the Company would be through a central bank. Within its framework the necessary capital can be raised in the shortest possible time via the existing large financial institutions by a simple process of consultation. It would have the distinct advantage that the billion marks—to stay with this amount for the moment—does not have to be fully available immediately. It would have the additional advantage, that the credit rating of these mighty financial conglomerates could be at the disposal of the enterprise. Many as yet unused political powers still lie slumbering in the powerful world of Jewish finance. The enemies of the Jews talk about the power of this financial clout as it could be potentially, rather than as it is in actuality. The poor Jews are aware only of the hatred which this financial power evokes, yet these poor Jews do not enjoy the advantages, the uses, the alleviation of their suffering, which this power should be able to bring them. The credit policies of the large Jewish financiers should be made to serve the idea of the people. These gentlemen may be quite happy with the present situation, but if we cannot get them to do something for their blood brothers who are always held responsible for the large wealth of a few, then the realization of this plan will provide the opportunity to draw a clear division between them and the rest of the Jewish community.

At any rate, the reserve bank will certainly not be required at all to make such a large sum available for reasons of charity. That would be a foolish expectation. Rather, the founders and directors of the Jewish Company should be offering a good business deal, and they will be in a position beforehand to assess what the chances are. The Society of Jews will have in its possession all the papers and data from which conclusions about the prospects of the Jewish Company can be drawn. In particular the Society of Jews will have researched in detail the scope of the new movement among Jews, and will be able to inform the founders of the Company with complete reliability what sort of participation can be counted on. By preparing a complete statistical data bank on the Jews, the Society of Jews will provide the Company with the facilities of a study group, such as happens in France, before the financing of a very large undertaking is decided upon.

Even so, the project may not attract the valuable support of the Jewish financial magnates. It is even possible that they use their secret vassals and agents to try to begin a secret struggle against our movement among the Jews. Like every other struggle which is forced upon us, we will fight this struggle with relentless severity.

The financial magnates may also perhaps content themselves to dismiss the project with a disdainful smile.

Would that be the end of it?

No.

The provision of finance would then enter a second stage: an appeal to the Jews of medium wealth. The Jewish trading banks would have to amalgamate to form an alternative formidable financial power to the central bank. That would entail the disadvantage that the whole affair would initially develop into a mere money concern, for the whole billion would have to be paid up at the start, otherwise you cannot start anything. As this money would only gradually be put to use, the first few years would be taken up with all sorts of banking and loan projects. It would not be beyond the realms of possibility that gradually the original objective would sink into obscurity; the medium-rich Jews would find a new big business outlet, and emigration among the Jews would stagnate.

We know that this idea of financial provision is not unrealistic. A number of attempts have been made to pit Catholic money against the central bank.* It has never yet been considered that the central bank can also be fought with Jewish money.

But imagine the crises which would follow all this: what harm would be done to the countries, where such financial wars were waged, how antisemitism would take over in the process.

So I do not like this idea; I merely mention it because it is a logical development of the general concept.

I do not know either whether the trading banks would tackle the project.

At any rate, the matter would not be finished even if the medium-rich were to reject it. It would merely add urgency to start the project well and truly.

For the Society of Jews, which does not consist of businessmen, can attempt the foundation of the company among the common people.

The working capital of the Company can be raised directly by subscription, without the mediation of the central bank or a syndicate of trading banks. Not only the poor little Jews, but also those Christians wanting to get rid of the Jews would participate, as only very small individual amounts would have to be subscribed. It could function as a new and unique form of plebiscite, in which everyone wishing to have a say in solving the issue of the Jews could be required to pay a limited deposit of money before stating his view. This condition would act like a guarantee. The remaining payment would only be due when the full amount needed for the project had been committed; otherwise the deposit would be refunded.

Should the entire amount necessary have been raised by a worldwide popular subscription, then every small amount is secured by the countless other small amounts.

We would need the express, decisive assistance of the participating governments.

Local Branches

THE TRANSPLANT

Up to now we have simply indicated how the emigration is to be effected without economic upheaval. However, such an emigration is also associated with strong, deep, personal disorientation. There are old customs, and memories which tie us people to specific places. We have cradles, we have graves, and we know the place of graves in the hearts of Jews. The cradles we will take with us—in them slumbers our smiling and rosy future. Our dear graves will have to be left behind—I believe this separation will weigh heavily on our possessive people. But it must be.

Economic distress, political oppression, and social hatred already separate us from our home towns and from our graves. Jews already leave one country for the next at every moment; a strong movement even leads overseas to the United States, where we are not welcome either. Where will we ever be welcome, so long as we do not have a country to call our own?

We, however, want to give the Jews a home country. Not by tearing them forcibly out of their present land. No, by lifting them carefully with all their roots and transplanting them into a better soil. Just as we want to create new conditions in the economic and political sphere, we will respect the sanctity of old ways in the cultural sphere. A few points about this. The greatest danger lies in this area, because people will think the plan purely fanciful.

And yet this, too, is possible and real; only it looks somewhat strange and helpless in reality. It can become sensible if we organize it properly.

Group Emigration

Our people should emigrate together in groups—in groups of families and friends. Nobody will be forced to be part of the group from the town in which he has lived up to now. Once his business has been liquidated, everyone will be able to go as he pleases, because he is going at his own expense, traveling in the class in rail or ship that he considers appropriate. Our trains and ships will probably only have one class. On such long journeys the difference in wealth will be a burden on our poor people. Even though we are not organizing a pleasure cruise for our people, there is also no need to spoil their enthusiasm on the journey.

Nobody will travel in misery. On the contrary, it should even be possible to provide an elegant level of comfort. Arrangements will be made well beforehand that the well-to-do emigrants join travel groups, for even in the most optimistic view it will take years before we will have single-class travel. People from the same network will travel together. We know that, apart from the very wealthiest, Jews have almost no contact with Christians. In many countries the situation is that, apart from those who support a few spongers, money lenders, or crawlers playing up to them, no Jews know any Christians at all. Internally, the ghetto is alive and well.

The middle classes will therefore prepare their departure carefully long beforehand. Every town forms its group. In the larger cities there will be a number of them, based on the various neighborhoods, who will keep in touch through elected representatives. This division into neighborhoods is in no way obligatory. It is merely designed to facilitate the departure of the less well-off, to make sure they are not uncomfortable or homesick during the trip. Everyone is free to travel by himself or to join the local group of his choice. The conditions are the same for everyone, depending on the class they travel. If an organized travel group is big enough, it receives a whole train from the Company and then a whole ship.

The Company office in charge of accommodation will look after the accommodation of the poor. At a later stage, when the more well-to-do come to emigrate, they will be received in free enterprise hotels that have been built in response to needs that can easily be foreseen. As well, the wealthier emigrants will have built their future homes while they were still in the old country, so that they merely have to move from the old, deserted home into the completed, new one.

This task does not have to occupy all of our intellectual capacity. Everyone involved in the national project will simply know how best to spread the news and be active in his own social circle. We will make a special appeal for the cooperation of our spiritual leaders.

Our Spiritual Leaders

Each group has its spiritual leader, who accompanies his congregation. Everyone may join a group freely. The local group is constituted around the rabbi. There will be as many local groups as there are rabbis. The rabbis will be the first to understand what we are about; they will be the first to be enthusiastic about the project and will inspire the others from their pulpits. There will be no need to call special meetings with all their idle talk. It will all be incorporated into religious services. That is how it should be. Only in the faith of our fathers can we recognize our common historical heritage, for we have already indelibly absorbed the languages of various nations long ago.

The rabbis will regularly receive information bulletins of the Society and the Company, and will broadcast and explain them to their congregation. Israel will pray for us, will pray for itself.

TRUSTED ELDERS OF THE LOCAL GROUPS

The local groups will form small committees of trusted elders under the chairmanship of the rabbi. These will consult and decide on practical matters and local needs.

Social service organizations will be transplanted freely by the local groups. Once over there, the foundations will remain within the control of the former local groups; the buildings should not be sold, in my opinion, but should be transferred to those needy Christians left behind in the towns. This will then be taken into account over there when the land is distributed, and local groups will be given gratis building allotments and every possible support when building.

The transplantation of the social service organizations provides us again with an opportunity, one of the many in this whole plan, to make a contribution to the well-being of all humanity. Our present confused private social service system does little good in comparison to the claims it makes for itself. Social service organizations can and must be brought together into one system, in which they will complement each other. In a new society these arrangements can be based on modern thinking and on the basis of our full social-political experience. This issue is most important for us, as we have so many beggars. The weaker persons in our community can easily be reduced to a beggar existence in the face of external pressure, which drains their courage, and of the soft-centered philanthropy of the rich, which spoils them.

In this context the Society, aided by the local groups, will devote the utmost attention to popular education. A fertile ground will be prepared for those with potential, who at present are just uselessly withering away. Whoever shows some goodwill should be put to good use. Beggars will not be tolerated. Whoever is not willing to work of his own free will shall be put into a common work shop.

On the other hand, we do not want to put the old into infirmaries. The infirmary is one of the most gruesome services which our foolish philanthropy has developed. In an infirmary the aged person slowly dies of shame and disease. He is really buried prematurely. We, however, want to leave an illusion of usefulness that is likely to bring consolation even to those at the lowest level of intelligence. Those unable to do physical work should get lighter duties. We have to take into account the atrophied poor of a generation which at present is already withering away. But the future generations will be brought up differently: in freedom, for freedom.

We will seek the moral blessing of appropriate work for all ages, for all stages in life. In this way our people will regain its moral fiber in the land of the seven-hour working day.

CITY PLANS

The local groups will delegate their representatives to the local elections. When the land is being divided, consideration needs to be given to maintaining what is right and best in the present setup.

City plans will be available from the local groups for inspection. Our people will be aware from the start where they are going, in which towns and houses they will live. I have already mentioned building plans and easy-to-understand drawings which will be distributed among the local groups.

The bureaucracy will be strictly centralized, but the local groups will be fully autonomous. Only under these conditions can the transplant be effected without pain.

I am not saying it is easier than it really is; but equally, it should not be made to seem more difficult.

THE EMIGRATION OF THE MIDDLE CLASSES

The middle classes will quite imperceptibly become involved in the movement. Some of them will have sons as officials with the Society or employees with the Company over there. Lawyers, doctors, technicians of all types, young merchants, restless old Jews who, tired of being oppressed, at present seek their fortunes in other parts of the world: all these will gather on the new soil so full of hope. Others have given their daughters in marriage to such ambitious people. Then our young people may make their brides follow them, or perhaps their parents and brothers and sisters. In new civilizations people marry young. That will only help the general moral standards. We will get a healthy new generation; not those weak children of fathers who married late, having already worn out their energies in life's struggles.

Each middle-class emigrant will pull others along with him.

The best of the new world belongs, of course, to the most courageous.

Now it seems as if the greatest difficulties in the plan lie in this area.

Even if we are successful in getting the issue of the Jews seriously discussed in international forums—

even if as a result of the present exploration it is recognized that the world in general is in serious need of a state for Jews;

even if we achieve sovereignty over a territory through the support of the Great Powers;

then how do we bring the masses of Jews without coercion from their present places of abode into this new country?

Surely the emigration is planned as a free movement?

THE PHENOMENON OF THE MASSES

It will hardly be very difficult to start the movement rolling. That much will be done for us by the antisemites. They only need to continue to do what they have done up to now, and the desire to emigrate will awaken in those Jews who have no such desire at present, and will strengthen where it is already present. The fact that Jews live in antisemitic countries is due mainly to the fact that we have never helped one another in our countless wanderings. Even people without a knowledge of history know that. If there were a land today where Jews were welcome and where they were offered even fewer advantages than in the projected Jews' State, there would immediately be a strong exodus of Jews to that country. The poorest, those who have nothing to lose, would drag themselves to that place. However, I maintain, as everyone well knows for himself, that the desire for emigration is present even in our well-to-do circles, because of the pressure which is such a burden to us. Because they are the strongest human resource for settlement, even the poorest among us would be sufficient to establish the new state; for large enterprises you need a bit of desperation.

As our desperadoes will raise the value of the land by their very appearance and their work, the better-off will gradually succumb to the temptation and follow suit.

Ever higher levels of our society will become interested in emigrating. The Society and the Company will lead the initial emigration of the poor, and will find support among the existing emigration societies and Zion societies.

How can a multitude be directed to go to a certain point without being ordered to do so?

There are a number of Jewish philanthropists in the big league, who want to alleviate the suffering of Jews through Zionist attempts. These philanthropists have already been concerned with these questions, and in the past they have thought to solve them by handing the emigrants money or work. The philanthropist has said: "I will pay the people to emigrate."

This approach is basically wrong; all the money in the world will not solve anything.

The Company will say on the contrary: "We do not pay them, we make them pay. But we offer them a bargain."

I want to use a light-hearted example to illustrate this. One of these philanthropists, whom we will call the Baron, and I myself, want to get a crowd on a hot Sunday afternoon on the fields of Longchamp* near Paris. The Baron promises to give each person 10 francs; he will have an outlay of 200,000 francs to get 20,000 sweaty unhappy people to the place. They will curse him for visiting this plague upon them.

Personally, however, I would put this 200,000 francs as first prize for the fastest horse, and then I let the people enter the race course. Whoever wants to get in, has to pay: 1 franc, 5 francs, 20 francs.

As a result I will get half a million people to go, the President of the Republic arrives à la Daumont,* the crowd is happy and finds its own amusement. Despite the sunburn and the dust, it is a happy trip into the country for most of them, and for the 200,000 francs outlay I have taken a million in entrance fees and betting money. I will get the same people there again whenever I want; the Baron will not, not at any cost.

I want to show the phenomenon of the multitude in a more serious context when it comes to earning your daily living. You should try sometime to broadcast loudly in the streets of a city: "Whoever wants to stand up all day in an iron hall in the depth of winter and in the heat of summer, talk to every passer-by and offer him smallgoods, fish or fruit, will get 2 guilders or 4 francs or whatever."

How many people would you get to go? Even if they are driven by hunger, how many days will they keep going? If they keep going, how diligently will they try to interest the passers-by in buying fruit, fish and small goods?

We go about things another way. At specific points where there is a lot of traffic—and we will be able to find these easily, because we are ourselves in charge of the traffic—at these points we build large halls and call them markets. We could even build these halls poorly and with disregard to health, and yet people would flock to them. But we will build them better and nicer, and put our whole soul into them. And these people, whom we have promised nothing, because if we want to be honest we cannot promise them anything, these courageous business people will develop a lively, light-hearted market-trade. They will tirelessly approach the buyers, they will stand for hours and hardly notice how tired they are. They will come back day after day to be the first there, and they will form unions, cartels and all sorts of societies to be able to practice this trade unhindered. Even when they realize at closing time that with all their good work they have only earned 1 guilder or 50 crowns or 3 francs or whatever, they will still face the next day with the hope that it will be better.

We have given them this hope.

Do you want to know where we get the goods which we need for the markets? Do I really still have to talk about this?

I have already demonstrated that we will produce fifteen times as much as now by using the *Assistance par le travail*. For one million, fifteen million. For one billion, fifteen billion.

Is this true on a macro scale as well as on a micro scale? Does not increasing the size of the capital progressively diminish earnings? This is true of capital that is slumbering and cowardly hidden away, but not of capital that is working. Capital which is put to work even increases its earning potential as it grows larger. That is the social issue.

Is it true what I say? I call on the wealthiest of Jews as witnesses. Why are they involved in so many industries? Why do they send people all over the world to extract coal for a meager wage and under terrible dangers? I do not think that is very pleasant, not for the owners of the mines either. I do not believe capitalists are heartless, and I do not want to speak as if I did. I do not want to stir up trouble, but I want to conciliate.

Do I still need to explain the problem of the multitude with reference to emigration motivated by religious considerations?

I would not want to insult the religious experiences of anyone by using words which could be interpreted wrongly.

I only quickly point out the phenomenon of the pilgrimage to Mecca in the Mohammedan world, the same with Lourdes* and so many other towns in the Catholic world, and the holy coat in Trier*, from where people return home consoled by their faith.

We, too, will establish shrines to satisfy the deepest religious needs of our people. Our clergy will be the first to understand us and go along with us.

Over there we would like everyone to gain his eternal happiness in his own way. That includes our precious free thinkers, our immortal army which will conquer ever new lands for humanity.

Nobody will be subjected to any force other than what is necessary to maintain the state and public order. This necessity will not be determined by the whims of one or a few persons who are always changing, but will be vested in water tight laws. If you wanted to conclude from the examples I have chosen that the multitudes may only be drawn temporarily to these drawcards of faith, commerce or pleasure, then this objection is easily countered. On its own, one such drawcard can certainly tempt the masses to come. All these attractions together, however, are needed to hold them and satisfy them in the long run. Together, these attractions form a great and long-sought unity, for which our people have never stopped longing, for which it has kept its identity, even in the face of pressures from outside: our free homeland. As the movement takes hold, we will follow the first groups, we will let others follow us, the third wave will be carried along, and the fourth will be pushed out of their country after us.

These latter groups, the hesitant latecomers, will have the toughest time when they are over there.

But the first ones, who go out full of faith, courage and enthusiasm, they will have the best positions.

OUR HUMAN RESOURCES

No people has had so many falsehoods said about it than the Jews. And through our historical sufferings we have become so oppressed and discouraged that we ourselves believe and parrot these falsehoods. One of these false claims concerns the inordinate trading propensity of the Jews. It is known that, where we are able to participate in the process of class advancement, we rush to distance ourselves from trade activity. By far the majority of Jewish merchants let their sons study. That is the cause of the so-called Judaization of the professions. But even among our economically weaker circles, our propensity to trade is not nearly as big as is commonly supposed. In the countries of Eastern Europe there are large masses of Jews who are not merchants and who do not resile from hard physical work. The Society of Jews will be in a position to prepare a scientifically accurate statistical compendium of our human resources. The new tasks and prospects, which await our people in the new country, will satisfy our present craftsmen and will transform many of our present traders into craftsmen.

A door-to-door salesman, who criss-crosses the country with a heavy pack on his back, is not as happy as his persecutors think. With the seven-hour working day these people can be turned into workers. These good people are at present misunderstood, and they suffer most of any. At any rate the Society of Jews will take over worker-education from the start. The desire to earn a living will be fostered in a healthy manner. The Jew is thrifty, flexible and most loyal to his family. Such people are suited to many ways of earning a living, and it will be sufficient to make the conditions for small traders unattractive to get the present salesmen to abandon their rounds. Providing favorable conditions for large-store trading would further encourage this trend. These large stores are already pushing small traders in towns out of business. In a new civilization they would simply prevent the establishment of small retail trading.

Establishing large stores from the start would have the added benefit of making the land attractive for people with advanced tastes and needs.

LITTLE CUSTOMS

Would it prejudice the seriousness of this paper, if I were to speak in passing of the little ways and everyday comforts of the common man?

I think not. Indeed, it is very important. For these little customs are like a thousand threads, each one thin and weak on its own, but together making up an unbreakable rope.

On this score, too, you must rid yourself of limited ideas. Those who have seen something of the world will know that at the present time the little everyday customs are transplanted quite easily to all sorts of places. Indeed, the technical achievements of our time, which this plan would like to put to use for all humanity, have been used up to now mainly in the context of these little things. There are English hotels in Egypt and on the mountain peaks in Switzerland, Viennese cafes in South Africa, French theaters in Russia, German opera houses in America and the best Bavarian beer in Paris.

If we do manage to leave Mizraim* once more, we will not forget the fleshpots.

In every local group each person can and will find his little customs again, only in a better, more beautiful and more pleasant form.

Society of Jews
and the Jews' State

NEGOTIORUM GESTIO

This paper is not addressed to professional lawyers; hence, like much else, I can indicate my theory of the legal basis of the state only in broad outlines.

Yet I must give some weight to my new theory, which I am sure will hold its own in any profesional discussion about the law.

Rousseau's conception of the social contract as basis of the state is today superseded. Rousseau* believes: "The clauses of the contract have been determined by nature in such a way that the smallest change would render them invalid and ineffectual. As a consequence, they have everywhere been adopted equally and recognized as a matter of course, even though this has not been specifically stated, etc."

The logical and historical refutation of Rousseau's theory is not difficult and has never been, even though this theory may have had both fruitful and terrible consequences. The question whether prior to the constitution there was already in existence in modern states a social contract "with not expressly stipulated, but unchangeable clauses," is devoid of practical interest. At this present time at any rate, the legal relationship between government and citizens has been fixed in writing.

However, before the establishment of a basic law, and when a new state is called into existence, these fundamental points do have practical significance. We well know that new states can still be founded today, and see this happen all the time. Colonies separate from the mother country, vassals tear themselves away from the sovereign, territories recently opened up are founded as free states straight away. At any rate the Jews' State is conceived as a quite unique new phenomenon attached to an as yet undecided territory. But a state is not constituted of pieces of land; rather, a group of people gathered under a sovereignty make up a state.

The people is the personal, the land is the concrete basis of the state. The personal basis is the more important of the two. There exists, for example, one sovereignty without a concrete basis, and it is the most esteemed sovereignty in the world: it is the sovereignty of the Pope.

In present day political philosophy the theory of the necessity of reason* is quite prominent. This theory is sufficient to justify the establishment of the state, and it cannot be refuted, like the social contract theory. Insofar as the establishment of the Jews' State is concerned, I am basing it in this pamphlet on the theory of the necessity of reason. The latter has nothing to say about the legal basis of the state. The theory of divine right,* the theory of superior power,* the theory of patriarchy,* patrimony,* and social contract are not in accordance with modern conceptions. The legal basis of the state is sought either exclusively in the person (superior power, patriarchy, contract theory), or exclusively beyond level of the person (divine right) or below the level of the person (concrete patrimonial theory). The necessity of reason leaves this question well alone, whether through laziness or caution. However, a question which has been the concern of the greatest legal philosophers of all times cannot be completely useless. In actual fact, the concept of state features a mixture of human and superhuman factors. A legal basis is indispensable to counteract the oppressive relationship that often exists between government and governed. I believe this basis can be found in the *negotiorum gestio*. The collectivity of the citizens should be seen as the *dominus negotiorum* and the government as the *gestor.*

The wonderful legal consciousness of the Romans created a noble masterpiece in the *negotiorum gestio*. When the property of one single obstructed individual is in danger, everyone may come in to save it. That is the *gestor*, the person in charge of the business of strangers. He has no mission, that is to say, no mission placed upon him by other human beings. His mission has been given to him by a higher necessity. This higher necessity can be expressed in the context of the state in different ways, and will be expressed differently depending on the levels of civilized society. The *gestio* is directed towards the well-being of the *dominus*, the people, to which in the final analysis the *gestor* himself belongs.

The *gestor* administers a realm of which he is also partly the owner. From his partial ownership he gets a sense of the particular emergency, which may necessitate involvement in war and peace, but at no stage does he give himself a genuine mission of his own accord. Even where circumstances seem clear-cut, he can only guess at the approval of his countless co-partners.

The state originates in a people's struggle for existence. In this struggle it is not possible to get a proper mandate all the time through complicated procedures. Indeed, all undertakings in name of the collectivity would be doomed to failure, if each time it was dependent on a direct majority vote. The inner division of the people would make it powerless to act in an external emergency. You cannot gather all heads under one hat, as the saying goes. So the *gestor* simply puts on the hat and leads the way.

The state *gestor* derives sufficient legitimacy if the common cause is in danger and the *dominus* is incapable of helping itself through lack of willpower or whatever.

But as he acts, the *gestor* gradually becomes indebted to the *dominus* as if a contract had existed between them, *quasi ex contractu*.

This represents the pre-existing, or rather the co-existing legal contract within the state.

The *gestor* must stand guarantor for every kind of negligence, including the culpable non-completion of projects once commenced, and the neglect of whatever is significantly related, etc. I do not want to say any more here about the *negotiorum gestio* or about its transfer to the concept of the state. That would get us too far away from our real subject. Only this should be mentioned in addition: "Through approval the business conduct becomes binding on the businessman in the same way as if it had occurred according to his commission in the first place."

And what does all this mean in our case?

The Jews are at present prevented by the diaspora from conducting their political affairs themselves as a people. This causes them greater or lesser hardship in a number of areas. They need a *gestor* above all else.

This *gestor*, however, should not be just a single individual. That would be ridiculous, or even despicable, for he would simply look after his own advantage.

The gestor of the Jews must be a moral entity in every sense of the word.

And that is the Society of Jews.

The Gestor of the Jews

This mouthpiece of the popular movement, whose nature and tasks we now turn to, will indeed be called into existence before everything else. Its origin will be very simple. This moral entity will be formed from the circle of brave English Jews, with whom I spoke in London about this plan.*

The Society of Jews is the central office of the developing movement among the Jews.

The Society has scientific and political tasks. The foundation of the Jews' State, as I see it, is based on modern scientific assumptions. If today we walk away from Mizraim, then this cannot be done in the naive manner of ancient times. We will have to consider our numbers and our power in a different light beforehand. The Society of Jews is the new Moses of the Jews. The enterprise of the old great *gestor* of the Jews in simple times compares with our own as a wonderful old *Singspiel** compares to a modern grand opera. We play the same melody with many more violins, flutes, cellos and basses; with electric light, decorations, choirs, sublime staging and with the top singers.

The present paper aims to open up the issue of the Jews to general discussion. Friends and foes will participate in this—I hope not in the form of sentimental defense and wild accusations. The debate should be conducted in a sober, magnanimous, serious and political manner.

The Society of Jews will gather all the information, both oral and written, from politicians, parliaments, communities of Jews, societies, featured in meetings, newspapers and books.

Thus the Society of Jews will learn and determine for the very first time whether the Jews want and need to emigrate to the Promised Land. The Society will obtain from communities of Jews all over the world the data to compile a comprehensive statistical compendium of the Jews.

The later tasks, such as the scientific exploration of the new country and its natural resources, the common overall plan of emigration and settlement, the preparatory work for the legislature and administration, will be developed intelligently from this statistical basis.

As I have already said in the general part of this paper, the Society must make an attempt to get recognition by the outside world as the legitimate agent in the formation of the state. It will gain the necessary authority vis-à-vis other governments from the freely-given support of many Jews.

Looking inward, that is, considering the condition of Jews as a people, the Society will create the indispensable institutions of the initial stages—the original cell, to use a term from the natural sciences—from which the public institutions of the Jews' State will subsequently be developed .

The immediate objective is, as already stated, to obtain internationally assured sovereignty over a piece of territory that is sufficient for our needs.

What has to happen after that?

SEIZING THE LAND

When peoples migrated in historic times, they were carried, pulled about, dragged on by chance factors. Like swarms of locusts they would settle anywhere at all, willy-nilly. In historic times, people had no knowledge of the world.

The new emigration of Jews must be based on scientific principles.

As recently as forty years ago, goldmining was done in an amazingly simple way. How adventurous things were in California. Following rumors, all the desperadoes in the world rushed there from everywhere, stole the earth, robbed one another's gold, and then squandered it just like robbers.

Today! Just consider goldmining in the Transvaal. No longer romantic vagabonds, but sober geologists and engineers are in charge of the gold industry. Appropriate machines separate the gold from the stones. Little is left to chance.

In the same way we must research the new land for the Jews with all modern instruments, and take possession of it.

As soon as the land has been secured for us, the conquering ship will sail to it.

On the ship will be the representatives of the Society, the Company and the local groups.

Those taking possession of the land have three tasks: (1) the exact scientific exploration of all natural characteristics of the land, (2) the establishment of a strictly centralized administration, (3) the division of the land. These tasks are interwoven and are to be carried out in accordance with clearly understood objectives.

One thing has not yet been made clear: how the possession of the land is to be effected, taking the local groups into account.

In America the occupation of newly opened-up land is still done in a most naive way. The occupiers gather together at the border and at the agreed time throw themselves forcibly onto the new land.

This is not the way it will be done in the new land for the Jews. The building allotments in the cities and the provinces will be auctioned. Not for money, but for achievements. Following the general plan, it has already been determined which roads, bridges, water installations are necessary for general commerce. All this is worked out according to provinces. Within the provinces urban building allotments will be auctioned in much the same way. Local groups take on the duty to do this in a responsible fashion. Costs are independently assessed. The Society will be in the position to make sure that no local groups carry burdens that are too great for them. Large areas are kept by the public authorities for their activities. Large donations will be rewarded with specific acknowledgements: universities, institutes of technical and higher education, experimental schools, etc.; and those institutes which need not be located in the capital city will be spread around the country.

The interests of the original settlers, or if need be the local authority, guarantee the proper management of the newly acquired land. We do not wish to abolish differences between individuals, and differences between local groups will also remain. Everything will fit together in a natural way. All acquired rights will be protected; every new development will receive sufficient room to unfold.

All these things will be clearly known to our people.

Just as we do not catch others unawares or deceive them, so we will not fool ourselves either.

From the start, everything will be determined according to plan.

Developing this plan, which I can only briefly indicate, will be the task of our best minds. In this context we will use all the sociological and technical achievements not only of the time in which we live but also of the future times which will see the difficult execution of the plan. All those fortunate discoveries which have been made, or which still await us, will be used. In this way it can become a historically exemplary form of colonization and state formation, with unprecedented chances of success.

THE CONSTITUTION

One of the large commissions to be established by the Society will be the Counsel of State Jurists. These must devise as good and modern a constitution as is possible. I believe the constitution must be reasonably flexible. In another book I have discussed which forms of government seem to be the best in my view. I maintain that the democratic monarchy and the aristocratic republic are the finest types of state. Types of state and principle of government must stand in symmetrical opposition to each other. I am a convinced friend of monarchical institutions, because they provide constancy in political life, and because they provide a mutual link of interest between the preservation of the state and the preservation of a historically famous family born to rule. However, our history has been interrupted for such a long time, that we can no longer tie in to such a development. Merely trying to do so would attract the curse of ridicule.

Democracy without the useful counterweight of a monarch has none of the limitations that are desirable, neither in what it approves nor in what it condemns; it leads to idle talk in Parliament, and to the ugly category of professional politicians. In addition, the peoples of today are not suited to unlimited democracy, and I believe they will be less suited to it as time goes on. Pure democracy presupposes very simple customs in a people, and our customs are becoming ever more complicated due to commerce and civilization. "*Le ressort d'une démocratie est la vertu,"** says the wise Montesquieu. And where does one find this virtue, I mean this political virtue? I have no faith in our political virtue, because we are no different from other modern peoples, and because the freedom would soon go to our heads. I hold the referendum to be an incomplete instrument, for in politics there are no simple questions that may be answered merely by yes or no. In addition, the masses are even worse than the parliaments in following every fad, in supporting every person making the most noise. When a people are in the process of gathering together, it is in no position to bother about external or internal politics.

Political activity has to be conducted from the top. Even so, nobody in the Jews' State will be oppressed, for every Jew who wants to can get to the top and will want to get to the top. Hence there will be an enormous development towards the top in our people. Every individual will think he is advancing himself, but as a result the whole society will advance. Political ambition is to be bound by moral considerations, useful to the state, serving the idea of the people.

That is why I am thinking of an aristocratic republic. That accords with the sense of ambition in our people, which at present has degenerated into foolish vanity. Many institutions in old Venice are on my mind; but everything that caused Venice to collapse must be avoided. We will learn from the historical mistakes of others, just as we will learn from our own, because we are a modern people already wanting to become the most modern among peoples. Our people, to whom the Society brings the new land, will also receive with gratitude the constitution which the Society offers it. However, should there be pockets of opposition, then the Society will break them. It cannot allow itself to be disturbed in its work by narrow-minded or malevolent individuals.

LANGUAGE

Someone may think that it will be a problem that we no longer have a common language. Surely we cannot speak Hebrew with one another. Who among us knows enough Hebrew to ask for a train ticket in this language? That is not possible. Yet the issue is very simple. Everybody hangs on to his language, which is the precious home of his thoughts. Switzerland is the ultimate example of the possibility of federalism in language matters. We will remain over there what we are now, just as we will not stop loving and longing for our dear home countries from which we were driven away.

We will accustom ourselves to drop the stunted and oppressed jargons, these ghetto-languages, which we use at present. They were the secretive languages of captives. Our teachers will address this issue. Soon the main language will be automatically the one which will serve best the needs of general social intercourse. Our community is specific and unique. Only the faith of our fathers makes us realize that we still belong together.

THEOCRACY

Will we end up having a theocracy? No! Faith will hold us together, science makes us free. We will not even allow the theocratic inclinations of our spiritual leaders to raise their ugly heads. We will know how to keep them in their temples, just as we will know how to keep our professional army in the barracks. Army and clerics will be highly honored, as much as is right and proper in the light of their beautiful functions. They have no say in the state which treats them with deference, for they will only conjure up external and internal difficulties.

Everybody is as free and unfettered in practicing his belief or unbelief as he is in his nationality. And should it come to pass that persons of other faiths or nationalities live among us, then we will accord them honorable protection and equality before the law. Tolerance we have learnt in Europe, and I am not even being sarcastic when I say this. Only in a few isolated instances can you equate modern antisemitism with the old religious intolerance. It is in most cases a movement among the civilized peoples, with which they want to ward off a ghost from their own past.

LAWS

As the realization of the idea of the state approaches, the Society of Jews will organize legal preparations through a college of jurists. For a period of transition the view should be accepted that each of the immigrated Jews from the different countries is to be judged by the laws of his country thus far. Soon a unified legal system should be the objective. Laws should be modern, the best from everywhere should be used. There is the potential for an exemplary legal code, permeated with all the justifiable social claims of the present time.

THE ARMY

The Jews' State is conceptualized as a neutral state. It only needs a professional army, though of course equipped with the full array of modern means of war, so that it may ensure external and internal order.

THE FLAG

We have no flag. We need one. If you want to lead many people, you must raise a symbol over their heads.

I am thinking of a white flag with seven gold stars. The white field symbolizes the new, pure life; the stars are the seven golden hours of our working day. Because Jews will enter the new land under the sign of labor.

RECIPROCITY AND EXTRADITION TREATIES

The new Jews' State must be established properly. Our future honor in the world is at stake.

Hence all the obligations we still have in our places of abode up to now must be met honestly. The Society of Jews and the Jewish Company will grant cheap fares and favorable settlement conditions only to those who can show an official certificate from their local authorities: "Departed in good order."

In the Jews' State it will be easier than anywhere else to bring to court all private legal claims brought over from the countries left behind. We will not even await reciprocity. We do this only to satisfy our own honor. In this way our later demands will find the courts more favorably disposed towards us, as may have been the case up to now.

After all I have said above, it goes without saying that until we are in a position to put into effect our penal law on the same basis as the other civilized peoples, we will extradite Jewish criminals more readily than every other state. So there is a transitional period in place, during which we will accept our criminals only after they have served their sentences. Once they have served their sentences, however, we will accept them without restriction. The criminals among us should also be able to start a new life.

Thus, for many Jews emigration could well turn into a crisis with a happy ending. The bad external conditions which have caused many a character to go astray will be lifted, and the lost ones can be saved.

I would now like to quickly tell the story which I found in an article about the gold mines of Witwatersrand. One day a man came to the Rand, settled down, tried a few things except digging for gold, finally founded an ice factory which prospered, and soon gained general respect through his good behavior. Years later he was suddenly arrested. As a banker he had been guilty of embezzlement in Frankfurt; he had fled and had started a new life there under a false name. When they took him away as a prisoner, the most reputable people went to the station, bade him a fond farewell and—see you again! For he will return.

This story says everything. A new life can even make criminals better. And yet we have very few criminals in our community, comparatively speaking. You may consult an interesting analysis about this, *Criminality among Jews in Germany*, compiled by Dr. P. Nathan in Berlin on the basis of official information, and commissioned by the Committee for the Defense Against Antisemitic Attacks.* Unfortunately, this paper like many other "Defenses" is based on the mistaken premise that antisemitism can be refuted by reasoned argument. I suspect we are hated just as much for our qualities as for our faults.

Advantages of Emigration among the Jews

I think that governments will give this paper some attention either of their own free will or under pressure from antisemites, and perhaps here or there they will start off showing some sympathy for my plan, which will in turn be directed to the Society of Jews.

Through the emigration of Jews I have in mind, there can be no economic crises. Rather, such crises which would have to come in the course of persecution of Jews would be softened if this plan were put into effect. A great period of prosperity would set in throughout the present antisemitic countries. For, as I have often said before, there will be an internal migration of Christian citizens into the positions which the Jews have evacuated slowly and according to plan. If they do not merely leave us alone, but even render us some assistance, the movement will have a beneficial effect everywhere. The concept that through mass migration of Jews countries will become poorer is narrow-minded, and has to be abandoned. Emigration as a result of persecution is a different thing insofar as it would bring with it the destruction of property, as what happens in the confusion of war. Peaceful free emigration of colonists is different, because everything can be finalized with respect to personal rights in a fully legal framework, free and open, in broad daylight, under the supervision of the authorities, and controlled by public opinion. Emigration of Christian proletarians to other parts of the world would cease in the wake of the movement of the Jews.

The states would further have the advantage of seeing their exports grow enormously, because the emigrated Jews would still be dependent for a long time to come on European products, and would have to buy them there. The local groups would coordinate this movement; for a while, their needs born out of custom should be satisfied solely with products from the places they have been used to.

One of the greatest advantages would be the lifting of social pressures. Social discontent could be ameliorated for some time to come, perhaps for twenty years or even longer—in any case, as long as the entire emigration among Jews would last.

How the social issue will shape up depends exclusively on the development of technology. Steam power has concentrated people into factories around the machines, where they are crowded together and are making each other unhappy. Production is enormous, unplanned, not freely decided; it is subject to continual serious crises, and leads both entrepreneurs and workers to their doom. Steampower has pressed people closely together, the introduction of electricity will probably scatter them again and perhaps lead to more favorable working conditions. At any rate, technical inventors, the true benefactors of mankind, will continue their work even after the start of the migration of Jews and hopefully continue to discover marvelous things as they have so far, perhaps even more marvelous ones.

Already the word "impossible" seems to have disappeared from the language of technology. If a man from the last century returned, he would find our new life full of magic incomprehensible to him. Wherever we moderns appear on the scene with our know-how, we change the desert into a garden. To construct cities we now need as many years as they needed centuries in former times—there are countless examples for this in America. The obstacle of distance has been overcome. The treasury of the modern spirit contains immeasurable riches which increase every day; a hundred thousand heads are busy thinking, exploring all points of the globe, and one individual's discovery belongs to the world the moment after.

In our new land for the Jews we ourselves will want to use and develop all the new experiments; we want to be an example to the whole world with our seven-hour working day; we want to lead the way in all things beneficial to humanity; and we want to turn our new country into an experimental country and a model country.

Following the emigration of the Jews, the enterprises which they created will remain where they were. The Jewish spirit of enterprise will not be absent where it is welcome. Mobile Jewish capital will continue to look for investment opportunities where its possessors know the conditions. Whereas, because of persecutions, Jewish capital at present searches out the most distant opportunities, after our peaceful solution it will return and contribute to the further betterment of the places where Jews have lived up to now.

Conclusion

So much has remained unexplained, so many limitations, harmful superficialities, and useless repetitions can still be found in this paper, which I have pondered long and deeply, and have revised often.

The reasonable reader, who is sensible enough to read between the lines, will not be repelled by the limitations. Rather, he will be encouraged to participate in this work and improve it with his perspicacity; it does not just belong to any one individual.

Perhaps I have explained what is self-evident and overlooked important reservations.

I have tried to refute some objections; I know there are many others, big ones and small ones.

One of the big objections is that the Jews' situation is not the only perilous one in the world. However, I think that we should nevertheless start to get rid of a bit of misery; even if it is our own for the time being.

It can further be said that we should not want to introduce new distinctions between people, or new boundaries; let us rather get rid of the old ones. I think those of that opinion are amiable enthusiasts, but the dust of their bones will already be blown in the wind without a trace when the idea of the fatherland will still be blooming. The general brotherhood of man is not even a beautiful dream. Only the presence of the enemy will bring the highest exertions of personality.

Yet how? Jews will not have even one enemy in their own state, and if they begin to grow weak and disappear in their prosperity, would the Jews as a people then really perish? I think the Jews will always have enough enemies, like every other nation. However, once they are situated on their own ground, they can no longer be dispersed over the whole world. The diaspora cannot be repeated, as long as the civilization of the world does not break down. That is merely the fear of the simpleton. Present-day civilization has enough of the instruments of power to defend itself.

The small objections are countless, just as there are more little people than great ones. I have tried to grapple with some limited conceptions. Whoever wants to march behind the white flag with the seven stars must help with this campaign of enlightenment. Perhaps initially the struggle must be waged against many a wicked, small-minded, limited Jew.

Will they not say that I put ammunition in the hands of the anti-semites. Why? Because I admit the truth? Because I do not maintain that we have only perfect persons in our community?

Will they not say that I point to a way which can lead to some harm? I dispute that most decisively. In my view, harm can be directed against us as individuals, or against groups of Jews—even those who are at present the most powerful among us, but it will never be done by the state, and never against all Jews at the same time. Once it exists, the legal equality of Jews can no longer be undone; for even initial attempts would drive all Jews, whether rich or poor, into the arms of the revolutionary parties. The very start of official discrimination against Jews is followed everywhere by economic crises. So, in effect, they can do little against us, unless they want to hurt themselves as well. So their hatred is growing bigger and bigger all the time. The wealthy do not notice that a great deal. But our poor people! Just ask our poor, who have fallen deeper into the proletariat since the renewal of antisemitism.

Will some of our well-to-do feel that the pressure is not yet big enough to start emigrating, and even forcible expulsions of Jews only confirm how reluctant our people are to go? Sure, for they do not know where to go. For they only go from one misery into another. But we show them the way into the Promised Land. The sublime power of enthusiasm will have to combat the terrible power of sloth.

Are the persecutions no longer as evil as during the Middle Ages? True, but we have become more sensitive, so that we do not notice a lessening in our suffering. The long persecution has strained our nerves to breaking point.

Will they still say: the enterprise is without hope, even if we get sovereignty over the land, because only the poor will join us? Those we need precisely first of all! Only desperadoes are useful in conquest.

Will someone say: yes, if it were possible, someone would have done it already?

Up to now it was not possible. Now it is possible. A hundred, even fifty years ago it would have been a fancy. Today all this is real. The wealthy, who have a satisfying overview of the whole spectrum of technological achievements, know very well that with money, everything can be done. This is what will happen: precisely the poor and the simple folk, who do not even suspect what dominion over natural forces man already possesses, will believe in the new message most strongly. For they have not lost the hope of the Promised Land.

There it is, Jews! No fairy tale, no deception! Everyone can convince himself, for everyone will carry a piece of the Promised Land in his luggage; one person in his head, the next in his arms, the next in the wealth he has acquired.

Now it could all seem to involve a long, drawn-out process. Even under the most favorable conditions the start of the establishment of the state is still many years away. In the meantime Jews will be hassled, insulted, scolded, beaten, plundered, killed in a thousand different ways. No, even if we just make a start with the plan, antisemitism will cease immediately everywhere. For that is the peace treaty. Once the Jewish Company is formed, the news will be carried within the day like lightning over our telegraph wires.

Immediately things will become easier for us. Our over-produced middle-range intellectuals will flow out of the middle classes into our first organizations; they will become our first technicians, officers, professors, officials, lawyers, doctors. Thus the project will continue, speedily and yet without major crisis.

In the temples they will pray for the success of the work. But in the churches, too! It is the solution to an old pressure which made everyone suffer.

But first our minds must be set alight. The idea must fly out and reach even the smallest unhappy town where our people live. They will awake from their gloomy brooding. A new meaning will enter the lives of our people. Everyone needs to think merely of himself, and the movement will become overpowering.

What fame awaits the unselfish fighters for the cause!

This is why I believe that a generation of wonderful Jews will grow out of the earth. The Maccabees* shall rise again.

Let me repeat my word from the beginning one last time: Those Jews who wish it will have their state.

We must at last live as free men on our own soil and die in our own homeland in peace.

By our freedom the world will be freed, by our richness enriched, by our greatness ennobled.

Whatever we will attempt over there for our own prosperity will have a powerful and life-enhancing effect on all humanity.

Glossary

à la Daumont   More correctly: *à la d'Aumont*, an adverbial expression. A style of riding by open carriage, where the carriage is drawn by four horses, two of which have a rider. The Duke of Aumont (1762–1831) introduced this style of riding to France in the years immediately after the fall of Napoleon.

(*Grand dictionnaire encyclopédique Larousse* 1982:I.830.)

Assistance par le Travail   The movement towards establishing working houses for the unskilled and unemployed had first gained momentum in the Netherlands and Belgium in the 1880s and had been copied by a number of municipalities in France by the early 1890s. In these working houses, usually run by the local municipal authorities, the unemployed were given simple tasks, in return for a very small wage or even coupons, which could be redeemed for food and clothing. Herzl had noted the existence of these establishments early in his stay in Paris, and had devoted a lengthy article to them in the *Neue Freie Presse* of 2 August 1893. In it he made particular mention of a working house in the Paris suburb of Batignolles-Monceau, which in the short space of two years had grown from catering for forty persons to catering for eight hundred. Herzl mentions that one of the specific tasks of the unemployed there was the cutting of *margotins*—small woodchips drenched in oil to light fires—a feature he also mentions in the *Jews' State*. He also mentions the truck system, which likewise finds its way into the *Jews' State*.

(Herzl 1893; Bein and Schaerf 1974:483–489.)

Catholics Against the Central Bank   In 1878, a number of right-wing Catholic political leaders in France established the *Union générale des Banques* with the express purpose of breaking the banking monopoly of the *Haute Banque en France*—a rather loose but powerful collection of Jewish and Protestant banks of which Rothschild's bank was the most important. The *Union générale* crashed in 1882 because of financial inexperience and mismanagement, and thousands of small Catholic subscribers lost their savings on that occasion. The Catholic leaders held Rothschild responsible for the crash, a charge he vigorously denied, and which investigations conducted after Herzl's death showed to be without foundation. Obviously Herzl himself did not know of these later investigations, and had no reason to doubt the complicity of Rothschild in the crash of the *Union générale*.

(Bein and Schaerf 1974:I.141.)

Colonization Companies   The final spurt of colonization by the European powers, the last European claims of as yet unclaimed land in Africa and the Pacific, occurred during the last two decades of the nineteenth century. Usually the initial claim was staked by private colonization companies, which were trading companies interested in the extraction of mineral wealth as well as in the settlement of targetted territories. Only when such settlement was already effective would the respective governments of the European powers take over and look after the legal aspects of such settlement.

The prototype of such a colonization company was the British South Africa Company, founded in 1889 by Cecil Rhodes, with the express purpose of securing the rich gold and diamond resources of Southern Africa for the British. However, by 1889, such companies had been part of the scene both in Britain and in Germany for some years already. The German colonialist Carl Peters formed his *Deutsch-Ostafrikanische Gesellschaft* (German East Africa Company) in 1885 which received a charter from the German government to appropriate land in Eastern Africa.

Herzl was most impressed by Cecil Rhodes' activities, and even sent him a copy of *The Jews' State* for his comment on 11 January 1902. He received no reply; hardly surprising as Rhodes by this time was already a very sick man, who was to die two months later in Capetown.

(Brockhaus 1966–1972 (articles on Rhodes, Peters, *Deutsch-Ostafrikanische Gesellschaft*, Schutzgebiete); Encyclopaedia Brittanica Micropaedia, Volume 10, 1988 (article on Rhodes).)

Cook System of Travel   Thomas Cook (1808-1892) was an English Baptist missionary who in 1841 persuaded the Midland Counties Railway Company to run a train between Leicester and Loughborough for a special group of participants at a temperance meeting. In 1844, the railways agreed to continue running special excursion trains for Cook if he provided the passengers. The idea caught on, and in 1855, Cook arranged for excursions between Leicester and Calais for the Paris Exhibition. In 1856 he organized the first Grand Tour of Europe, and during the next decade he became an agent for the sale of personal transport tickets as well as postal services. His firm Thomas Cook and Son survives to this day.

(*The New Encyclopaedia Brittanica, Micropaedia*, 1994, Volume 3.)

Darwin's Expression "Chromatic Function"   Herzl's meaning is quite clear here, although his reference to Darwin is obscure. By encouraging those Jews who find it difficult to assimilate to emigrate to the Jews' State, the Jews that remain behind would find it easier to integrate into their respective mainstream societies. They are now in a position to adopt the latter's salient characteristics or colors. This happens in the natural world, too, during cell division or mitosis when the nuclei of cells resolve into small bodies known as chromosomes, which have the capacity to become colored when stained by certain dyes. As part of cell division, chromatids, or part of chromosomes, "cross over" to the new cells, thus giving the new cells certain characteristics of the parent cells. Herzl attributes the use of the term to Darwin, but there is no reference to the term or concept in Darwin's work. In fact, chromosomes were not observed until twenty years after the publication of *The Origin of Species* by the German scientist Walter Flemming in Kiel (1879). Herzl simply suggests that, by analogy, a "chromatic function" is also operative in the realm of society.

(Kalmus 1954.)

Divine Rights of Kings   The divine rights of kings theory is one of a number of variants of the ideology that kings have absolute power to rule. In the words of C. H. McIlwain (in Seligman and Johnson, Volume 5, 1959:176), "under the theory of the divine right of kings the monarch is not in person divine, but he does enjoy and exercise a personal right to rule in virtue of his birth alone and not of his office, a right based not merely upon national and customary law but found in the law of God and of nature. Under it no king can de facto have any legitimate authority: all true kings must be kings de jure; under the law of God and the law of nature they succeed by heredity alone to the rights of their ancestors, who in the beginning were divinely appointed to rule. They are never the creatures of the people, their authority does not come from the people's law, and their powers are not derived from their predecessors in the royal office but from their ancestors alone." The king's right to rule therefore does not reside in the office of kingship, but in the incumbent's personal status as having been given the right to rule by God. In England divine rights claims have been dismissed since the Glorious Revolution of 1688, in France since the French Revolution, but in Herzl's time the divine right was still claimed as a matter of course by the Czar, and at times by Kaiser Wilhelm II.

(Seligman and Johnson Volume 5, 1959.)

"Don't Buy from Jews," "Away with the Jews"   These two slogans, which were to get such notoriety during Nazi times, were already well-known in Germany during the time of Herzl. Philippson reports that in February 1889 a band of some four hundred to five hundred youths roamed the streets of the southeastern suburbs of Berlin, chanting the slogan "*Juden raus*, [Away with the Jews]" and plundering Jewish shops (Philippson, 1910:II.43). In a number of towns in northern Germany during the Christmas season of 1892 leaflets were distributed with the text "*Kauft nicht bei Juden* [Don't buy from Jews]" (Philippson, 1910:II.48).

(Philippson 1910:II.43, 48.)

Dr. Paul Nathan   Paul Nathan (1857–1927) lived and worked in Berlin as freelance publicist and politician. For many years he was the chairman of the local Committee to repulse antisemitic attacks (*Komitee zur Abwehr antisemitischer Angriffe*), and in this capacity published a number of articles and pamphlets about the Jews and their place in German society. Together with James Simon, Nathan established the *Hilfsverein der deutschen Juden* [Society to Assist German Jews] in Berlin on 28 May 1901, "to advance the moral, spiritual and economic development of our co-religionists" (cited in Rinott 1986:294), or more specifically, to promote Jewish education in Palestine. Until the foundation of the *Hilfsverein*, German Jews had participated in the work of the *Alliance Israélite Universelle*, based in Paris, in establishing educational institutions in Palestine. But in Germany the work of the *Alliance* had increasingly come under suspicion of being more concerned with spreading French civilization and political influence in Palestine than with promoting Jewish communal life (Jonas, 1923:419), so from its very inception, the *Hilfsverein* sought German government protection for its schools in Palestine—in vain, as it turned out (Rinott, 1986:294–296). The most lasting monument to the work of the *Hilfsverein* is the foundation of the Technion in Haifa. (Patai, 1971:502)

Nathan published the pamphlet *Die Kriminalität der Juden in Deutschland* in 1896, the first in a series sponsored by the *Komitee*. In it he examines the claim of German antisemites *"daß die Juden durch eine ganz besondere Anlagung zum Verbrechen eine Gefahr für jene Länder seien, in denen sie sich aufhalten* [that the Jews are a danger to those countries where they live, because of their particular propensity to crime]" (Nathan, 1896:VII). After a close examination of population and crime statistics for the years 1882–1892, Nathan concludes that in terms of their proportion of the German population, the crime rate for the Jews in Germany is roughly 20 percent less than that of the general population (Nathan, 1896:VIII). A particularly interesting section of the report is Nathan's examination of the crime rate in Saxony, which is reportedly almost *judenrein* (Nathan himself uses the ominous expression, 1896:VIII); hence the incidence of crime in Saxony cannot be acribed to any Jewish influence.

Herzl takes note of Nathan's paper, but doubts whether it can achieve its aim of alleviating antisemitism by reasoned argument.

(Herlitz 1930:IV/1, 412–413; Jonas 1923; Nathan 1896; Patai 1971; Rinott 1986.)

Establishment   There is some controversy attached to the terminology here. Herzl uses the term *Herstellung*, which d'Avigdor translated as *restoration*. This translation has been picked up uncritically since then in a number of English versions of *Der Judenstaat* (e.g. Haas, 1904; Cohen, 1934), and later critics have based their work on this concept of restoration (e.g. Hertzberg, 1977:204, Laqueur, 1984:6). Yet, as Desmond Stewart (1974:217 note and 361, note 8) discusses in his biography of Herzl, the German word denotes *creation, establishment, preparation*, but there is no element of *restoration* contained in the German word. This is evidently the view of Harry Zohn, who in his translation (Herzl, 1970:27) uses the word *establishment*. The French translation of Claude Klein (Herzl, 1990:15) suggests *création*, and Gino Servadio in his Italian version opts for *costituzione* (Herzl, 1955:55). Had Herzl had the concept of restoration in mind, he would have used the word *Wiederherstellung*, the prefix *wieder* to *again* or referring (Messinger, 1981:783). The maintenance of the concept of *restoration* with respect to *Herstellung* adds an ideological dimension to the concept in English, which Herzl's own terminology cannot reasonably carry.

Internal evidence from *The Jews' State* as well as external evidence from the diary supports this interpretation. Herzl talks about the new Jews' State in terms not of a restoration, but of a *Neubildung* [new formation], even a "unique" (*eigentümliche*) new creation; he mentions the *Entstehung des Judenstaates* [formation] as well as the *Entstehung* of the Society of Jews; the creation of the state is seen in terms of a *Gründung* [foundation], which cannot be linked with the old Jewish state of biblical times:

> *Die Gründung des Judenstaates, wie ich mir sie denke, hat moderne, wissenschaftliche Voraussetzungen. Wenn wir heute aus Mizraim wandern, kann es nicht in der naiven Weise der alten Zeit geschehen. Wir werden uns vorher anders Rechenschaft geben von unserer Zahl und Kraft.*

The foundation of the Jews' State, as I see it, is based on modern scientific assumptions. If today we walk away from Mizraim, then this cannot be done in the naive manner of ancient times. We will have to consider our numbers and our power in a different light beforehand.

There is even clearer evidence from the diary that Herzl dissociates himself from any thoughts that his Jews' State should be seen as a restoration of the biblical Jewish entity. William Hechler may have written a pamphlet about *The restoration of the Jews to Palestine according to the prophets* (Chouraqui, 1970:106), but at the audience Herzl and Hechter had with the Grand Duke of Baden at Bregenz on 2 September 1898, he distances himself from Hechler's views:

> *Ich machte überhaupt darauf aufmerksam, daß mit den Juden ein deutsches Kulturelement in den Orient käme. Beweis dafür: deutsche Schriftsteller—wenn auch von jüdischer Abstammung—führen die zionistische Bewegung. Die Kongreßsprache war die deutsche. Die überwiegende Mehrheit der Juden gehört der deutschen Kultur an.*
>
> *Wir brauchen ein Protektorat—das deutsche wäre uns demnächst das liebste . . . Hechler mischte sich ab und zu mit prophetischen Bemerkungen über the return of the Jews ein. Der Großherzog hörte ihm milde lächelnd zu, nickte aber mir Beifall zu, als ich sagte: "Diese Dinge entziehen sich meiner Beurteilung. Ich kann nur davon sprechen, was ich sehe." Der Großherzog sagte hierauf: "Ja, wir wollen die Sache nur als eine weltgeschichtliche, nicht als eine theologische betrachten." (3 September 1898; BT2:606–607)*

I drew his attention to the fact that with the Jews a *German* cultural element would come to the Orient. Evidence of this: German writers—even though of Jewish descent—are leading the Zionist movement. The language of the Congress is German. The overwhelming majority of the Jews are part of German culture. We need a protectorate—accordingly, we would prefer a German one . . . Hechler occasionally broke in with prophetic remarks about *the return of the Jews*. The Grand Duke listened to him with a benign smile, but nodded approval to me when I said: "Such things are beyond my judgment. I can only speak of what I see." At this the Grand Duke said: "Yes, let us consider the matter only as a world-historical matter and not as a theological one." (P2:658–659)

This is not to say that the concept of *restoration* was unknown in Jewish circles in Vienna in the 1890s. A comparison between Herzl and Nathan Birnbaum in this context is instructive. In one of the early issues of Birnbaum's journal *Selbstemanzipation* (15 September 1885) he editorializes that "*die antisemitischen Drangsäle sind die Wehen, die der Wiedergeburt unserer Nation vorangehen*" [the anti-semitic hardships are the pains which precede the rebirth of our nation] (my italics), and in 1893 he published a pamphlet entitled *Die nationale Wiedergeburt des jüdischen Volkes in seinem Lande als Mittel zur Lösung der Judenfrage* [The national rebirth of the Jewish people in its country as means of solving the issue of the Jews]. Herzl knew Birnbaum well, and Birnbaum was for a time extremely active in the organization that preceded the First Zionist Congress; he even worked for a time on Herzl's paper *Die Welt*. Herzl was well aware of the *restoration* issue but chose not to go that path himself (c.f. the discussion in Gaisbauer, 1988:44–45); in his own words:

Will man heute ein Land gründen, darf man es nicht in der Weise machen, die vor tausend Jahren die einzig mögliche gewesen wäre. Es ist töricht, auf alte Kulturstufen zurückzukehren, wie es manche Zionisten möchten.

If you want to establish a country in this day and age, you cannot do so in the only way that might have been appropriate a thousand years ago. It is foolish to want to hark back to old concepts of culture, as many Zionists are keen to do.

Stewart (1974:217 note) may well be correct in hinting that ideological preoccupations have been at the basis of the "subtle" altering of the meaning of *Herstellung* "in modern Zionist texts" to become *restoration*. Against this, however, it needs to be said that the denotation *restoration* is used by Sylvie d'Avigdor in her translation of *Der Judenstaat* as early as 1896, and that, certainly in England, the concept of *restoration* has had currency in both Jewish and non-Jewish writing ever since the end of the seventeenth century (Gelber, 1927:126). Gelber, for instance, cites an anonymous treatise dating from 1746 entitled *A treatise of the future restoration of the Jews and Israelites to their Owen [sic] land* (Gelber, 1927:294, note 82), and Nahum Sokolow (1969:I.127) offers an article published in *The Times* of 17 August 1840 headlined "Syria—Restoration of the Jews," which cites a ministerial paper that begins: "What are the feelings of the Jews you meet with respect to their return to the Holy Land?" Rather than burden d'Avigdor with ideological preoccupations about changes of meaning, the explanation of the original mistranslation may be a simpler one. D'Avigdor had come to live in Britain from Belgium; she may have confused the meaning of the German word *Herstellung* with the Dutch word *herstel*, which indeed means *restoration* (Bruggencate, 1983:II.325). The two words, although superficially related, are fundamentally different in meaning. The German word consists of a stressed separable prefix *her* (*upright*) combined with the noun *Stellung* (*placement*); hence the meaning of the word *establishment*. The Dutch word consists of the *inseparable unstressed* prefix *her* (*re-, again*; Bruggencate, 1983:II.320) with the noun *stel* (*placement*); hence *restoration*. It is of some interest that Cohen-Slijper's Dutch version of *Der Judenstaat* (1919) also mistranslates *Herstellung* with *herstel*.

It must be stated that there is one reference in English by Herzl in the diary to *Jewish restauration* [sic] (13 June 1901; BT3:299, P3:1160).

(Bruggencate 1983; Gaisbauer 1988; Gelber 1927; Hertzberg 1977; Herzl 1896, 1904, 1919, 1934, 1955, 1970, 1990; Messinger 1981; Laqueur 1984; Sokolow 1969; Stewart 1974.)

Experiments in Belgium and England   The English social legislation to which Herzl here alludes is the batch of legislation enacted by Disraeli's last ministry in 1875. During his younger days, Disraeli had written of the "two nations" into which England was increasingly being divided as the Industrial Revolution took its course, and he believed that the paternal interest of his Conservative party in the workers was the best guarantee for the alleviation of their misery. The year 1875 saw the passing of a number of laws to give effect to this philosophy: the Artisans' Dwellings Act and the Public Health Act which aimed to improve the sanitary conditions in which workers lived and worked; the Conspiracy and Protection of Property Act which legalized strikes and peaceful picketing during a strike; the Employers and Workmen Act, which freed workmen from criminal prosecution for breach of contract if they went on strike; and the Factory and Workshop Act, which provided uniform regulation of working hours throughout the country. The successor ministries to Disraeli were less interested in further social legislation, although in 1891 elementary education was made free and universal. The second great wave of social legislation, based on the example of Bismarck's pioneering insurance laws in Germany in the 1880s and encouraged by David Lloyd George, came only after Herzl's death (Small Holdings Bill, 1907; National Insurance Bill, 1911).

Unimpeded economic liberalism remained the ruling social ideology in Belgium well into the 1870s, supported both by the liberal and clerical parties in government, and attempts to alleviate the misery of workers—such as to fix the minimum age for child labor—were thrown out of parliament as late as 1878. A wave of serious strikes erupted in Belgium in March 1886, "*la vague de grèves la plus violente et la plus massive qu'ait jamais connu la Wallonie* [the most violent and massive wave of strikes that the French-speaking part of Belgium has ever experienced]" (Witte and Graeybeckx, 1987:104). In Liège and Verviers, factories were destroyed. The army managed to break the initial strikes, but there were dozens of fatalities and there was a second outbreak of strikes in May 1887. It was now obvious to the government that the traditional organs of conciliation were not suited to tackle the grave differences between workers and employers. So Prime Minister Beernaert's government instituted a *Commission du Travail* to examine the situation of Belgian workers. Its recommendations were subsequently enshrined in a series of social laws enacted between 1887 and 1889, which in its scope rivals if not surpasses both Disraeli's legislation and the Bismarck packages of 1881–1882 in Germany. For a start, in 1887 the government outlawed the payment of workers in kind (and in alcohol) rather than money. In 1889 a number of laws followed. The working day was limited to twelve hours. Conciliation boards between employers and employees were established, and the old condition that workers must be at work before conciliation can be effected was abolished. The government instituted *Conseils de l'industrie et du travail* to monitor relations between employers and employees in the workplace. A law on women and child labor stipulated the minimum age for women to work in the coal mines at twenty years, and children below twelve years of age were not allowed to work. Minimum standards were set by the government for workers' housing. Compulsory labor was abolished; workers could withhold their labor under certain conditions. A second wave of social legislation between 1905 and 1909 came too late for Herzl to take notice of.

(Beer 1969; Read 1994; Trevelyan 1965; Witte & Graeybeckx 1987.)

Gestor   The passage in Justinian's *Institutes* (Book 3, title 27) is as follows:

> *Post genera contractuum enumerata dispiciamus etiam de his obligationi-*
> *bus, quae non propriae quidem ex contractu nasci intelleguntur, sed*
> *tamen, quia non ex maleficio substantiam capiunt, quasi ex contractu*
> *nasci videntur. Igitur cum quis absentis negotia gesserit, ultro citroque inter*

eos nascuntur actiones, quae appellantur negotiorum gestorum: sed domino quidem rei gestae adversus eum qui gessit directa competit actio, negotiorum autem gestori contraria. quas ex nullo contractu proprie nasci manifestum est: quippe ita nascuntur istae actiones, si sine mandato quisque alienis negotiis gerendis se optulerit: ex qua causa ii quorum negotia gesta fuerint etiam ignorantes obligantur. idque utilitatis causa receptum est, ne absentium, qui subita festinatione coacti nulli demandata negotiorum suorum administratione peregre profecti essent, desererentur negotia: quae sane nemo curaturus esset, si de eo quod quis impendisset nullam habiturus esset actionem. sicut autem is qui utiliter gesserit negotia habet obligatum dominum negotiorum, ita et contra iste quoque tenetur, ut administrationis rationem reddat. quo casu ad exactissimam quisque diligentiam compellitur reddere rationem: nec sufficet talem diligentiam adhibere, qualem suis rebus adhibere soleret, si modo alius diligentior commodius administraturus esset negotia. (Moyle, 1896:461–463)

Having dealt with types of contracts, let us consider also those relations which, strictly speaking, are not deemed to be derived from a contract, yet seem to be quasi-contractual, since they are not based on a crime. Thus, when anyone undertakes the affairs of another person, there occur between these men mutual proceedings which are called management of affairs; but, indeed, to the principal is due a proceeding against the man who has managed the affair, and on the other hand to the manager of affairs an opposing proceeding is due. It is obvious that, strictly speaking, these proceedings do not derive from any contract, for they arise if anyone presents himself as manager of the affairs of another without being commissioned to do so; and in this situation those whose affairs have been undertaken are under an obligation—even if they did not know about the action. This [principle] has been accepted for the sake of expediency, lest the affairs be abandoned of men who are away, forced to go abroad in sudden haste without entrusting the management of their affairs to anyone; and he would have no action if no one took care of these affairs, even though someone had already expended effort on the matter. However, just as the man who has managed the affairs beneficially holds the principal under an obligation, so also he in turn is bound by an obligation to render account of his management. In this event each party is obliged to give an account with very precise care; and it is not sufficient to [merely] apply such care as he usually applies to his own affairs: he must undertake another's affairs more assiduously and more favorably.

In his French edition of *The Jews' State*, Claude Klein provides the best modern commentary on the concept of *negotiorum gestio* (Herzl, 1990:91, note 28). Klein notes that the concept is equally a feature of the French Civil Code (articles 1371–1381), and comments that it concerns the rights and obligations of a person who involves himself in the affairs of another without having obtained the express permission of this latter party to do so. He advances the classical case of a person who may have to deal with damage which has occurred to the property of a neighbor who is absent and is therefore in no position to take the necessary measures himself, yet who has left no permission to another person to cover such eventuality. As Herzl comments, by analogy he sees himself as the *gestor* of the Jewish people, who are not in a position to look after themselves. Evidently, Herzl's legal training at the University of Vienna shows up here. One of the law professors at Vienna while Herzl was a student, Moritz Wlassak, had published a book on the very subject in 1879, entitled *Zur Geschichte der Negotiorum gestio, eine rechtsgeschichtliche Untersuchung* [The history of the *negotiorum gestio*—a legal-historical examination].

(Herzl 1990; Moyle 1896.)

Giro   Giro refers to a system of banking whereby monetary credits are transferred between banks and post offices. In the giro system, the post office is able to take on the functions of banking that have to do with the transaction of checks, but it cannot deal with other banking functions, such as issuing loans. Checks are the normal way of transacting money in this system; and the giro system represents the only system within which the post office is able to issue and transact checks. In Herzl's time this system of banking was not in vogue in England, but it was well-known in Europe, and especially popular in Germany, where this system of banking linked the Reichsbank and the Reichspost (Westminster Gazette, 17 September 1910).

(Simpson and Weiner, Volume 6, 1989.)

Huguenots   The Huguenots were the community of Protestants which had grown up in France since the Reformation. Their status in French society was always precarious, swinging between times of religious freedom and their persecution in civil wars and individual bloodbaths (St. Bartholomew's night, 1572). Their freedom was guaranteed under the Edict of Nantes (1598), which was repealed in 1685 by Louis XIV. The vast majority of the Huguenots then left France for England, Holland and Prussia, and with their trading and artisan skills contributed significantly to the prosperity of England and Holland during the 18th century.

The Jews from Hessen   The strong economic development in Germany after 1870 was encouraged by the substantial war reparation monies which flowed into Germany from France in the aftermath of the Franco-Prussian War. This also led to a number of financial difficulties and scandals, which were often ascribed to dark Jewish machinations. There were the occasional outbreaks of anti-semitic violence all over Germany as a result, but it seems that the region of Hessen was a special case. Until 1870, Hessen had been a particularly backward part of Germany, and such Jews that lived there had been active in the small retail trade and in the cattle trade. In the wake of the economic difficulties of 1870, small peasants often had to take out loans to keep their heads above water, often from Jewish financiers. When they continued to have difficulties with payments, their economic plight was often ascribed to the Jews. As a result, there were a number of civil disturbances in Hessen in the 1880s involving Jews, the local government refused to appoint Jews in official positions, and when the federal Reichstag elections of 1890 yielded four antisemitic deputies, they all came from Hessen.

(Philippson 1910:II.1–69.)

Jude   The word *Jude* occurs in the text as a noun on its own (149 times), as the first noun in a compound noun connected with 24 other nouns (85 times), as the second noun in a compound noun once (*Finanzjuden*), as the first noun connected with an adjective once (*judenfeindlich*) and 27 times as the adjective *jüdisch*. Neither the single noun *Jude* nor the adjective *jüdisch* were associated with negative connotations in Herzl's day, and their literal renderings into English do not present undue difficulties. Translation of the compound nouns featuring *Jude* presents, however, a number of problems; some of these have to do with different denotations of the literal translation into English; others with the fact that compound nouns in German, of which *Jude* forms a part, often carried with them negative connotations, which Herzl plays with in order to reinforce the points he is making. These negative connotations have been the subject of intensive historico-semantic investigation by Nicole Hortzitz (1988). The question of how to render the term *Judenstaat* has already been addressed in the introduction. The traditional rendering of the term *Judenfrage* (15 times) as "Jewish question" carries with it misleading connotations about the locus of the question, and where responsibility of the problems engendered by the question lies. In Herzl's view, it is not a question that is the responsibility of the Jews: the Jews know perfectly well what they want and what their social position in the various states should be. Rather, it is an issue for the non-Jewish mainstream populations of the countries where Jews reside, and the issue these various populations, governments and institutions have to deal with is what the relationship between them and the Jewish populations in their respective states should be and why. Hence, paradoxically, it would be more in the spirit of Herzl to render *Judenfrage* as *gentile question*—a question for the mainstream societies. To incorporate this meaning into Herzl's concept, I have rendered Herzl's word as *issue of the Jews*. Similarly, *Judenhaß* (3 times) can hardly be rendered "Jewish hatred"; rather, we are talking about *hatred of the Jews*. As already noted in the introduction, compound nouns featuring *Jude* are apt to carry pejorative connotations, of which Herzl is well aware, but which he uses with the express motive of challenging the world. Heading the list of these is the term *Judenknecht* (2 times), which can hardly be rendered as "Jewish servant" as it refers in antisemitic parlance to non-Jews who have sunk so low as to have to be servile to Jews. Hortzitz (1988:222ff) has discussed in detail how the term *Jude* in compound nouns referring to finance carries "*negative Assoziationen des Inhalts 'unlauter im ökonomischen Verhalten'* [negative associations connoting 'unclean economic behaviour']"; this needs to be borne in mind in Herzl's use of the terms *Finanzjude* (once), *Judengüter* (once) and *Judengeld* (once): terms that in the present century were to get such notoriety, and that are inadequately rendered by terms incorporating the adjective "Jewish." *Judenvolk* (6 times), normally rendered as "Jewish people," is more accurately rendered as "Jews as a people." The pejorative meaning is still there, though less so, in the term *Judenfreund* (once). The vicious term *Verjudung* (Judaization), so beloved of antisemites (see our citation from Eugen Dühring in the commentary), occurs once in *The Jews' State*, and even Herzl, though ever ready to throw out a challenge, feels the need to qualify it with the adjective *so-called.*

(Hortzitz, 1988.)

Le Ressort d'une Démocratie est la Vertu   The passage in question occurs at the start of Book 3, chapter 3, of Montesquieu's *De l'esprit des lois*, and is as follows:

> *Il ne faut pas beaucoup de probité pour qu'un gouvernement monarchique ou un gouvernement despotique se maintienne ou se soutienne. La force des lois dans l'un, le bras du prince toujours levé dans l'autre, règlent ou contiennent tout. Mais, dans un État populaire, il faut un ressort de plus, qui est la* VERTU. *(Montesquieu/Gressaye, 1950:56)*

> There is no greater share of probity necessary to support a monarchical or despotic government. The forces of laws in one, and the prince's arm in the other, are sufficient to direct and maintain the whole. But in a popular state, one spring more is necessary, namely, virtue. (Montesquieu/Nugent, 1962:20)

For a discussion of the influence of Montesquieu on Herzl's concept of the form of the state, see the introduction.

(Montesquieu/Gressaye 1950; Montesquieu/Nugent 1962.)

Lessing—*Nathan der Weise*   Gotthold Ephraim Lessing (1729–1781) was arguably the most important poet of the German Enlightenment period. He wrote theoretical works on the theater as well as of dramas, of which *Nathan der Weise* (1779) is the most enduring. It is a treatise on tolerance. Set in the Palestine of Crusader times, its three main protaganists are the Jewish merchant Nathan, the Christian Templar who saves Nathan's daughter from a housefire, and the historical Saladin who previously had spared the Templar in combat. Saladin summons Nathan to his palace, ostensibly in order to ask for a loan of money, but in the event he confronts Nathan with the question: Which of the three monotheistic religions is the true one? Nathan answers by way of the parable of the three rings. A family posesses a magic ring, the bearer of which is favored by God and man as a good man. The ring is passed on from father to favorite son, who then assumes his place as head of the family. This particular father in question had three sons, whom he loved equally, and, feeling his death approaching, did not know to which of his sons to pass on the ring. So he had two extra copies made of the ring, and just before his death gave each of his sons one of the rings. No sooner had the father died, but an argument erupted between the three sons about which was the genuine ring, and a judge had to be called on to decide. The decision was that as the true ring had the power to instil goodness and wisdom in its bearer, each son should strive in his way to full humanity, and in this way the prophecy of the ring would be fulfilled for each of them, thus illustrating Nathan's earlier statement to the Templar: "Despise my people as much as you wish. Neither of us had a hand in choosing our people. Are we our people? What does it mean, people? Are Christian and Jew first Christian and Jew and only then human being? Oh, how I wish I have found someone in you who is satisfied with being a human being" (Act 2, scene 5).

The model for the character of Nathan was the German-Jewish philosopher Moses Mendelssohn (the grandfather of the composer Felix), a friend of Lessing, whose intelligence and generosity of spirit were much admired by him.

The play as a plea for tolerance is generally considered one of the pinnacles of eighteenth-century German literature. "*Nathan der Weise* remains today the most beautiful tradition: . . . because he represents the idea of humanity, the most noble aim of Christian and Jew and Moslem, the highest task of man" (Drews, 1962:144). Herzl himself for a moment considered inserting an adaptation of the parable of the three rings, a "hat parable," into *The Jews' State* (20 June 1895, BT2:146, P1:122). Characteristically, Herzl's admiration for Lessing was not so generally shared in his time of Christian-imperialist optimism. Wilhelm Marr (1879:19) was particularly upset that Lessing had shown such nobility of character in a person who was both *Jude* and *Geldmensch* [Jew and money-maker]. A popular German literary history text in general use in universities and senior secondary schools wrote: "There is no denying that Lessing has not given equality of treatment to positive Christianity compared to Islam and Judaism, for in the play he has given it a less than worthy representative" (Heilmann, 1909:67).

(Lessing 1779; Drews 1962; Heilmann 1909; Marr, 1879.)

Liberals in Hungary   The cooperative relationship between the Liberals of Hungary and the Jewish community to which Herzl alludes here went back to the *Ausgleich* [Compromise] of 1867, which divided the Habsburg Empire into a Dual Monarchy, consisting of an Austrian Empire and a Hungarian Kingdom. Both halves of the new Dual Monarchy proceeded to enact new constitutions, which both stipulated the irrelevance of religious belief as a prerequisite for holding public office. It was this stipulation which Josef Wertheimer celebrated in such glowing terms in Vienna. There had been previous attempts at emancipation of the Jews, both in Austria and in Hungary following the 1848 revolution, but these had been revoked in the 1850s. The emancipation of the Jews in Hungary now went ahead in two stages. Traditionally, the three main Christian denominations—the Catholics, the Calvinists and the Lutherans—had enjoyed a peculiar legal status as *rezipierte* [received] religions, which meant that they had certain quasi-political functions and privileges, among which were the conducting and registering of marriages, and the registering of births. These functions were of immense significance to the churches, as they enabled them to influence the choice of partners in prospective marriages, and put pressure of families on occasions of baptisms. The first stage of Jewish emancipation was therefore to give the Jewish congregation equal *rezipierte* status. The Minister of Culture after 1867, Joszef Eöstvös, therefore called on the Jewish communities to organize themselves into a body to whom *rezipierte* status could be accorded.

Jewish groups held a number of conferences between 1868 and 1870, and it transpired that there was no unity among them. Three camps emerged: the Orthodox, the Modernists (called Neologs), and a group who wished things simply to remain as they were (McCagg, 1989:137–139). These three groups could not agree about how to organize themselves into a body capable of receiving *rezipierte* status, so in the end the government accepted that there were to be three Jewish communities in Hungary, each of them with *rezipierte* status. The second stage of Jewish emancipation occurred in the early 1890s with the Liberal government's desire to secularize the functions the religions had had due to their *rezipierte* status: this concerned specifically the introduction of civil marriage and a civil personal register. The churches, especially the Catholic Church, could see their control in these areas disappear, and a bitter struggle ensued between the churches and the government, the Catholics even going so far as to take their fight to the Pope, who issued a special encyclical *Constanti Hungarorum* condemning the Liberal plans in the strongest terms. In the end, however, the Liberals, against the wishes of the Catholic Church and in the face of opposition of the king Franz Joseph, pushed through the new arrangements which became law on 10 December 1894. It is this law which Herzl refers to. One of the effects of this law was that the religious authorities, whether Jewish or Christian, largely lost the control they previously had over mixed marriages, and that it became easier for Christians and Jews to intermarry. It therefore functioned as an agent of assimilation.

In terms of the social situation of the Jews in Hungary, the 1894 arrangements simply confirmed and codified what had been developing since 1867. The government since 1867 had been in the hands of the Liberals, consisting of the aristocratic landowners. By virtue of the Compromise, the markets in the western part of the Dual Monarchy became open to the Hungarians, and there was a huge potential for economic development and investment. The landed gentry, often impoverished, relied for capital and know-how on the Jewish community of Hungary, whose initiatives were received with open arms. The Jewish community saw in this development an opportunity to intermarry on a large scale with the higher echelons of Hungarian society and improve its social status (Mc-Cagg, 1989:192). It was a significant movement: by 1914, 346 Jewish merchants and bankers had obtained a title, and a fifth of the large landed estates belonged to Jews (Hoensch, 1984:45). The increasing waves of antisemitism so characteristic of Vienna at this time, where Lueger took to cursing the *Judäomagyaren*, were largely absent in Hungary; many Jews emigrated and worked in Hungary: in 1910, Jews constituted twenty-three percent of the population of Budapest (Hoensch, 1984:40). It has been remarked that as a corollary, early Zionism hardly made any inroads into Hungary; indeed, only seven of the delegates to the First Zionist Congress were Hungarians (Hoensch, 1984:40; McCagg, 1989:194).

(Hoensch 1984; McCagg 1989.)

Longchamp   Famous horse-racing track in Paris, opened in 1857.

(*Grand Larousse Universelle* 1994:IX.6381.)

Lourdes   A small French town situated in the Pyrenees Mountains. From 11 February until 16 July 1858, according to Roman Catholic tradition, a local fourteen-year-old girl, Bernadette Soubirous, experienced a series of apparitions by "*quelque chose de blanc, comme une petite demoiselle* [something white, like a little lady]," who gave her a set of instructions, among them to strike a spring from a rock nearby and to build a church at the location. On the second last apparition the lady identified herself as the Immaculate Conception, i.e., the Virgin Mary; the doctrine of the Immaculate Conception of Mary having been declared by Pope Pius IX just four years previously. Bernadette's reports of the incidents were tested by the local bishop, who declared on 18 January 1862 that the Roman Catholic Church was satisfied that miraculous appearances by the Virgin had occurred (Lille, 1896). On some of the later occasions that the Virgin appeared, Bernadette had been accompanied by groups of the local faithful, thus beginning a tradition of pilgrimages to the location. The first official pilgrimage took place on 4 April 1864, long before a church was finally completed on the spot in 1901. Between 1867 and 1908, so roughly during Herzl's lifetime, there were 5,297 pilgrimages that brought 4,919,000 pilgrims to Lourdes (Herbermann, 1910:389-390).

Pilgrims to Lourdes were (and are) often sick people who believed devotions at the spring and the location could work miraculous cures. Between 1858 and 1908 it was claimed that 3,962 recoveries took place at the shrine (Herbermann, 390); later, more sober estimates put the number of miracles associated with the shrine during the first hundred years of its existence at 58 (CathEnc, 1967:1032). From the very beginning, a body of scientific literature, both supportive and critical, has sprung up about the shrine. For nearly fifty years during Herzl's time (1879–1925) the priest L. Cros investigated claims about the shrine (*Notre Dame de Lourdes, documents inédits* (1879), *Histoire de Notre Dame de Lourdes d'après les documents et les témoins* (1925), both Paris, Gabriel Beauchesne). Joris Karl Huysmans, after his conversion to Catholicism, wrote supportively in *Les foules de Lourdes* [The crowds of Lourdes]. Emile Zola was an early critic (*Lourdes*, 1894). Others, like the Jewish headmaster of the school in Nancy, Bernheim (*Hypnotisme, Suggestion, Psychothérapie*, Paris, 1903, 2nd edition) ascribed the cures to autosuggestion (Helbermann, 1910:390). Herzl himself had written an early article on Lourdes for the *Neue Freie Presse* in 1891 (Pawel, 1989:141).

(Centre Interdisciplinaire des Facultés catholiques de Lille Volume 7, 1975; Glazier and Hellwig 1994; Herbermann Volume 9, 1910; *The*

New Catholic Encyclopedia Volume 8, 1967; Huysmans, n.d.; Pawel 1989.)

Maccabees   The Maccabees were a Hasmonean Jewish family, whose story is related in the two biblical books of the Apocrypha. They led the Jews to independence during the final stages of the Hellenistic era. The earliest known member of the family was the aged priest Mattathias, who had five sons. The title Maccabee, meaning *hammer*, was first given to Judas, third son of Mattathias, on account of the bitter blows with which he defeated his enemies. The Maccabean era is usually taken to start with Judas' revolt against the Syrians in 168 B.C.E. He reconquered and rededicated the Temple in Jerusalem in 165 B.C.E. Jewish independence under the Maccabees came to an end when after a period of internecine Jewish strife the Romans under Pompey conquered the Jewish tribes in 63 B.C.E.

(Davis 1944; Nave 1969.)

Mizraim   Mizraim is the usual word for Egypt found in the Bible. In this sentence, Herzl alludes to the exodus of the Jews from Egypt under Moses, and specifically to Exodus 16:2–3: "The Israelites complained to Moses and Aaron in the wilderness and said, 'If only we had died at the Lord's hand in Egypt, where we sat round the fleshpots and had plenty of bread to eat! But you have brought us out into this wilderness to let this whole assembly starve to death.'"

(*The New English Bible* 1970:I.93; Davis 1944; Nave 1969.)

Panama   By the time Herzl was writing *The Jews' State*, the construction of the Panama Canal already had quite a history, and had shaken the very foundations of the French Republic. In the late 1870s, the builder of the Suez Canal, Ferdinand de Lesseps, by then already a man of advanced years, had started to propagate the idea of him building a canal across the Panama isthmus, and by 1881 he had received permission from the Colombia Government to build the canal. The building was to be financed by private enterprise, and the amount of seventy million dollars had been obtained initially by public subscription, which was far too little when compared to the final cost of the Suez Canal, which had been so much simpler to build (EncAm, 25:845). It soon became evident that Lessep's company was overreaching itself, both in terms of engineering expertise and financial management and resources. There were physical problems with the nature of the terrain, as well as with the persistent yellow fever. In the course of excavations, which took place between 1881 and 1889, several hundred French engineers died. In terms of available finance, Lesseps's Company had overshot its budget and run out of funds as early as 1883. The directors turned to speculators and crooks, among whom some were Jewish. The main men, Baron Jacques de Reinach and Cornelius Herz, both baptized Jews, obtained government subsidies by bribing politicians, organized ever new subscriptions, bought off the press by bribery (Pawel, 1989:170). Eventually the Company went into receivership in 1889 and Lesseps resigned a broken man (EncAm, 347).

The whole scandal was then brought to light by Edouard Drumont of *La libre parole*. Reinach committed suicide, Herz left the country in a hurry for England. The government decided to prosecute Lesseps and his son Charles; the trial ran from November 1892 until May 1893. It brought to light much government incompetence, bribery and corruption, and considerable Jewish involvement in the scandal (Pawel, 1989:171). The trial shook the French republic to its very foundations, and also brought to the surface a considerable level of anti-Jewish feeling in France. Herzl covered the trial for the *Neue Freie Presse*. The French government then made an effort to salvage the plan and formed the *Compagnie nouvelle du Canal de Panama* in 1894, but when the United States government intervened with the declaration that French government involvement would breach the Monroe doctrine, French interest in the venture quickly dissipated. By 1898 the French had pulled out and the Canal was eventually completed under United States auspices in 1914 (EncAm, 347).

(Pawel 1989; *The Encyclopedia Americana,* Volumes 21 and 25.)

Patrimony, Patriarchy   Herzl is here talking about states based on estates, like the *ancien régime* in France. The estates were communities of interests (the third estate), fixed since time immemorial and legitimated by the passage of time, which as estates performed the functions of government under a benign ruler. Estates were considered stable entities, deriving "their validity of custom considered as inviolable by reason of the sanctity of what had always been," with the sovereign representing "the eternal yesterday" presiding over the whole state (Freund, 1970:241). The individual subject did not directly participate in the state; his concerns were first mediated through the estate, which then brought them up in government at the appropriate time. Patrimonial authority was based on fealty and subjection of both estate and individual to the sovereign, who ruled over his charges as a father rules his children. There was no sense of an objective administrative structure, no division between the private and public spheres; administration was personalized, and the only criterion of power was the "confidence the sovereign placed in his favorites" (Freund, 1970:241). Romantic theorists in Germany in the early part of the nineteenth century, exploring a return to a glorious past (Fichte and Görres), played with these sorts of ideas which Herzl rejects. After Herzl's death, Max Weber was to deal extensively with patrimonial authority, both in political and social relations, in his *Wirtschaft und Gesellschaft* [Economy and Society].

(Freund 1970; Weber 1978.)

People Herzl Spoke to in London   Herzl made a trip to London in November 1895 to discuss his ideas with a number of prominent members of the Jewish community there. During his stay in London he first met Israel Zangwill; he also called on the Chief Rabbi of London, where he drinks *"einen leichten Rotwein aus einer Zionskolonie* [a light red wine from a Zion-settlement]" (23 November 1895; BT2:283, P1:279), and Sir Samuel Montague, a Jewish member of parliament (24 November 1895; BT2:284, P1:280). He also made a day trip to Wales to meet a colonel Goldsmid, a Jew who had been brought up a Christian, only to discover his Jewishness subsequently, and to revert back to Judaism (Stewart, 1974:274).

(Stewart 1974.)

Physiocrats   The Physiocrats were a school of French political economists in vogue in the second half of the eighteenth century; the word itself was invented by one of them, Dupont de Nemours, in 1758. Their thinking was based on the premise that the only true index of the wealth of nations was the food supply these nations were able to engender. As a school they were a reaction to the theories of mercantilism, which had seen the true wealth of nations as being based on the maintenance of favorable trade balances, which were to be maintained by cutting national imports to the bone and encouraging the export of manufactured goods. The physiocrats represented a necessary reaction against the theories of the mercantilists, but made the mistake of undervaluing manufactures almost as much as the mercantilists had overvalued them. Their most lasting contribution to economic thought lay in showing the advantages of a policy of laissez-faire, as compared with a system of state interference.

(Baldwin 1925; Robert 1962.)

Rip van Winkle   Rip van Winkle is the hero of the story by Washington Irving (1783-1859), *The Legend of Sleepy Hollow*, which first appeared in Irving's collection *The Sketch Book of Geoffrey Crayon, Gent.* (1819–1820). Irving's story is a retelling of the archetypal tale in which the central character awakens after a period of supernatural slumber to find himself in a strange new world. The narrator's purpose is invariably to point the contrast between one era and another. In another related group of legends, the sleeper is a great hero awaiting his country's time of need when he will return as a deliverer.

The story takes place in the Catskill Mountains of New York during colonial times. Rip, an unsuccessful farmer, goes hunting one day to escape his wife's continual nagging. In the woods, he chances upon Hendrik Hudson and the crew of the *Half Moon* playing ninepins in a secluded valley. He falls asleep after tasting their liquor and awakes to find himself an old man with a foot-long beard. His sleep has only lasted the moderate period of twenty years, but meantime the American revolution has taken place and all is changed. His wife has died, his children have grown, and the colonists have won their independence. At first, everyone laughs at Rip's story. But then he is recognized by some old friends in his village who confirm his story. He becomes famous for his unusual adventure and lives out his natural span in his daughter's home.

Herzl must have been quite impressed by the Rip Van Winkle legend, because he uses a variation of the theme as a structural device for his novel *Altneuland*, with the variation that the hero Friedrich does not die, but spends twenty-five years away from civilization on an island in the South Seas before he comes back to the world, visits the new Jews' State, and has occasion to be astounded by all the developments that have taken place there.

(Chambers, Volume 11, 1968; Howe 1988; World Book, Volume 16, 1988.)

Rousseau   This passage contains a paraphrase by Herzl of a paragraph in chapter 6 of Rousseau's *Du contrat social*, which deals with the social compact. The full passage in Rousseau is as follows:

> *Les clauses de ce contrat sont tellement déterminées par la nature de l'acte, que la moindre modification les rendrait vaines et de nul effet; en sorte que, bien qu'elles n'aient peut-être jamais été formellement énoncées, elles sont partout les mêmes, partout tacitement admises et reconnues, jusqu'à ce que, le pact social étant violé, chacun rentre alors dans ces premiers droits, et reprenne sa liberté naturelle, en perdant la liberté conventionelle pour laquelle il y renonça. (Rousseau, 1975:243)*

The clauses of this contract are so completely determined by the nature of the act that the slightest modification would render them null and void. So that although they may never have been formally pronounced, they are everywhere the same, everywhere tacitly accepted and recognized, until the social compact is violated, at which point each man recovers his original rights and resumes his natural freedom, thereby losing the conventional freedom for which he renounced it. (Rousseau/Masters, 1978:53)

For a discussion of Herzl's attitude toward Rousseau's philosophy on the state as compared with Montesquieu's, see the introduction.

(Rousseau 1975; Rousseau/Masters 1978.)

Sachsengängerei   Herzl here uses the term *Sachsengängerei*. A *Sachsengänger* was an itinerant agricultural laborer, usually coming from the Polish regions of Czarist Russia, who used to go to Saxony every year to help with the harvest of the sugar beets (cf. Wahrig, 1978:3102). It was a rather chaotic annual movement of peasant laborers; the suffix -*ei* gives the word a slightly pejorative meaning. Herzl sees in it a possible basis for the organization of itinerant labor in his own projected state.

(Wahrig 1978.)

Singspiel   The *Singspiel* (literally: play with songs) is a genre of comic opera, developed in Germany in the second half of the eighteenth century. It aimed to have popular appeal among the common people, in contradistinction to the *opera seria*, which dealt with elevated subjects of interest to the educated classes. The language of the *Singspiel* was normally German, the language of opera being Italian. The orchestration of the *Singspiel* was considerably lighter than that of opera proper, and it is to this feature of the *Singspiel* that Herzl draws attention. Mozart wrote two famous *Singspiele*, *Die Entführung aus dem Serail* [The Abduction from the Seraglio] (1781) and *Die Zauberflöte* [The Magic Flute] (1791)

Sir Thomas More   Sir Thomas More was born on 7 February 1477 and died on 6 July 1535. After studies in law, More became undersheriff of London on 3 September 1510. He received his first royal commission from Henry VIII on 25 October 1515 to the Low Countries. After long consideration he entered the royal service in 1518, and was a royal counselor until 1529. More's professional life centered on the court from 1518–1529. He was Lord Chancellor of England from 1529–1532. He incurred the displeasure of Henry VIII for refusing to approve of the King's divorce from Catherine of Aragon, and was beheaded in 1535. More began his literary career in 1503 with the *Lamentation for the death of Queen Elizabeth*. *Utopia* is his fourth work. The full title of the book is *Libellus . . . de optimo reipublicae statu, deque nova insula Utopia*, and it was published in Leuven in 1516. It contains an idealized description of a brave new world, seen through the eyes of a mysterious traveller, Raphael Hythloday. *Utopia* is a romance, less concerned with realistic description than with playing with ideas and ideal states. The book has been the inspiration for countless "utopias" written since More's. The adjective *utopian* has become synonymous with conceptions of impractical idealized states, and it is in this connection that he is mentioned by Herzl in *The Jews' State*: as distinct from More, Herzl claims he is concerned about writing a realistic treatise that can be achieved in practice, not about playing an intellectual game with ideas.

(*New Catholic Encyclopedia*, Volume 19, 1966; *Encyclopaedia Britannica*, Volume 15, 1970.)

Theodor Hertzka   Theodor Hertzka was born on 13 July 1845 in Budapest. He studied economics in Budapest and Vienna, then became a journalist. From 1872 until 1879 he was the editor of the scientific and economic supplement to the *Neue Freie Presse*, the paper for which Herzl was to work ten years later. Hertzka branched out on his own by establishing the *Wiener Allgemeine Zeitung* [Vienna General Paper] in 1880, which he later sold, and the *Zeitschrift für Staats- und Volkswirtschaft* [Journal of State and National Economy] in 1889. In 1901 he became the chief editor of *Magyar hirlap* [Hungarian Newssheet] in Budapest. Hertzka died on 22 October 1924 in Wiesbaden.

During the late 1880s Hertzka published a number of books on economic subjects. In *Die Gesetze der sozialen Entwicklung* [The laws of social development] (1886) Hertzka proposed his blueprint for an ideal society. This philosophy was further developed in the novel *Freiland, ein soziales Zukunftsbild* [Freeland, a picture of future society], which was published in 1890. *Freiland* was a considerable success, and had run to ten editions by 1896. Hertzka believed that the contemporary social problems stemmed from capital and land taxes, because taxes on goods, land tax, and profits were responsible for limiting the demands for goods among the lower classes, and thus inhibited further technological development and industrial productivity. So in Hertzka's ideal society, private landownership is to be abolished. The status of land is to be like the status of air: it is neither privately nor publicly owned, but to be available freely for development by freely constituted associations. These associations become the producers of social goods, are self-governing and divide their profits among members. Joining or leaving such associations is a matter of free choice for members. The state lends these associations the necessary capital without interest; it has to be paid back over a number of years.

Freiland is a utopian description of an ideal society, in the tradition of Sir Thomas More. In the latter half of the nineteenth century a number of utopias had appeared, of which the most recent had been *Looking Backward* by the American Edward Bellamy in 1888, a socialist utopia, which was very influential, and Bellamy societies sprang up.

Similarly, after the publication of *Freiland*, a number of Freiland societies were established to put into practice the economic ideas of Hertzka. An attempt to realize Hertzka's ideas in Kenya failed in the face of difficult conditions and British distrust.

In *The Jews' State* Herzl is at pains to stress the practicality of his own proposal for a state for Jews, and wants to distinguish his work from other utopian descriptions like Hertzka's.

(Mumford 1959; *Neue deutsche Biographie*, Volume 8, 1969; *New Catholic Encyclopedia*, Volume 14, 1967.)

Theory of the Necessity of Reason (*Vernunftnotwendigkeitstheorie*)

Herzl here alludes to the philosophy of Immanuel Kant, who, in his *Kritik der reinen Vernunft* [Critique of Pure Reason] (1781) had developed the theory that human reasoning was necessary to discover the laws of nature, and that the latter were based on reason. In his *Grundlegung zur Metaphysik der Sitten* [The Basis of the Metaphysics of Morals] (1785) he then extended his theory by suggesting that human reasoning was also necessary to regulate the area of human conduct: his categorical imperative was the important outcome of the application of human reason to morality. In *Zum ewigen Frieden* [Eternal Peace] (1791) Kant finally applied these principles to the conduct of states, speaking both of the conduct of governments toward their citizens as well as of the conduct of governments among each other: "*Trachtet allerst nach dem Reiche der reinen praktischen Vernunft und nach seiner Gerechtigkeit, so wird euch euer Zweck (die Wohltat des ewigen Friedens) von selbst zufallen* [For a start, aim to conquer the realm of pure practical reason and its justice, and your objective—the benefit of eternal peace—will come to you as a matter of course]" (Kant, 1947:53).

(Kant 1960, 1947.)

Theory of Superior Power   The idea of the state as power found its most influential proponent in Heinrich von Treitschke, professor of history at the university of Berlin from the 1870s until his death in 1896. From 1874 until 1896 he held an annual series of lectures entitled *Politik*. Basic to Treitschke's conception of the state was the belief that power is the supreme defining characteristic of any state:

> *Ist der Staat eine Persönlichkeit, so folgt daraus weiter die notwendige und vernunftmäßige Vielheit der Staaten.... Nur darum ist der Staat Macht, um sich zu behaupten neben anderen ebenso unabhängigen Mächten...*
>
> *Der Staat ist keine Akademie der Künste; wenn er seine Macht vernachlässigt zugunsten der idealen Bestrebungen der Menschheit, so verleugnet er sein Wesen und geht zugrunde. Die Verleugnung der eigenen Macht ist für den Staat recht eigentlich die Sünde wider den heiligen Geist; sich aus Sentimentalität einem fremden Staate anzuschmiegen, wie wir Deutschen es oft den Engländern gegenüber getan haben, ist in der Tat eine Totsünde.* (Treitschke, 1915:12–15)

As the state is a *persona*, it follows that a multiplicity of states is both reasonable and necessary. The state is power only so that it can maintain itself in the face other powers who are likewise independent.

The state is no academy of fine arts; if it neglects its power in order to pursue the ideals of humanity, it denies its very nature and will collapse. The denial of its own power is for the state truly the sin against the Holy Ghost; it is a mortal sin to curry favor with a foreign state for reasons of sentiment, as the Germans have done so often with the English.

A state merely confirms its continued existence by waging war against other states: peace is a curse (*Unsegen*, Treitschke, 1915:20), and war is the only medicine for sick peoples (Treitschke, 1915:27). The European peoples have to put their stamp on the barbaric colonial countries (Treitschke, 1915:34). Implicit in Treitschke's conception of the state is the rejection of any mechanism that inhibits the power of the state, whether this mechanism operates between states or within the one state. International arbitration is incompatible with the sovereignty of the state; treaties between states do not have binding status (Treitschke, 1915:17); the idea of a common humanity is loathsome:

> *Daher ist die Idee eines Weltreiches hassenswert; das Ideal eines Mensch-heitsstaates ist gar kein Ideal. (Treitschke, 1915:12)*

> That is why the idea of a worldwide state is hateful; the ideal of one state for all humanity is no ideal at all.

In addition, Treitschke had no time for the democratic mechanisms within a state; he condemned democracy, workers' aspirations, trade union activity.

Largely due to Treitschke's influence, these ideas were common currency in German academic and political life in the three decades before the outbreak of World War I. Herzl himself, although by and large he does not ascribe to them, is nevertheless not entirely immune. These ideas may not be "in accordance with modern conceptions," but he, too, ascribes to the contemporary European ethos of the Jews' state leaving a European stamp on Palestine against the "barbarism" of Asia, and he, too, maintains that the ideal of a brotherhood of man "is not even a beautiful dream."

(Samuel 1963; Treitschke 1915.)

Trier   A city in Germany on the river Mosel, close to the borders between Germany, Luxemburg and France. It is the seat of the Catholic diocese of Trier, which is the oldest diocese in Germany. In Roman times, Trier was the capital of Belgica Prima, a division of the Roman empire as reorganized by Diocletian. There were Christians among its population from the second century onward, and the first authenticated bishop was Agricius, who took plart in the Council of Arles in 314. The most important church of the diocese is the Cathedral, the oldest church of a Christian bishop on German soil. The oldest section of the church goes back to the Roman era. It was sponsored and endowed by St. Helena, mother of Constantine the Great, early in the fourth century. Throughout her life Helena sponsored the building of a number of important churches, including in the Holy Land the Church of the Holy Sepulchre in Jerusalem and the Church of the Nativity in Bethlehem. Among the Christian relics she discovered in her travels in the Holy Land was the mantle of Jesus mentioned in John 19:23: "The soldiers, having crucified Jesus, took possession of his clothes, and divided them into four parts, one for each soldier, leaving out the tunic. The tunic was seamless, woven in one piece throughout; so they said to one another, "We must not tear this; let us toss for it"; and thus the text of Scripture came true: "They shared my garments among them, and cast lots for my clothing." Helena gave this mantle to the church in Trier. In Herzl's time, the mantle was exhibited publicly in 1891 as an occasion to demonstrate against the effects of Bismarck's *Kulturkampf*, and a number of miracles were supposed to have happened during that exhibition, described in the book by Michael Korum, *Wunder und Gnadenerweise, die sich bei der Ausstellung 1891* *zugetragen haben* [Miracles and signs of grace, which happened during the exhibition of 1891] (Trier 1894), which Herzl may have known.

(Attwater 1983; Herbermann Volume 15, 1912; The New English Bible 1970:II.188.)

Truck   Truck refers to a system of employer-employee relations, where the employee is not paid for his labor by money (wages), but by other commodities, such as credits or other goods. There was an Act of Parliament passed in England in 1886 regulating the practice of truck.

(Simpson and Weiner, Volume 18, 1989.)

Bibliography

Works and
Translations of
Theodor Herzl

Herzl, Theodor. *Der Judenstaat*. 13th edition. Jerusalem: The Jewish Publishing House, Ltd., 1975.

———. *Wenn ihr wollt, ist es kein Märchen: Altneuland/Der Judenstaat*. Ed. by Julius Schoeps. Kronberg: Jüdischer Verlag, 1978.

———. *Der Judenstaat*. Zürich: Manesse.

———. *A Jewish State*. Trans. by Sylvie d'Avigdor. London: David Nutt, 1896.

———. *A Jewish State*. Trans. by Sylvie d'Avigdor, ed. by Jacob de Haas. New York: Maccabaean Publishing Company, 1904.

———. *The Jewish State*. Rev. by Israel Cohen. London: Central Office of the Zionist Organisation, 1934.

———. *The Jewish State*. Trans. by I. V. Lask. Tel Aviv, 1954.

———. *The Jewish State (Der Judenstaat)*. Trans. by Harry Zohn. New York: Herzl Press, 1970.

———. *The Jewish State*. Based on the trans. by Sylvie d'Avigdor. New York: Dover Publications, 1988.

———. *De joodsche staat*. Trans. by V. Cohen-Slijper. Book and brochure department of the Dutch Zionist League, 1919.

———. *Lo Stato Ebraico*. Trans. by Gino Servadio. Rome: La Rassegna Mensile d'Israel, 1955.

————. *L'état des Juifs.* Trans. by Claude Klein. Paris: Éditions de la Découverte, 1990.

————. "Arbeitshilfe." *Neue Freie Presse,* 2 August 1893, pp. 1–2.

————. "Dr. Güdemanns Nationaljudentum." *Österreichische Wochenschrift,* 23 April 1897, pp. 346–348.

————. "Protestrabbiner." *Die Welt,* 16 July 1897.

————. *Briefe und Tagebücher.* Ed. by von Alex Bein, Greive, Schaerf, and Schoeps. Vienna: Propyläen, Berlin: Frankfurt am Main, Ullstein, 1983–1996.

————. *The Complete Diaries of Theodor Herzl.* Ed. by Raphael Patai. Trans. by Harry Zohn. New York: Herzl Press and Thomas Yoseloff, 1960.

————. *Vision und Politik: Die Tagebücher Theodor Herzls.* Ed. by Gisela Brude-Firnau. Frankfurt am Main: Suhrkamp, 1976.

Reference Guides

Attwater, Donald. *The Penguin Dictionary of Saints*. Harmondsworth: Penguin, 1983.

Baldwin, James Mark. *Dictionary of Philosophy and Psychology*. Gloucester (Mass): Peter Smith, 1925.

Berger, Adolf. *Encyclopedic Dictionary of Roman Law*. Philadelphia: The American Philosophical Society, 1953.

Brockhaus Enzyklopädie in Zwanzig Bänden. 17th ed. Wiesbaden: F. A. Brockhaus, 1966–1974.

Bruggencate, K. Ten. *Engels Woordenboek*. 18th ed. Groningen: Wolters-Noordhoff, 1983.

Centre Interdisciplinaire des Facultés Catholiques de Lille *Catholicisme. Hier, aujourd'hui, demain*. Paris: Letouzey et Ané, 1975.

Chambers's Encyclopedia. London: George Newnes, 1959–1964.

Davis, John D. *The Westminster Dictionary of the Bible*. London: Collins, 1944.

Encyclopaedia Britannica, Macropaedia. Chicago: William Benton, 1970.

Encyclopedia of Zionism and Israel. Ed. by Raphael Patai. New York: Herzl Press/McGraw-Hill, 1971.

Glazier, Michael, and Hellwig, Monika K. *The Modern Catholic Encyclopedia*. Newtown (New South Wales): Dwyer Press, 1994.

Grand dictionnaire encyclopédique Larousse. Paris: Larousse, 1982.

Grand Larousse Universelle. Paris: Larousse, 1994.

Herbermann, Charles G. et al. *The Catholic Encyclopedia*. New York: Robert Appleton, 1910–1912.

Herlitz, Georg, and Kirschner, Bruno. *Jüdisches Lexikon: Ein enzyklopädisches Handbuch des jüdischen Wissens in vier Bänden*. Berlin: Jüdischer Verlag, 1927–1930.

Hertzfeld, Hans. *Geschichte in Gestalten*. Frankfurt am Main: Fischer, 1963.

International Encyclopedia of the Social Sciences. Ed. by David L. Sills. London: Collier–Macmillan, 1972.

Messinger, Heinz. *Langenscheidts Grosswörterbuch: English–Deutsch*. Berlin: Langenscheidt, 1981.

Neue deutsche Biographie. Ed. by the Historische Kommission bei der Bayrischen Akademie der Wissenschaften. Berlin: Duncker & Humboldt, 1959–1969.

Robert, Paul. *Dictionnaire alphabétique et analogique de la langue française*. Paris: Société du nouveau Littré, 1962.

Seligman, Edwin R. A., and Johnson, Alvin. *Encyclopaedia of the Social Sciences*. New York: Macmillan, 1959.

Simpson, J. A., and Weiner, E. S. C. *The Oxford English Dictionary*. Oxford: Clarendon Press, 1989.

The Catholic University of America, Washington. *New Catholic Encyclopedia*. San Francisco: McGraw-Hill, 1967.

The Encyclopedia Americana: International Edition. Danbury (Connecticut): Grolier.

The Jewish Encyclopedia. Ed. by Isidore Singer, et. al. New York and London: Funk and Wagnall, 1904–1910.

The New Encyclopaedia Brittanica: Micropaedia. Chicago: Encyclopaedia Brittanica, 1994.

The New Encyclopaedia Brittanica: Micropaedia. Chicago: The University of Chicago, 1988.

The World Book Encyclopedia. Chicago: World Book, Inc., 1988.

Wahrig, Gerhard. *Deutsches Wörterbuch*. Gütersloh: Bertelsmann Verlag, 1978.

Newspapers
and Journals

Die Neuzeit. Vienna. 10 January 1868.
Die Welt. Vienna. 1897ff.
Jüdische Zeitung. Vienna. 1906ff.
Jüdisches Volksblatt. Breslau. 1910ff.
Österreichische Wochenschrift. Vienna. 1883ff.
Selbstemanzipation: Zeitschrift für die nationalen, sozialen und politischen Interessen des jüdischen Stammes. Vienna. 1885ff.
Wiener Allgemeine Zeitung. Vienna. 1 March 1896.

Books and Articles

Avineri, Shlomo. *The Making of Modern Zionism: The Intellectual Origins of the Jewish State.* London: Weidenfeld and Nicolson, 1981.

Barissia Prague. *Protokoll des 1. Zionistenkongresses in Basel von 29. bis 31.* Prague: Jüdisch-nationale akademisch-technische Verbindung, 'Barissia,' 1911.

Beer, Samuel. *Modern British Politics.* London: Faber and Faber, 1969.

Bein, Alex. *Theodor Herzl: A Biography.* Philadelphia: Jewish Publication Society of America, 1962.

Bein, Alex, and Schaerf, Moshe. *From Boulanger to Dreyfus: A Collection of Herzl's Articles from the Neue Freie Presse* (in Hebrew). Jerusalem: Zionist Library, 1974.

Beller, Steven. "Herzl und Wien." *Das jüdische Echo,* vol. 43 (October 1994).

Beller, Steven. "Fin de Siècle Vienna and the Jews: The Dialectics of Assimilation." *The Jewish Quarterly,* 33(3), 1986.

Bericht der vierten Generalversammlung. Vienna: Verein zur Abwehr des Antisemitismus, 1894.

Birnbaum, Nathan. *Die Assimilationssucht.* Vienna: D. Löwy, 1884.

———. *Die Nationale Wiedergeburt des Jüdischen Volkes in Seinem*

Lande als Mittel zur Lösung der Judenfrage. Vienna: Selbstverlag des Verfassers, 1893.

Bracher, Karl Dietrich. *The German Dictatorship: The Origins, Structure, and Consequences of National Socialism.* Harmondsworth: Penguin, 1971.

Bülow, Bernhard Fürst von. *Denkwürdigkeiten.* Edited by Franz von Stockhammern. Berlin: Ullstein Verlag, 1930.

Bunzl, Matti. "Surveying Jewish Austria." Review of "Austrians and Jews in the Twentieth Century: From Franz Joseph to Waldheim." *The Jewish Quarterly, 41(1).* London: Macmillan, 1994.

Bunzl, John. "Der Zionismus und die jüdische Nation." *Das jüdische Echo,* vol. 43, 1994.

Carneiro, Robert L., ed. *The Evolution of Society: Selections from Herbert Spencer's "Principles of Sociology."* Chicago: University of Chicago Press, 1974.

Chouraqui, André. *A Man Alone: The Life of Theodor Herzl.* Jerusalem: Keter Books, 1970.

Clare, George. *Last Waltz in Vienna: The Destruction of a Family 1842–1942.* London: Pan Books, 1982.

Darmesteter, James. *Les Prophètes d'Israel.* Paris: Calmann Lévy, 1892.

Dethloff, Klaus, ed. *Theodor Herzl oder der Moses des fin de siècle.* Vienna: Böhlau, 1986.

Drews, Wolfgang. *Lessing.* Reinbek bei Hamburg: Rowohlt, 1962.

Dühring, Eugen. *Die Judenfrage als Frage des Rassencharakters und seiner Schädlichkeiten für Existenz und Kultur der Völker.* 6th ed. Leipzig: O. R. Reisland, 1930.

Ernst, Ludwig. *Kein Judenstaat sondern Gewissensfreihit.* Leipzig and Vienna: Literarische Anstalt August Schulze, 1896.

Fichte, Johann Gottlieb. "Reden an die Deutsche Nation." In *Sämtliche Werke.* Berlin: Veit, 1846.

Freund, Julien. *The Sociology of Max Weber.* London: Allen Lane Penguin, 1970.

Gaisbauer, Adolf. *Davidstern und Doppeladler: Zionismus und jüdischer*

Nationalismus in Österreich 1882–1918. Vienna: Böhlau Verlag, 1988.

Geehr, Richard S. *"I Decide Who Is a Jew!": The Papers of Dr. Karl Lueger*. Washington: University Press of America, 1982.

Geehr, Richard S. *Karl Lueger: Mayor of Fin de Siècle Vienna*. Detroit: Wayne State University Press, 1990.

Gelber, N. M. *Zur Vorgeschichte des Zionismus: Judenstaatprojekte in den Jahren 1695–1845*. Vienna: Phaidon Verlag, 1927.

Gobineau, Arthur de. *Essai sur l'inégalité des races humaines*. Paris: Firmin-Didot, 1855.

Goldmann, Nahum. "Ich habe Israel und die Juden gewarnt." *Der Spiegel*. Hamburg, 27 January 1975.

Güdemann, Moritz. *Nationaljudentum*. Leipzig and Vienna: Max Breitenstein, 1897.

Haas, Jacob de. *Theodor Herzl: a Biographical Study*. New York: Brentano, 1927.

Heer, Friedrich. *Gottes erste Liebe: Die Juden im Spannungsfeld der Geschichte*. Munich/Berlin: Herbig, 1981.

Heilmann, Karl. *Deutsche Nationalliteratur und Poetik*. 6th ed. Breslau: Ferdinand Hirt, 1909.

Heine, Heinrich. "Zur Geschichte der Religion und Philosophie in Deutschland." *Heinrich Heines Sämtliche Werke*, vol. 4. Edited by Ernst Elster. Leipzig: Bibliographisches Institut, 1834.

Hellendal, F. "Heinrich Heine: Poet and Prophet." *The Jewish Quarterly*, 21, 1973.

Hertzberg, Arthur (ed.) *The Zionist Idea: A Historical Analysis and Reader*. New York: Athenaeum, 1977.

Hoensch, Jörg K. *Geschichte Ungarns 1867–1983*. Stuttgart: W. Kohlhammer, 1984.

Hortzitz, Nicoline. *"Früh-Antisemitismus" in Deutschland (1789–1872)*. Tübingen: Max Niemeyer, 1988.

Howe, John. *Rip Van Winkle, by Washington Irving*. Boston: Little Brown, 1988.

Huysmans, Joris Karl. *The Crowds of Lourdes*. Trans. by W. H. Mitchell. London: Burns, Oats and Washbourne.

Israel Pocket Library. *Zionism*. Jerusalem: Keter, 1973.

Jellinek, Adolf. *Rede zur Feier des siebzigsten Geburtstages des Herrn Josef Ritter von Wertheimer.* Vienna: Jacob Schlossberg, 1870.

Jonas, Hans. "Das Jüdische Schulwesen in Palästina." In *Zionistisches Handbuch*. Edited by Gerhard Holdheim. Berlin: Berliner Büro der zionistischen Organisation, 1923.

Vienna Kadimah. *Festschrift zur Feier des 100: Semesters der Akademischen Verbindung Kadimah*, 1933.

Kalmus, H. *Genetics*. Harmondsworth: Penguin, 1954.

Kant, Immanuel. *Zum ewigen Frieden. Ein philosophischer Entwurf.* Leipzig: Reclam, 1947.

————. *Auswahl*. Edited by Hans-Georg Gadamer. Frankfurt am Main: Fischer Bücherei, 1960.

Kaser, Max. *Das Römische Privatrecht*. Munich: C. H. Beck, 1971.

Kraus, Karl. *Frühe Schriften*. Edited by Joh. Braakenburg. Munich: Kösel, 1979.

Laqueur, Walter, and Rubin, Barry (eds.). *The Israel-Arab Reader*. London: Penguin, 1984.

Leser, Norbert. "Der zeitgeschichtliche Hintergrund des Wien und Österreich im Fin de Siècle." In *Theodor Herzl und das Wien des Fin de siècle*. Edited by Norbert Leser. Vienna: Böhlau Verlag, 1987.

Lessing, Gotthold Ephraim. "Nathan der Weise." In *Dramen*. Frankfurt: Fischer Bücherei, 1962.

Marr, Wilhelm. *Der Sieg des Judentums über das Germanentum*. 2nd ed. Berne: Rudolph Costenoble, 1879.

Marrus, Michael R. "The Theory and Practice of Anti-semitism." In *Commentary*, 74(2), August 1982.

McCagg, William O. *History of Habsburg Jews, 1670–1918*. Bloomington/Indianapolis: Indiana University Press, 1989.

Montesquieu. *De l'Esprit des Lois*. Edited by Jean Brethe de la Gressaye. Paris: Société les Belles Lettres, 1950.

Montesquieu, Baron de. *The Spirit of the Laws*. Trans. by Thomas Nugent. New York: Hafner, 1962.

Moss, George L. "Jews and their Enemies." Review of *From Prejudice to Destruction: Anti-semitism 1700–1933*, by Jacob Katz. In *Commentary*, 70(6), December 1980.

Moyle, J. B. *Imperatoris Iustiniani Institutionum*. Oxford: Clarendon Press, 1896.

Mumford, Lewis. *The Story of Utopias*. Gloucester (Mass): P. Smith, 1959.

Nathan, Paul. *Die Kriminalität der Juden in Deutschland*. Berlin: Siegfried Cronbach, 1896.

Nave, Orville J. *The New Nave's Topical Bible*. Grand Rapids (Michigan): Zondervan, 1969.

Nordau, Max. "Ein Tempelstreit." In *Die Welt*, 11 June 1897.

Nordau, Max. *Zionistische Schriften*. Berlin: Jüdischer Verlag, 1923.

Pauley, Bruce F. *From Prejudice to Persecution. A History of Austrian Antisemitism*. Chapel Hill: The University of North Carolina Press, 1992.

Pawel, Ernest. *The Labyrinth of Exile: A Life of Theodor Herzl*. London: Collins-Harvill; New York: Farrar Straus & Giroux, 1989.

Philippson, Martin. *Neueste Geschichte des jüdischen Volkes*. Leipzig: Gustav Fock, 1910.

Pinsker, Leo. *Autoemanzipation: Mahnruf an seine Stammesgenossen von einem russischen Juden*. Brünn: Jüdischer Buch- und Kunstverlag, 1913.

Pross, Harry (ed.). *Die Zerstörung der deutschen Politik 1871–1933*. Frankfurt am Main: Fischer, 1960.

Pross, Harry (ed.). *Deutsche Politik 1803–1870*. Frankfurt am Main: Fischer, 1963.

Read, Donald. *The Age of Urban Democracy*. London: Longman, 1994.

Reinach, Theodor. *Histoire des Israélites depuis l'époque de leur dispersion jusqu'à nos jours*. Paris: Hachette, 1884.

Rinott, Moshe. "Capitulations: The Case of the German-Jewish Hilfsverein Schools in Palestine 1900–1914." In *Palestine in the Late Ottoman Period: Political, Social, and Economic Transformation*. Edited by David Kushner. Jerusalem: Yad Izhak Ben-Zvi, 1986.

Rousseau, Jean-Jacques. *Du Contrat Social et autres oeuvres politiques.* Paris: Garnier, 1975.

Rousseau, Jean-Jacques. *On the Social Contract.* Trans. by Judith R. Masters. Edited by Roger D. Masters. New York: St. Martin's Press, 1978.

Samuel, Richard H. "The Origin and Development of the Ideology of National Socialism." In *Richard H. Samuel: Selected Writings.* Edited by D. R. Coverlid. Melbourne: Melbourne University Press, 1963.

Schenk, H. G. *The Mind of the European Romantics.* London. Constable, 1966.

Schnitzler, Arthur. *Der Weg ins Freie.* In *Gesammelte Werke von Arthur Schnitzler.* Berlin: S. Fischer, 1898.

———*Arthur Schnitzler Tagebuch 1893–1902.* Vienna: Verlag der Österreichischen Akademie der Wissenschaften, 1989.

———*Jugend in Wien. Eine Autobiographie.* Vienna: Fritz Molden, 1968.

Schoeps, Julius H. "*Moderne Erben der Makkabäer: Die Anfänge der Wiener Kadimah,*" 1882–1897. In *Theodor Herzl und das Wien des fin de siècle.* Edited by Norbert Leser. Vienna: Böhlau Verlag, 1987.

Shklar, Judith N. *Montesquieu.* Oxford: Oxford University Press, 1987.

Simon, Maurice (ed.). *Speeches, Articles, and Letters of Israel Zangwill.* London: Soncino Press, 1937.

Sokolow, Nahum. *History of Zionism 1600–1918.* Selected and arranged by Israel Solomons. New York: KTAV Publishing House, 1969.

Sondheimer, H. *Jüdisch-geschichtlicher Religionsunterricht.* Lahr: Moritz Schauenburg, 1906.

Stewart, Desmond. *Theodor Herzl: Artist and Politician.* London: Hamish Hamilton, 1974.

The New English Bible. Cambridge: Oxford and Cambridge University Press, 1970.

Treitschke, Heinrich von. *Deutsche Politik: Gedanken von Heinrich von Treitsche.* Leipzig, 1915.

Trevelyan, George M. *British History in the Nineteenth Century and After: 1782–1919*. Harmondsworth: Penguin, 1965.

Vital, David. *The Origins of Zionism*. Oxford: Oxford University Press, 1975.

Wagner, Nike. "Theodor Herzl und Karl Kraus." In *Theodor Herzl und das Wien des fin de siècle*. Edited by Norbert Leser. Vienna: Böhlau, 1987.

Wagner, Richard. *Gesammelte Schriften und Dichtungen in zehn Bänden*. Berlin: Deutsches Verlaghaus Bong.

Weber, Max. *Wirtschaft und Gesellschaft: Economy and Society*. Edited by Günther Roth and Claus Wittich. Berkeley: University of California Press, 1978.

Weiser-Varon, Benno. "Anstelle eines Nachworts." In *Theodor Herzl und das Wien des fin de siècle*. Edited by Norbert Leser. Vienna: Böhlau, 1987.

Weizmann, Chaim. *Trial and Error: The Autobiography of Chaim Weizmann*. New York: Schocken, 1966.

Wistrich, Robert S. *The Jews of Vienna in the Age of Franz Joseph*. Oxford: Oxford University Press, 1989.

Wistrich, Robert S. *Antisemitism: The Longest Hatred*. London: Thames Mandarin, 1995.

Witte, Els, and Graeybeckx, Jan. *La Belgique politique de 1830 à nos jours*. Brussels: Editions Labor, 1987.

Zmarzlik, H. G. *Wieviel Zukunft hat unsere Vergangenheit*. Munich: R. Piper, 1970.

Zohn, Harry. "Die Rezeption Herzls in der jüdischen Umwelt." In *Theodor Herzl und das Wien des fin de siècle*. Edited by Norbert Leser. Vienna: Böhlau, 1987.

Zogby, James. "Palestinian Human Rights in the Context of the Historical Development of the Zionist Movement." In *Question of Palestine: Legal Aspects*. New York: United Nations, 1991.

Zweig, Stefan. *Die Welt von Gestern, Erinnerungen eines Europäers*. Vienna: Bermann-Fischer, 1948.

Index

About the Author

Henk Overberg was born in the Netherlands, emigrated to Australia as a teenager, and completed studies of literature, history, and anthropology at Melbourne and Monash Universities. He has lectured in the anthropology of minority groups at various institutions and has published extensively about the Dutch community in Australia. His interests in early Zionism date back to a sabbatical in Israel in 1975, where he studied the reception of immigrant children in Israeli schools. This sabbatical was followed by regular study trips to Israel and the Middle East. He has been a senior lecturer in Middle Eastern Studies at Deaken University, Melbourne, since 1992. *The Jews' State* is his first publication in the field of Zionism. He is married, with three children.